Memories of Resistance

Memories of Resistance, *W*omen's Voices from the Spanish Civil War

Shirley Mangini - Gonzalez,

Yale University Press   New Haven & London

For Donna, who fought bravely for so many years and taught all of us about life and death

Published with assistance from the Program for Cultural Cooperation between Spain's Ministry of Culture and United States Universities.

Designed by Deborah Dutton.

Set in New Caledonia text and Futura display types by Rainsford Type, Danbury, Connecticut.

Printed in the United States of America by Edwards Brothers, Inc., Ann Arbor, Michigan.

Library of Congress Cataloging-in-Publication Data

Mangini González, Shirley, 1946–
    Memories of Resistance : women's voices from the Spanish Civil War
    / Shirley Mangini.
        p.   cm.
    Includes bibliographical references and index.
    ISBN 0-300-05816-0 (alk. paper)
    1. Spain—History—Civil War, 1936–1939–Women.   2. Women—Spain—
History—20th century.   3. Spain—Politics and government—20th
century.   I. Title.
    DP269.8.W7M36   1995
    946.081—dc20   94-29752
                                                            CIP

A catalogue record for this book is available from the British Library.

The paper in this book meets the guidelines for permanence and durability of the Committee on Production Guidelines for Book Longevity of the Council on Library Resources.

10 9 8 7 6 5 4 3 2 1

Contents

Preface

Given the geographic, historical, and social factors that dictated the subservience of women on the Iberian Peninsula, scant attention has been given to the role of Spanish women in the annals of history. Certainly the same is true of women before, during, and after the Spanish civil war (1936–1939), one of the most important events of contemporary European history and the main focus of this study.

I examine here the social condition of women in the late nineteenth and early twentieth centuries, the sociohistorical factors that were to provoke the war, and their effect on Spanish women of, particularly, the Second Spanish Republic (1931–1936) and those who were part of the leftist resistance to the Franco regime (1939–1975). By hearing the voices of women—from their memoirs, oral testimonies, and other documents—we can understand their function in the Republic, the war, and its aftermath, and comprehend how they perceived themselves. As Gerda Lerner has explained in *The Majority Finds Its Past* (Oxford University Press, 1979, p. 160), "Women's history must contain not only the activities and events in which women participated, but the record of changes and shifts in their perception of themselves and their roles." *Memories of Resistance* proposes to provide that record.

I am grateful to the Fulbright Commission, which enabled me to begin the research for this book in 1985–1986; to the Women's Studies Program at Yale University, which launched me on my journey in search of the memory texts of Spanish women; to California State University, Long Beach, for supporting my work; to the National Endowment for the Humanities, Nancy K. Miller, and my colleagues at the 1991 Summer Seminar on Autobiography at the City University of New York (CUNY) Graduate Center; and finally, to John Chambers and the fellows at the Center for Historical Analysis at Rutgers University, who gave me space for my final ruminations.

My friends Angel González, Mari Carmen and Paco Ignacio Taibo, Charo and Manolo Lombardero, María Luisa Fernández and Agripino Tomás gave me my first visions of Spain's tragedy through their accounts as "children of the civil war." I am deeply indebted to them.

Special thanks go to those who listened, read, and corrected: to Lorraine Holmes for her enormous help and equally enormous sense of humor, and to Grinor Rojo, Wilma Gregory, and Barbara Solomon for their generous time and insightful remarks. I am grateful to Sharlene LaForge and Catherine Lewis-Ida at Interlibrary Loan, who saved my bibliographic life, and to Signal Hill Supper Club members, Chris Campbell and Mary Oliphant, who tore me away from my work and impelled me to cook gourmet dinners as night fell on my computer. At Yale University Press, for their saintly patience and invaluable help, many thanks go to Charles Grench, who always believed, and to Otto Bohlmann. And, finally, my heartfelt thanks are extended to those brave women who shared their lives with me and who have never stopped fighting political injustice, especially the wrongs committed against women in war.

Part One *S*panish Women in the
Nineteenth and Twentieth Centuries

Chapter 1   The Awakening to Rebellion

In the late fifteenth century, the marriage of the Catholic rulers Isabella of Castille and Ferdinand of Aragon united the two wealthiest regions of Spain. The power of the two sovereigns was bolstered by the riches acquired during the so-called discovery of America and by the control exerted over Spanish citizens by means of the Royal Inquisition. Throughout the ensuing centuries Spain was controlled by an all-powerful monolith composed of the monarchy, church and military officials, landowners, and other sectors of the aristocracy.

Through serfdom, the empire continued to maintain both financial and ideological control over its citizens, even after the waning of its world power in the seventeenth century. In this largely agrarian society, the uneducated, landless masses were taught obedience to God and country, while the land-holding minority lived a life of excess. Women of the humble class were doubly bound by patriarchy and poverty: their minds were controlled by their confessors, and their bodies were controlled by their men. Women lived a life of abnegation and invisibility; they were ravaged by childbearing, excessive work, and general mistreatment.

Only in the late nineteenth century did a middle class begin to emerge, and with it a questioning of the social inequities that had prevailed since the formation of modern Spain. The year 1868 marks the timid beginning of ideological modernization for a cluster of liberals announced a revolution intended to overturn the reigning monolith and to achieve the secularization of the state. The first Spanish Republic lasted only from 1873 to 1874. Although the monarchy was quickly restored, the seeds of dissent had been planted.

A group of intellectuals known as the Krausists emerged.[1] In spite of persecution by the government, these thinkers managed to make significant contributions toward liberalizing education in Spain (which until then had been completely controlled by the church). They founded the Institución Libre de Enseñanza (Liberal Teaching Institute, or ILE); because the institute was not government funded, the Krausists were able to teach as freethinkers. The ILE would later influence the ideologues of the Second Spanish Republic, and the chasm created by the liberals and the reactionary monolith would lead Spain to its destruction during the years of the Spanish civil war.

The ILE made the first changes in Spanish attitudes about women, acknowledging—with reservations—the potential of the female mind. In 1868 Fernando de Castro, dean of the University of Madrid, established the "Sunday Lectures for the Education of Women," a remarkable feat in a country where in 1870 only 9.6 percent of women could read and write. The lectures revolved around women's roles as mothers and wives, but de Castro was also responsible for establishing the Ateneo for Women and the School for Female Teachers in 1869, both clearly designed to prepare women for public life.

The Krausists, ostracized in their ivory tower, managed to educate only a small number of women whose fathers had financial means and who were part of the freethinking minority. As the twentieth century began, the plight of unmarried, uneducated females was still deplorable. Prostitution was legal and white slave traffic plagued the country. The alternatives were working in the fields, serving in wealthy homes, or performing sweatshop labor alongside young boys. Wages for all of these jobs were meager; women could not afford to nourish themselves and therefore could not avoid the illnesses caused by substandard working conditions. A primarily rural country, Spain was divided into two classes. In his book on the causes of the Spanish civil war, Gerald Brenan writes of the first third of the century: "The first thing to notice is that Spain is one of those countries with an underdeveloped, primitive economy which is divided by a fairly definite line into two sections. Above are the upper and middle classes, say one-fifth of the population, who vote, read newspapers, compete for Government jobs and generally manage the affairs of the nation. Beneath are the peasants and workmen, who in ordinary times take no interest in politics, frequently do not know how to read and keep strictly to their own affairs."[2]

Little had changed from past centuries. In the 1930s landless laborers continued to make up three-quarters of the population. Brenan tells us that at that time wages in rural areas dropped to nearly half their previous level--and existed only when there was planting and harvesting to be done, a few months out of the year.[3] Nearly 60 percent of the working women of Spain in the early 1900s labored at agricultural tasks. But by the 1930s, industrial development had finally come to Spain and there was a tremendous shift of population from the countryside to the city. Approximately 40 percent of working women moved into domestic service. In industry, women worked primarily in textiles—especially in Barcelona, which had the most important textile industry in the country.

For an assessment of the general condition of working women, the textile industry provides a clear picture: women's salaries were roughly half those of men.[4] Women were ignored by the unions, and there was no allowance for pregnancy and childbirth. Even in the workplace women were expected to be subservient to men or to be "macho" to impress their male and female coworkers. Female farm workers received no wages, but instead were provided with meals that barely kept them on their feet to perform the grueling tasks of the field.

Women were still thought fit only for housewifery. In the early 1920s there was validity in Emilia Pardo Bazán's sarcastic indictment of "the queen of the home," whom she describes as "innocuous, ignorant . . . without culture or personality," whose house is full of "dirt and abandonment," and who knows only "the letters that the grocery clerks dispense for alphabet soup."[5] In 1919 and 1920 there were just 439 women in Spanish universities, a mere 2 percent of the student population.[6] The famed Generation of 1898 writers, which according to the canon was composed of males only, did not advocate a change of attitude. Even José Ortega y Gasset, the major thinker of early-twentieth-century Spain, maintained that women were not equipped for the real world.[7]

In the interim years between the First and Second republics (1873 to 1931), despite the struggle for power between the two Spains—that archconservative sector of church and state supported by the upper classes and the military, and the liberals who now were joined by a growing socialist and anarchist proletariat—the tradition of the ILE somehow survived and grew. In 1907 the Junta para Ampliación de Estudios e Investigaciones Científicas (Council for the Diffusion of Scientific Studies and Research) was created in keeping with the reformist ideals of the ILE. Francisco Giner de los Ríos and Manuel Cossio wished to continue the ILE tradition by bringing together a board of directors under the histologist and Nobel Prize Winner Santiago Ramón y Cajal, to promote scientific research abroad (mostly in Europe) for promising scholars. It was an endeavor that sought to internationalize study for Spaniards and to overturn the stagnation within the university system that afflicted both professors and students.

The junta was also instrumental in establishing the Residencia de Estudiantes in 1910 to house male students from the provinces. The residence became the hotbed for the most important intellectual activity in Spain from the 1910s to the 1930s. At various times many of the writers and other artists who today have acquired great fame lived there.[8]

In 1915 the Residence for Young Ladies was created under the auspices of the most active feminist and pedagogist of the early twentieth century in Spain, María de Maeztu. In 1913 she had begun a collaboration with the International Institute for Young Ladies in Spain. Maeztu was a central figure in the education of women and in the founding of cultural organizations until the outbreak of the civil war.

In 1926 Maeztu, in cooperation with members of the International Institute, organized the Lyceum Club; it was the first women's club in Madrid.[9] She became president, and other illustrious figures were elected vice presidents: for example, Isabel Oyarzabal de Palencia (1881–196?; pen name Beatriz Galindo)[10] and Spain's first female lawyer, Victoria Kent (1897–1987). The wives of many of Madrid's principal political and literary figures participated in the club's activities, which were primarily literary and scientific discussions and lectures. By 1930 there were some five hundred members and the club had a branch in Barcelona. The women were often the target of male ridicule and were described as a group of frivolous women taking tea and putting on airs. They were, above all, criticized because the club was "a real calamity for the home and a natural enemy of the family, and above all, of the husband. . . . The moral ambience of the street and the family would gain a great deal by hospitalizing or confining these eccentric and unbalanced females."[11] Because of their interest in literary and other cultural pursuits, they were considered "madwomen" who belonged "in the attic."[12] One wonders how any woman of those times had the energy to combat such relentless misogyny and patriarchal hysteria.

The writer María Teresa León recalls the ambience of the late 1920s in Madrid during the final years of the monarchy and the Primo de Rivera dictatorship:[13]

Spanish women! I think they moved around Madrid without much organization, without forming a battlefront except for a few feminist events— almost always seen as a joke by imprudent men. The international Residence for Young Ladies, directed by María de Maeztu, had been born and the institute had inaugurated its coed classes, which made the hair of the reactionary prudes stand on end. But women did not find a center until the Lyceum Club appeared.

In those years the eclipse of Primo de Rivera's dictatorship began. In the assembly rooms on Infantes Street there were conspiracies among the conferences and the teacups. That unusual female independence was furiously attacked. The scandal was taken to the pulpit; political bells were rung to destroy the rebellion of the skirts. . . . But others supported the experiment, and the Lyceum Club became the hard bone to chew with regard to feminine independence. . . . Those were the days when mockery and subversion were spreading through the streets of Madrid. The capricious monarchy of the times sustained the jolly dictator so that he would block entrance to something that was approaching. The Lyceum Club was not a gathering of women dancing with fans. It had challenged itself to advance the hands of Spain's clock.[14]

The critic Janet Perez, points out that the women were indeed beginning to change their views of themselves, as seen in their writings:

As a group, these women display a certain tendency to demythologization, modifying traditional views of women and of motherhood or rejecting them altogether. Theirs is a restrained,[15] but nevertheless determined nonconformity, no longer limited to noncommital presentation of injustices of the feminine condition. They express more audible dissent, not only portraying women who work or seek options beyond matrimony, but who reject patriarchally inscribed definitions of womanhood or deliberately transgress the patriarchally defined boundaries. The feminist movement per se makes its fictional debut in their works, and social criticism becomes a significant preoccupation.[16]

These organizations reflected the changing times, which would eventually result in the new democracy and freethinking of the 1930s. Female suffrage became, under the dictatorship of Primo de Rivera, for the first time an issue to be debated. It was proposed that women—except married women and prostitutes—be given the right to vote, though that law was never implemented during Primo's governance. He did, however, ask thirteen women to join the National Assembly—which had been founded to prepare a new constitution— and gave a number of women posts in the city council.[17]

Also in 1926, the Feminine Socialist Group of Madrid was convened to discuss women's rights. The well-known female lawyers Victoria Kent and Clara Campoamor (1888–1971) were among the lecturers. Even earlier, in 1920, the Feminine Youth University Group was formed. It later became the Spanish Association of University Women. An affiliate of the International Federation of University Women, which held its first conference at Bedford College in London in 1920 and its twelfth conference in Madrid in 1928,[18] the organization still exists today.

The feminist consciousness that had taken root in industrialized societies, especially the United States and England, was not the same in Spain. Still, several other women were advancing the destiny of Spanish women from a liberal or leftist viewpoint. Among these intellectuals was María Cambrils, a militant in the Socialist party in the 1920s who produced an anomalous document entitled *Feminismo socialista;* in the introductory note she politely requested that men permit their wives to read the book, so that "they can clearly recognize the freedom of citizenry."[19] The prologue to Cambrils' book was written by Clara Campoamor, a lawyer in the College of Madrid with a doctorate in law, who in the 1930s was to be the outstanding defender of female suffrage under the Second Spanish Republic. Carmen de Burgos (1867–1932) was another outspoken feminist, although her writing was until recently ignored by scholars,[20] as was the more political and sociological work of Cambrils, Campoamor, and Virginia González (one of the founders of the Communist party in Spain).

By 1920, according to Campo Alange, there were other "feminist entities": the woman of the Future and Feminine Progressive in Barcelona, the Spanish League for the Progress of Women, and the Concepción Arenal Society in Valencia. In 1920 the Feminine Social Action group met in Madrid.

These advances at the turn of the century reflect the attempt of women to empower themselves in the public sector. Yet the members of these organizations were largely of the middle class and represented a minority of women. The battle for educational equality in Spain would not change significantly until the 1970s. The attitudes of patriarchy would thwart and nullify women's efforts, as we shall observe in later chapters.

Several of the Spanish women who lived through the civil war period and testified to their experiences provide insights into the treatment of women in the early twentieth century. Educated or cultivated women consistently express the embarrassment experienced by their families because they read books or wished to have a career. As they describe their childhood, their education, and the social inequality in their country, they speak explicitly or implicitly of their rebellion. In fact, the remarks of the few well-known female writers in Spain during the nineteenth century are very similar to those of women in the twentieth century.[21] Even women who remained conservative throughout their lives and condoned the insurgent rebellion and subsequent civil war comment on the intolerable situation in which female children, teens, and adults were forced to live.

For instance, Mercedes Fórmica (1918–), who was born in the archconservative southern region of Andalusia and who later became a lawyer and activist in the Sección Femenina,[22] speaks of her childhood in the first volume of her autobiography:

> The fact that a female student of the Sacred Heart School would prepare herself for the university caused surprise and disgust, and I will always remember the scandalized gestures of my schoolmates in singing class when a lay sister called us "the college girls." The "college girls" was only one of us, the one who is writing this, who walked across the room feeling like a strange beast. It was a miracle that I didn't get a horrible complex at that time.[23]

Later she tells us:

> When my mother confided in her [Formica's teacher, a nun] that she wanted us to have a career, Mother Paul was perplexed. Since she cared a great deal for my mother, she tried to dissuade her, assuring her that if we went to the university we would never be able to marry in Seville. The female students occupied an ambiguous place as far as society was concerned; we seemed to be a mixture of prostitutes and comedy actresses.[24]

We will have occasion to remember the equation "intelligent female = prostitute" when we discuss activist women who were treated like whores. In essence, women protagonists of any situation were considered unacceptable and were made to feel like misfits because they had transgressed the societal rules that required women to remain in the shadow of men. And, of course, the most ignominious misfit was a whore.

María Teresa León in *Memoria de la melancolía,* which deals primarily with her experiences in exile, also describes her childhood in the early twentieth century. The daughter of an army colonel of noble ancestry, León from her earliest days displays a liberal streak. Her somewhat Joycean narrative style depicts her as she watches her life pass before her. For instance, she describes a conversation with a grade-school classmate who asks her incredulously about books she has read (all of which seem to cause a scandal, since novels were traditionally considered filth, no matter what their topic):

> You read Dumas? The girl told that María Teresa León read prohibited books. No! Yes! And Victor Hugo? I've also read him. Of course, your mother supervises you so little. . . . And that uncle of yours! And I shouted, And my aunt! My aunt was the first woman in Spain to study in a university! Too bad for you. The devil's work. Don't be stupid, you

nun. I'm not yet, but I will be. Nice future. And you will be . . . a mother, right? This girl. Silence was imposed on us. The teacher came by. "Why are you crying, María Teresa?" I stood up like a wounded virgin. "Because I read Alexander Dumas." "Who?" "Alexander Dumas." Well, sit down. They asked their confessor if it was a sin.[25]

León succeeds in presenting the ignorance and fanaticism that constituted a young girl's education at the turn of the century with comicality, unlike most of the other writers, whose tone is primarily critical.

Pilar Jaraiz Franco, born in 1916, niece of the dictator Francisco Franco, became a lawyer and later a professor. Her autobiography[26] describes her strict childhood, her sympathy toward her uncle's politics (she even spent time in a Republican prison during the war), and her gradual, remarkable move toward socialism in the post-Franco era. With irony she sums up the situation of women of her class in the early part of the century:

> Women . . . lived highly conditioned by certain taboos, some of which and their outcomes have unfortunately still not disappeared completely. What could a señorita do who belonged to the privileged class of the navy[27] in a city like Ferrol besides busy herself with housework, dream of her Prince Charming in the form of a lieutenant, and pray for the salvation of an unhealthy child-king who could provide hope and save our endangered country?[28]

Later, referring to the wars with Morocco[29] at the beginning of the twentieth century; she says:

> While all this was happening, life continued in Ferrol, routine and peaceful, women at home or at church. . . . My mother, Pilar Franco, studied teaching, and the fact that a woman from a good family studied was not at all normal in those times. We all know that women in Spain were educated to marry and that was it. The instruction that the daughters of comfortable families received then was, in the best of situations, about managing the home, notions about cooking, sewing, and a thing or two that one learned in school in those days.[30]

In María Lejárraga's autobiographical text about the collaborative effort she and her husband carried out in the world of the theater, she says: "My mother had received a sublime education, abnormal in her childhood. She had not gone to school—a horror in the mid-nineteenth century—but she had had French female professors."[31]

Constancia de la Mora is the most "scandalous" female dissident in contemporary Spanish history. The granddaughter of Antonio Maura, one of Spain's major conservative political statesmen, de la Mora was eventually to rebel against her aristocratic upbringing, divorce her philandering husband, remarry, and become a Communist. Her autobiography gives many examples of the strictures of Spanish society in the first third of the century. Born in 1906, de la Mora describes her early years, underlining the oppression that dictated the lives of young women of her class. She tells us of her childhood days when the family summered in a fashionable resort in the Basque country.

In Zarauz I became a rebel against my heritage. Although it took twenty years and more to develop, I remember distinctly that my first feeling of hostility to my surroundings, my people, my life, was born in Zarauz. For this summer resort was almost exclusively peopled by the Spanish aristocracy with a sprinkling of the diplomats accredited to the Court. . . . And although I played every morning on the beach and every afternoon in the various parks of the Villas with small children bearing the beautiful and sonorous great Spanish names, I always felt, even as a child, something unutterable that kept me from really liking them or being one of them.[32]

Her description of the schooling of upper-class Spanish women is the most enlightening treatise available about this period, yet her autobiography has generally been ignored by historians. She indicts the church repeatedly for shaping and maintaining the rigid social mores over the centuries. She speaks of the education received in the upscale Handmaidens of the Sacred Heart School in Madrid, which opened in about 1915 "for the daughters of the rich and great."[33] It was a Jesuit school, the counterpart of the most progressive boys' school of that time. De la Mora notes that nuns were only slightly familiar with the subjects taught—geography, religion, English literature, history, and art. She remarks that Spanish literature was virtually untouched, which is not surprising; the church had always considered the country's literature innately heretical because much of it provoked critical thinking about Spanish institutions.[34]

De la Mora also describes the school's taboo against making intimate friendships. She tells us, "I always wondered what the nuns meant when they said that the devil stood between two people—even two twelve-year-old schoolgirls—when they talked alone."[35] Yet this school was a paradise compared to the boarding school where Constancia was sent when her mother became pregnant. (The family considered it scandalous for Constancia to witness the swelling of her mother's belly and the biological process of maternity.)

After six years of unhappiness in the boarding school, de la Mora was finally sent off to a convent in Cambridge. Permitted to have close friends and to study literature, she remarks: "I stayed in England from 1920 to 1923 without once returning to Spain. It was the one happy period of my life my parents gave me."[36] Freedom was limited, she notes, but included coed activities; and the English nuns did not regard most activities as leading to mortal sin. She later adds: "As the time grew nearer for my final return to Spain, I became more and more gloomy. I felt like a prisoner going to his execution rather than a young girl preparing for her debut."[37] De la Mora made one last attempt to remain in England; she wrote her parents asking for permission to remain there to work in a dress shop. She was quickly rescued by her horrified mother, who took her to Paris to buy clothes for her coming-out party.

In her text, she intersperses anecdotes about her personal life with constant judgments about the political situation in Spain. De la Mora returned to a country that was already in a state of ferment. In the midst of the Primo de Rivera dictatorship and with the bloody defeat in Morocco in 1921, the government was tottering. But de la Mora would continue the course plotted by her parents for a few more years.

My coming-out was the first step in the life my parents had planned for me. After that, for a year or so, I could flirt, and dance and go to parties—always at my mother's side of course. Then my father would examine the social and financial position of my beaux. At nineteen, I would be officially engaged to a solid, sensible gentleman with money and position. At twenty, I would have a great church wedding, a Paris trousseau, and a three months' wedding trip.

And after that—well, but after that there was nothing to talk about. My life would be secure, settled, begun and ended at the same time.

My mother met me in England with considerable excitement. She was to be the general of the delicate maneuvers of the next three years of my life. I had been brought up like all rich children of Spain by nurses and governesses and stewards and nuns. My mother hardly knew the child called Constancia. But now that I was officially an adult, now that I was ready to enter the Madrid marriage market, my mother took up the reins of my life. Only middle-class people sent their daughters out with old crones, chaperons hired by the hour to trot behind the girl on the streets. My mother, as befitted a lady of the aristocracy, became, from the moment she met me in Cambridge until the day of my marriage, very nearly my constant companion. Without my mother I would not be able to set foot on the streets—only by her side could I go to those parties and dances which would make my life gay. We were to be inseparable, my mother and I—and the truth of the matter was that neither of us really liked the other. I had been taught in school to love and obey my parents. All I could do was to try to obey my mother—for she was nearly a stranger to me—a stranger with queer tastes, strange values, irritating habits.[38]

The estrangement of upper-class parents from their children was customary in those days, inasmuch as the children were brought up by nannies and nuns and sent off to boarding schools. They were, nevertheless, brought home to conform to the social mores of parents and relatives. Although this routine seemed to be meekly accepted by most upper-class young women, Constancia de la Mora was to prove a great disappointment to her parents when she rebelled against their conservative politics and lifestyle.

Isabel Oyarzábal de Palencia was born in 1881, decades before most of the other women discussed here, who were still teenagers or young adults when the civil war broke out. Isabel's father was from a prominent Andalusian family and her mother was Scottish—and though she became a Roman Catholic years after her marriage to Oyarzábal, she did not exhibit the repressive tactics of the Spaniards in her child-rearing techniques. Yet Palencia was sent to a Catholic boarding school, like most children of upper-class families. She describes the source of her "unhappiness" in detailing the daily routine of school.

The rules of the convent were very strict. We rose at a quarter to six and were taken down to chapel for Mass and meditation. Then we were given one quarter of an hour for breakfast and sent up to our classrooms for lessons or study until eleven-thirty when we had our dinner, followed by our first half hour of recreation outside. Then two hours of sewing while someone read aloud from the lives of the saints. More study and another half hour's recreation, followed by studies until our six o'clock supper, after which we had one hour of supposedly free time, but we had to employ it in singing or joining in a sort of general conversation under the control of the nun on duty.

She goes on tell us that life would have been more bearable if they had been permitted to "speak to each other at least during meals. But talking was strictly forbidden all day, and the slightest infraction was punished with a bad mark or with having to kiss the floor in public."[39]

Palencia longed to be at home with her brother. She was bored with her classes, although she excelled (except in lacemaking). Palencia describes an epiphanic moment in her life, which would later catapult her into activism against her own class. Unaware of the poverty that had plagued her country for so many centuries, she recounts a conversation she had with one of the overseers at her aunt's latifundio in Andalusia. When she questioned him about the hungry look of the people who worked the land, he replied: "How do you wish them to be, señorita? . . . They are hungry. Just hungry, day in and day out they are always the same." . . . "I looked at him with astonishment. I had never before realized that hunger could be something more than a passing discomfort." When Palencia questioned him about why he as overseer did not help them, he retorted: "But, how can I feed a family of six with fifty centimos a day? I work from sunrise to sunset for fifty centimos. We just manage to get a plate of gazpacho once a day."[40]

This conversation, Palencia explains, prompted her to begin to do charity work, traditional among wealthy women in Spain. Also traditional was the price for those who received it if they had "revolutionary" political convictions. On one occasion, while visiting a sick widower with four small children, Isabel was cautioned that she had to extort a promise that the individuals to whom she gave would go to church and take the holy sacraments. She says that her father remarked: "You may take all you want from the house for anyone who needs it, but you must take care not to encourage people who are undisciplined. That man is probably a socialist."[41]

Isabel's desire "to do something" with her life—other than become a nun like her sister—was thwarted by her father's sentiment: "You don't need to. . . . You can have all you want at home."[42] He was, of course, referring to the fact that they had no financial problems. Spanish women of standing were prohibited from working because it was considered a reflection on the father's ability to provide for them.[43] After her father's death, though, Palencia still entertained thoughts of being an actress or a writer. She hid a half-written manuscript, in order not to be caught in such a shameful endeavor. "Through it all I felt I was doing what would finally estrange me from the people I knew. At times I was frightened and would ask myself if it would not be better and safer not to try to swim against the current. But the answer was always 'No.' "[44]

When Palencia was invited to study acting in Madrid, the opposition of friends in her archconservative town, Málaga, and that of her family, created a great deal of pressure. The stage was still considered immoral for women.[45] As we have seen, any sort of prominence was taboo, and the stage provided the most radical form of prominence. Her mother, an exceptional woman who did not oppose Palencia's search for her identity and for visibility, accompanied her to Madrid to study; but Palencia became bored with the stage and turned back to writing. She founded a women's magazine and describes her fear of appearing too daring in her writing: "I realized, of course, that it would be necessary to use caution so as not to frighten our future readers or their censors. *La dama,* as we decided to call the magazine, must be frivolous enough to be attractive, deep enough to achieve its purpose, and subservient enough to custom not to provoke criticism."[46]

It is obvious that the need to be both frivolous and subservient to avoid the wrath of male critics would not make for a particularly enlightening magazine for women. But her apprenticeship work on the magazine led her to a job as a correspondent in a news bureau, which further stimulated her political consciousness. Like de la Mora, Palencia describes her personal development alongside her intellectual and political awakening (circa 1910):

> Undoubtedly, I owed much to this new work, for through it I began to understand for the first time what Spain really was, how and where she stood in relation to the rest of the world and, above all, what new developments were taking place within her frontiers.
>
> I discovered that small party politics, and the interjection of the church and army into public life, had kept the country in an abject state of poverty and ignorance. Over fifty-two per cent of the population was illiterate. The wages, especially for workers of the land, were disgracefully low. There was no limit to working hours, and living conditions even in the capital were a disgrace. Child mortality in Spain was among the highest in the countries in Europe, and as for an outside policy, it did not exist. Meanwhile in Madrid the conservative and liberal parties succeeded each other in a poor imitation of British Whigs and Tories. Every time there was a change of cabinet, a legion of civil employees lost their posts to the new arrivals and went home to twiddle their thumbs and hope for a prompt defeat of their political opponents.
>
> The only hopeful sign was to be found in the labor movement. Under the guidance of Pablo Iglesias the workers were being organized into unions and were fighting corrupt politicians while they strove to better conditions for the people. The words "general suffrage" had until then meant nothing, but every new election brought a change, at least in the big cities where the seats were strongly contested and often won from nepotists in power.[47]

Palencia's description of Spanish social conditions is very similar to those found in texts written about the 1930s. The major difference after some twenty years was that socialist leader Pablo Iglesias' efforts had born fruit and the syndicated workers' organizations—with the reluctant blessing of the liberal Republican government—had already begun to frighten the church, state, and military factions, setting the stage for war.

The Countess María Campo Alange (1902–) became an accomplished writer of historical and sociological studies, especially about Spanish women. Married to an aristocrat, she was a strict traditionalist and left Spain during the war, returning when the bloodbath had ended. Her description of her childhood in Seville is enlightening. She begins her autobiography with a dialogue between herself as an adult and herself as a child. The adult self asks the child why she considers herself ignorant. The child replies: "Because they don't want me to study, or read, or know anything about anything. . . . Also I see things everywhere that are prohibited, prohibited, prohibited. The truth, the truth is that they don't want me to learn to think critically. Mother, who is very intelligent, and my confessor, who is a stupid idiot, are in agreement that knowledge would be bad for me."[48]

Campo Alange then talks about her life in Seville: "The world of my youth—like that of my childhood—was populated with guardian angels and devils lying in wait, souls in purgatory. . . . In society, two different languages were used: language men used when they were alone or in the company of prostitutes . . . the other, men's language when they were with 'respectable' or respected women, was also the normal one among these latter women."[49]

It is curious that the role of prostitutes is clearly defined, whereas among the upper classes she suggests that there were women who were either considered respectable because of their social class or were truly respected because of their virtue. This confirms de la Mora's suggestion that hypocrisy was flagrant among women of the upper classes, though among the lower classes a woman was either a saint or a whore and was treated without ambiguity. The rules of patriarchy were set in stone only for poor women, who were the slaves of upper-class men *and* women.[50] Campo Alange adds: "On another level of things, the masculine criteria reigned, while the feminine were paltry and inoperative. Old age is premature with our present criteria and sexual repression strong. Result: hypocrisy and fanaticism."[51]

María Lejárraga, a prolific creative writer of dramatic works and essays, was also one of the few "modern" feminists in Spain. She championed the rights of women in most of her literary work, as is visible throughout *Una mujer por caminos de España,* which she wrote under the name María Martínez Sierra while on political campaign tours in 1933 and 1936.[52] Lejárraga incessantly laments the difficulty of making women aware of the need for education and the right to vote. Unlike the other early writers, she came from an enlightened family of liberals. She was educated at home until she went to school to prepare herself for a career, which was extraordinary for a Spanish woman in those days. Even as a young child, she noticed the extreme division between rich and poor, for her father was a country doctor (though he barely managed to feed his large family). Still, it was not until Lejárraga became a teacher in the poor section of Madrid that she came to grips with the real meaning of poverty.

It was in my youth, from age twenty-three to thirty-three, as a teacher in the working-class neighborhoods of Madrid, that I came to know profoundly, through the children, the black misery of Madrid's proletariat of those times. I remember that once I proposed to my students (girls of seven to fourteen) a composition with the following theme: "What would you like to do during one whole day that would make you completely happy?" And I also remember—and my heart is torn as I recall it—that 70 percent of the participants responded, "I would go to a cafe and eat steak and potatoes." "I would go to brunch and eat breaded filets and fried fish and egg custard." "I would eat ham and omelets and lamb chops and many pastries." I still remembered, when the civil war broke out, those yellowed sheets of school paper on which, with bad handwriting and uncertain spelling, the Madrid children confessed to their hunger because what else, in the midst of daily, hopeless hunger, can produce the dream of happiness like a steak, a filet, or a lamb chop?[53]

Lejárraga's book is, to some extent, a political treatise on Spain's injustices, as are Palencia's and de la Mora's works. But Lejárraga is not just a spectator, as she tells us. Hers is also a theoretical and practical treatise, which shows her personal knowledge of socialist materialism and its tenets; she puts all her observations in that context, often with great emotion. Her remarks about poor Spanish women in the countryside illustrate this very well. Speaking of the hungry, retarded condition of children at the onset of the Republic, she adds: "That was the Spain we found on the birth of the Republic! . . . These emaciated and aged women—who knew if a woman from the Castilian or Andalusian countryside was twenty-five or two hundred fifty?"[54]

In another passage, Lejárraga dwells on the plight of the hungry agrarian population:

The women atrophied and aged in their efforts to continue their incessant maternity. "It's the only luxury the poor have," Santiago Rusinol[55] has said, bringing children into the world and burying them, sending them, as the women say, like angels, to heaven. The men crushed beneath the double weight of hard and badly paid work and forced idleness . . . and all of them, women, children, men, consumed by the chronic fever of slow hunger, of interminable hunger.[56]

She constantly comments on the condition of women in the family and hopes that when women begin to write about women, they will have a better chance to improve their condition. In one of her campaign speeches, she says: "Mothers have been talked about a great deal, about the abnegation of the mothers, the love of mothers for their children. Mothers have become the familiar idol simply because until recently, men have made literature, but when women begin to write!"[57] Lejárraga obviously views herself not only as the spokesperson for the Socialist party, but also as the single most important writer and orator championing women's rights in Spain at that time.

The texts cited above were written by aristocrats and cultured, middle-class women. Most maintained the same social and political standing all their lives (such as Campo Alange, in spite of her indictment of the hypocrisy motivated by the double standards of the Catholic church), while a precious few (such as de la Mora and Palencia) rebelled.

When the women of the lower classes speak, their stories are obviously from radically different viewpoints; their socioeconomic and religious experiences were not the same as those of the upper-class women. Precisely because they had grown up within a class embattled with conservative institutions, they frequently escaped the pedagogical oppression of the church. They were often awakened to the injustice of their poverty through political indoctrination, as we shall observe through the quintessential example of Dolores Ibárruri, the Communist leader known as La Pasionaria. They frequently received some sort of education within their political groups. And in contrast to the wealthy women, their fathers often did not oppose their rebellion, but encouraged it.

Given the widespread illiteracy of women before the 1930s and their strict social roles, there is little possibility that a proletarian woman would have written down her life story before that time. The only writings by women of the working class were provoked by the Spanish civil war and the need of these women to tell their stories of activism and subsequent imprisonment and exile.

Soledad Real, who became an activist as a teenager and spent sixteen years in Franco's prisons, describes the contrast of her conservative, religious mother and her politicized father, who indoctrinated her. In her autobiographical *Las cárceles de Soledad Real,* transcribed by the journalist Consuelo García, we find:

> For political and religious reasons there was constant quarreling in my house. My mother, in her religiousness, felt very alone because none of the three of us turned out religious. But my mother made the mistake of people in her era of trying to impose it on us, and my father won the game in this because he never imposed anything on us. The three of us became revolutionaries because we all took after our father, since we ad-mired him more.[58]

Real's education ended at age seven, when she was sent home from school. Because it was a charity school, according to Real, it was typical that once a child had taken Holy Communion, the school authorities felt that they had provided that child with a basic education. Real began to work at age nine. She was literally the "breadwinner;" that is to say, her tiny contribution per-mitted her family to buy bread for the week. But at age sixteen, Real became politicized. Her education came from the streets, where she was awakened to social injustice and her own needs as a woman, especially as a woman of the lower class.

Juana Doña's *Desde la noche y la niebla* is also about life in Franco's pris-ons. She was given the death sentence, which was later commuted to thirty years; she spent eighteen years altogether in prison. Unlike most of the girls in her working-class neighborhood, Doña went to a tuitioned school:

> I was in that school till I was fourteen. And then my parents decided I knew enough: I could read and write. . . . But I became a Communist at fourteen. It was because of my father. He wasn't a Communist, he was a "fellow traveler." When I joined in 1933, there were a hundred militants in Madrid. Seven were women. I was the eighth to join the youth group. My father subscribed to a traveling library. There was Marxist literature and, more important, the Communist songs of those times—"The Inter-national," "The Young Guards." When I would hear the part about the "pariahs of the land," I'd cry. I didn't know what that meant, but I knew it was something awful. There was a young Communist on my street; he belonged to the Communist party. I asked him to explain about the pari-ahs. He gave me a tremendous lecture about them and I said, from that moment on, "I'm a Communist." He took me to sign up for the youth group. I was an integral Communist from the very beginning. I left child-hood from that moment on. I became an activist twenty-four hours a day.[59]

The simplicity and naiveté with which Doña describes her embracing of Communist ideology is typical of most of the activists who have written their stories or given testimony.

In her unpublished and untitled autobiography, Marisa Bravo, who also spent several years in prison, describes her politicization and how, as a child, she was embroiled in political activities because of her father. Bravo's incomplete work reveals many lapses in her memory, shows a rudimentary ability to write, and suggests a bout with mental illness after prison. In addition, in discussing her work with her, I learned that even after Franco's death her family disapproved of her memoirs; in fact, she kept the manuscript hidden and only pulled it out from under a pillow when I asked if I could make a copy, expressing fear that her daughter would arrive at any moment and try to destroy the document.

Bravo could remember no formal education as a child except for the typical seamstress school that so many poor teenage girls attended. Her education, like that of many others, was derived from the political activities she witnessed and experienced in the street and in her family life. Yet in her later years she served as an instructor of small children, probably under the auspices of the Communist party, in which she remained active until her mysterious death at the end of the 1980s.

Rosario Sánchez was a well-known *miliciana*[60] in Spain. She lost a hand on the battlefield at the start of the war and was known as Rosie the Dynamiter. Sánchez became politicized through her sewing class in Madrid. She emphasizes that even before she left her hometown for the big city, her father, the town blacksmith, made her aware of social injustice.

> In my home there was constant talk of politics. My father was always
> there with friends talking of politics. And I was always listening, of
> course. My father had this funny quirk: he'd go around at night and
> change the street names that were named after reactionary political fig-
> ures to ones like "Mariana Pineda." I can remember the poor, poor, poor
> farm laborers, who had nothing but themselves and maybe a donkey—
> not even a horse! They would go out with their donkeys and collect a
> faggot of wood, wood that was city property. And because of that misera-
> ble bundle of wood, for which they would earn a few pennies, the Civil
> Guards would be there waiting to burn it! I suffered so much. I was just
> a child. How I suffered! And I thought, "But my father charged this man
> more just to fix his farm tools than this bundle of wood is worth!"[61]

Even though in the 1920s and 1930s it was the child of the Left who was more likely to become indoctrinated politically through family and friends, female children were usually raised according to the church's teachings because of their mother's influence. Maruja Cuesta tells us that she questioned her staunch Catholicism when she found it necessary to rebel against the social injustices that the church either condoned or ignored. She felt, for instance, that her education had been truncated because of financial inequalities in Spain.

I come from a middle-class family in which my parents worked very hard to raise their children. So that the life we have lived, the times we lived in—such hard times! My father had a shoe repair shop. My teacher wanted me to study, but I wasn't able to finish, precisely because of the hard times. And then the war came. I was a young girl then who had very Catholic inclinations, but because of my sense of justice, I rebelled against a lot of things I didn't like. . . . I wanted to study and couldn't. My professor was a Catalonian woman, a magnificent teacher who dedicated herself completely to her students, and she especially liked me and wanted me to have a career. If my father hadn't been a shop owner, I could have had a scholarship to study. But he didn't make enough money to pay for a daughter's career. Consequently, my teacher fought many battles; she wanted me to go to live with her and her family in Madrid. The problem was that I would have had to pay room and board, and my parents couldn't do it. This was in February of 1936.[62]

Nieves Torres, in discussing women's development during the war, remarks on her education before that time:

The war prepared women little by little. Courses were organized for them by people with more education. For instance, in a workshop if there was a woman who had studied, she gave classes to the others. There were a lot of illiterates then. At that time, most studied until the age of twelve, starting at age six. Well, you can imagine the kind of education you ended up with. If you were lucky enough to have a good teacher . . . but if you were from a small town like mine, where the teacher spent most of her time cooking for her husband and children, who gave us tasks to do while she ran home—well, I mean, you learned next to nothing. I learned to read, write, multiply, and divide, but Spanish history, for example, nothing—don't ask me anything about history! I never missed one day of class because for me and my parents, that was sacred. Then my father died when I was twelve, and everything changed. People thought women didn't have to know even how to read and write. They only had to know how to mend sheets. What ignorance! But that's what the capitalists and some men continue to think: that women are just for the kitchen and the bedroom.[63]

The Hegelian "secularization of spirituality," which had begun in the latter part of the nineteenth century in Spain, became more obvious in the twentieth century as the lower classes grew more rebellious toward the church's teachings of humility and poverty—teachings that were not prescribed for the ruling classes. This fault line between rich and poor would become wider in the 1930s with the Second Spanish Republic. As we shall see, for more than five years the forces would clash. Finally, as if victim to the apocalyptic nature of an earthquake, Spain would be plunged into an irrevocable nightmare of violence and destruction.

Chapter 2   Visible Women of the Second Spanish Republic

The beginning of radical social and political change in Spain came in 1931 with the establishment of the Second Spanish Republic. A secular, democratic government, during its short five-year life it attempted to initiate sweeping social and political reforms. At first, the majority of the population acquiesced to the new government (labeled the "Niña Bonita": literally, the cute girl), since it appeared to be a rather benign change. The king and queen had gone into exile, profoundly disconcerted by the lack of loyalty displayed by their subjects. A cluster of "liberals"—Republicans of center or left-of-center politics and Socialists—dominated the government, many of whom had been influenced by the ILE. The minister of war, Manuel Azaña, a confirmed anticlericalist, hastily orchestrated a separation of church and state and created a land-reform policy that produced immediate consternation among members of the power monolith.

The government clamored for reform in the military and, of course, a secular and improved educational system. Efforts along these lines had begun a century before, but (with the exception of the examples we have cited) had been undermined by the policies of both church and state. The final outcome of the separation of church and state dispute was the cancellation of the state subsidy for the church and the loss of ecclesiastical power in government affairs. In addition, the church was dominated by the state, since Catholic education was eliminated and public events sponsored by the church had to be authorized by the state.[1] Aniceto Alcalá Zamora, the interim prime minister and a staunch Catholic, relinquished his post and Azaña took over in October 1931. The response by the church was immediate: the primate of Spain published a letter accusing the Republic of communism and atheism, and other important members of the church hierarchy followed suit. Churches and convents were burned and the polarization of Spain, brewing since the nineteenth century, became more radical. By 1932 General José Sanjurjo had attempted the first military coup against the Republic.[2]

All of the reforms that the Republic strove for required large sums of money. Although Spain had been affected less by the 1929 Wall Street crash than other countries, it was not in good shape financially; the peseta, after a slow rise, dropped when foreign interests did not show confidence in the Niña Bonita. The wealthy, of course, wished no change at all; the proletariat and farm workers, of course, wanted hasty and visible reform. Stanley Payne succinctly describes the "precocious liberalism" phenomenon that took place in Spain during the Republic:

> The Second Spanish Republic represented an attempt at democratization in the very moment that the direction of political change in the rest of Europe was toward authoritarianism, whether conservative, fascist, or communist. It ended with the dismal spectacle of the only country in the history of the twentieth century whose polity completely broke down into revolutionary/counterrevolutionary civil war without experiencing major involvement in foreign war, colonialism, or outside intervention.
>
> This was the fault neither of clericalism nor of anticlericalism but of two other aspects of the Spanish situation. One of these was the inherent conflict between the country's political precocity—combined with the advanced cultural and institutional norms of its modern elites—and its social and economic backwardness. A maximally explosive combination was produced: optimal freedom and opportunity for the development of sociopolitical conflict contrasted with very limited means for its deflection or resolution.[3]

The church and its constituents began to mobilize, and the outcome was the creation in 1933 of CEDA (Spanish Confederation of Autonomous Rightist Groups). The confederation was led by a young law professor, José María Gil Robles, who immediately became a hero of the archconservative Catholics in Spain. The division between the "two Spains" became more and more apparent as the privileged fought for the status quo and the poor clamored for change through strikes, assassinations, and uprisings.

In spite of Spain's downward spiral in the 1930s, some changes significant to women were initiated by the "precociously liberal" and well-meaning government. The first authentic social reform that would affect women was implemented. Divorce was legalized. Republican and leftist women's organizations flourished. Beginning with the suffrage debate in Parliament in 1931, during which female suffrage became a constitutional right, women gained more national attention than ever before. The Republican scenario was to prepare women—both visible women, who were serving in the public sector, and invisible women, who had previously never ventured out of their private domain—for the challenge of the civil war, turning them into public citizens of new dimensions and new identities. As the battle over the issue of female suffrage ensued, the three women in Parliament, the Radical Socialists Victoria Kent and Clara Campoamor and the Socialist Margarita Nelken (1896–1968) were closely monitored by the press and by all Spanish citizens who had any political orientation. Many women's organizations rallied to their cause. Campoamor created the Female Republican Union, to promote the vote for women; María Lejárraga, with Campoamor and Regina García, established the Foundation for Women. The National Association of Spanish Women (ANME), created in 1918 and headed by the activist María Espinosa, also lobbied for female suffrage, as did the more liberal Union of Spanish Women (UME) and the Lyceum Club.[4] Out of the National Association grew the Superior Feminist Council of Spain, also headed by Espinosa.

Whereas Campoamor championed women's suffrage wholeheartedly, Kent and Nelken concerned themselves more with party politics—as did most of the visible women during the Republic and the Spanish civil war. They were against giving women the vote at that moment in history. They saw women as a group to which they did not really belong, believing that their education and experience had made them exceptional. If we analyze their arguments on suffrage, it becomes clear that Kent and Nelken took the political position of their male counterparts. Their rationale was obvious; they felt that, given the possibility of voting, women would not think for themselves because of their scant sophistication in political matters, but instead would let their husbands and confessors decide their votes.

The strong ties between the church and the majority of females in Spain until the civil war had truncated the possibility of feminism or any semblance of independent, critical thinking. For the church advocated not only women's innocence in pedagogical matters, but also their subservience to males—priests, husbands, fathers, or any other male relative who was responsible for the chastity[5] of his female charges. As Margarita Nelken had pointed out in the 1920s: "Doubtless . . . if women were to intervene in our political life, they would be inclined very sensitively toward the reactionary spirit, since women here—the majority of them, even before they are Christians, even before they are religious beings—are meek disciples of their confessors, who are, we must not forget, their mentors."[6]

By 1931 Nelken had not substantially changed her opinion; she was, after all, a dyed-in-the-wool anticlericalist. Speaking of the feminist movement among the middle class, she remarked, "There are still fewer women who are

spiritually emancipated today than there are women who would ask their confessor for orders or who would let themselves be guided with docility by those
who exploit their natural feminine conservatism in the home."[7] Nelken purported to have done her homework in this area, and stated categorically that
"there is not a single women who will confess that she has not been interrogated by her confessor about her political ideologies."[8]

Kent claimed that women in 1931 were not yet educated enough to vote.
In a key statement that shows her desire to have the suffrage question post-
poned, she says:

> I express myself in this fashion in renunciation of my feminine ideal be-
> cause that is what the health of the Republic requires. Because I have
> committed myself to serving the Republic, I rise to beg the chamber to
> arouse the Republican conscience and to delay the granting of the femi-
> nine vote. I request this not because I am trying to diminish the capacity
> of women in the least; no, deputies, it is not a question of capacity, it is a
> question of opportunity for the Republic.[9]

Ultimately, it is clear that Kent's reaction emanated from the same issue
that concerned Nelken: that women would vote conservatively because of pres-
sures at home and at church. Kent spoke again on this topic: "If Spanish women
were all workers, if Spanish women had gone to the university and had become
liberated, I would stand up in front of the entire chamber to ask for the feminine vote."[10] In contrast, Campoamor accused the members of Parliament of
attempting to defeat the suffrage proposal for purely political reasons and of
disregarding the human rights question. She argued that only those "who think
that women are not human beings could deny their equal rights with men."[11]

The final suffrage debates were considered amusing by many of the four
hundred sixty-seven male members of Parliament. They jested about the three
female members, especially the feminist Campoamor. She was described as "a
wounded lioness . . . a colorful figure in the masculine Assembly, shouting in
the desert."[12] The journalists wrote that the feminist groups who waited outside
Parliament to cheer Campoamor on to victory were "picturesque." Kent was
described in this fashion: "She speaks like a man; no, more like a political boss.
But her speech, cold, empty, praises her party and the radicals."[13] Campoamor
lobbied, fought, and won, after several attempts by other members to limit or
postpone the decision. Nelken did not attend on the day of the vote. The
conservatives had supported female suffrage, astutely confident that confessional politics would bear fruit in 1933.

Of the women visible in the political arena at the time, only Campoamor and the playwright María Lejárraga had been in favor of female suffrage. In 1933 the conservatives won the elections, and the "disaster" was attributed to the female vote. Lejárraga comments negatively on this matter in one of the strongest indictments of the church's control of women:

Spanish women will have in their hands the ability to vote, which until today has interested them very little. Our campaigns without a doubt have reached a few selected middle-class groups in Madrid, but the enthusiasm of the members of the Lyceum Club or the Feminine Association of Civic Education—the homes of our feminism—are nothing but—why fool ourselves?—a type of polished snobism.

The organizations of female workers in the big industrial cities have prepared their members better through union action, but in general the Spanish female is accustomed to considering political activity as one more vice, or at least as a waste of time typical of men. A little more than thirty months of Republic have not been able to cure this prejudice. The great amorphous masses, the women of the provincial middle class, the women who work in union organizations, the female farm laborers, are not at all prepared to exercise their right to vote; they don't have any idea of what it means to vote.

On the other hand, the Spanish clergy has mobilized its followers, has put its formidable means into action, and each parish, each confessional, is a forum for fiercely anti-Republican propaganda.

This makes one quite afraid of the result of the female vote. It's not that Spanish women are too Christian. Their clergymen have kept them in a state of such ignorance over the centuries that, to tell the truth, there are few Spanish women . . . who know how to recite the creed. . . . The only religious duty that is universally understood by the devout Spanish female is to do whatever the priest says.[14]

Campoamor was not reelected to Parliament, although she had been the most active female member. Her outspoken nature and her unpopular causes were the chief reason for her ostracism from the political front lines. Perhaps the most ironic blow was the fact that Campoamor had sacrificed her career by championing the right to female suffrage, yet women did not vote for her in subsequent elections. They had been trained to vote against their own liberation.

During her term in office, particularly after her defense of the divorce law (which Nelken also had supported) and then female suffrage, Campoamor was constantly heckled and interrupted by her colleagues, especially when she brought up questions dealing with the civil rights of women and children. Yet she was undaunted by the relentless badgering of her peers. If we contemplate the odds against her, Campoamor was enormously successful. Listen as she discusses the treatment she received:

> When those memorable sessions of masculine nervousness spun out of control, a state of parliamentary aggression, in the form of attacks, was showered on me; not on my principles or objectives, but instead personal, sometimes insultingly humorous remarks about my interventions. I don't know if they were hoping that the interruptions, the jokes, and the sarcasm would silence me. They did not understand my resoluteness, placed at the service of a cause, just as they did not understand themselves. In spite of the fact that their attitude hurt me, an attitude that I do not hesitate to call desperate—and it did hurt me—I was not ready to sacrifice my legitimate rights to the others, my personal dignity, even my own political future, and the rights and interests of all Spanish women, whom I had the sorrow or the satisfaction of defending in those stormy sessions.[15]

Campoamor continued to be very active after she lost in the 1933 elections. She was appointed head of public welfare, though she resigned from that post and left the Radical party after observing the devastation inflicted by the government during the Revolution of Asturias in 1934.[16] In 1935 she headed the Pro-Infancia Obrera group, which had been organized to help the families of the Asturian miners wounded or jailed when government and colonial troops marched in to quell the rebellion.

Campoamor made attempts to join the Republican Left in these years before the war but was summarily rejected. The attitude of male politicians had not substantially changed. Campoamor's "mortal sin," as she called it, was her undaunted feminism and defense of women's suffrage. In 1938 she went into exile in Argentina. In Buenos Aires she abandoned all political activity and dedicated herself to literature. At the end of the forties and in the early fifties she made several attempts to return to Spain, but was warned that she would have to stand trial in Franco's courts for her status as a female Freemason during the 1930s. She went instead to Switzerland, where she lived in oblivion until her death in 1972.[17]

Campoamor was perhaps the most obvious scapegoat because of her feminism, but Kent and Nelken also suffered discrimination in this obstinately male-dominated system. Nelken, though born in Spain, had a German Jewish father and a French mother. When she was elected to Parliament in 1931, she was forced to go through special bureaucratic procedures to become nationalized. Her political interests were accepted with uneasiness by no less than Manuel Azaña, who wrote in his diary: "The very idea that Nelken has opinions on political topics infuriates me. She is indiscretion in person. She has spent her life writing about painting, and I never imagined that she had political ambitions."[18]

Nelken was thirty-four years old when that passage was written; she had been an art critic since she was fifteen and had written a precocious treatise on the social condition of Spanish women when she was about twenty-one. She lived a bohemian life as a student in Paris, and when she returned to Spain she started teaching children in the proletariat sections of Madrid. When she created a small orphanage, the church protested because it controlled all charities. Nelken was launched into the Socialist party and its union, the UGT (General Union of Workers), after giving a speech at the party's cultural center, thus becoming its feminist leader. Clearly, she had been concerned about sociopolitical matters for many years before she became a member of Parliament. Her feminism, though, seemed to instill fear in male politicians. Nelken wrote for several newspapers and magazines, including the still-popular gossip weekly *Blanco y negro*, until she was elected to Parliament. Although she continued to be involved in the art world, she was immersed in the political life of Spain during the Republic and her journalistic work revolved almost entirely around that topic. Reelected in 1933, she wrote outspokenly in *El socialista*, for which she was constantly attacked in the press and criticized by her colleagues.

Nelken was also ridiculed in the courts, and endured frequent racist references to her foreign background. Azaña notes with satisfaction that even though she acted "as though she were a character of some importance," the Socialists often managed to stifle her comments and obliged her to retreat to the hallways.[19] The historian Robert Kern claims that because of Nelken's alleged involvement in the 1932 Castilblanco affair[20] she was never given more than a trusteeship on the board of the Prado Museum, whereas Kent and Campoamor were given more responsible positions.[21]

It is clear that Nelken irritated the male members of Parliament almost to the same degree that Campoamor did. Yet she was the only woman elected to Parliament by the Socialist party in the Republic's three elections—1931, 1933, and 1936. In 1937 she had a change of heart and joined the Communist party. Matilde de la Torre (1884–1946), a Socialist member of Parliament elected in

1936 who wrote about her experiences in the war years, speaks ironically of Nelken's transformation:

> In the noisy cliques, the session's incidents are commented on. Margarita Nelken has abandoned the insistent use of impertinent remarks that had designated her as having an inquisitorial personality. Now she uses some lovely eyeglasses that give her a rather doctoral air. She shows me a photo of her son in his officer's uniform. He is at the Madrid front. . . . Anyway, Margarita Nelken's opinions no longer show the almost fighting, independent spirit that used to cause unease among her enemies and even among her cohorts. Now Mrs. Nelken is a Communist, and she has to moderate her judgments with an iron will.[22]

Most historians who comment on Nelken's move to the Communist party feel that she hoped for a more energetic organization and a more prominent role for herself. But according to Mariá Gloria Nuñez Pérez, Nelken's feminism had not been welcomed by the Socialists and she was impatient for changes for women. After a trip to the Soviet Union in 1934, she became convinced that the Russians had succeeded in liberating women and she began to embrace communism.[23] She wrote several books on her political experiences, one on Parliament, and another on the Revolution of Asturias, yet she did not write any autobiographical works that would explain her change of heart.[24]

The Anarchist leader Federica Montseny, who shared the difficult and passionate days defending Madrid at the onset of the war, explains Nelken's political shift as a desire for more public recognition:

> Margarita Nelken's error was her move from the Socialist to the Communist party; perhaps because she knew that she was a better writer, a better speaker, and more educated than Pasionaria,[25] she thought that she would become the number one woman of the party. But the number one spot was already occupied by Dolores Ibárruri, who was a deep-rooted myth difficult to displace. The Socialists never pardoned what they saw as treason, and the Communists always looked at her with a certain mistrust and suspicion. That was, for me, Margarita Nelken's tragedy. But the Margarita Nelken art critic, the Margarita Nelken journalist, the Margarita Nelken in any field, was a really exceptional jewel and a brave woman at all times and in all situations. Perhaps that is why, because she was an exceptional woman, silence has fallen over her like a heavy stone slab.[26]

Montseny perceives Nelken's "exceptionality" as her tragic flaw, her ticket to anonymity in the annals of history, just as Campoamor sees her own exceptional feminist stance in the same way. Montseny points out another more personal reason for Nelken's relative invisibility: "One also has to recognize the fact that Margarita Nelken had a very 'free' lifestyle, which clashed with all the prejudices of that period. She was married, but I think her second son was not her husband's. She had a free sexual life, and that bothered people profoundly." Montseny continues:

I know that men whom I have admired and whom I have appreciated greatly for their personal value, like Largo Caballero, were categorically opposed to having women intervene in politics . . . and since Margarita Nelken, la Pasionaria, and I myself appeared in the forefront so often, all this created a special, somewhat rarefied climate. Dolores Ibárruri was lucky in that the Communist party needed a feminine banner and they found it in her. Also, she was well received in the international leftist context: a Spanish woman, dressed in black, who gave moving speeches, who pronounced epic slogans such as "They shall not pass"—in addition to her comrades putting up with her as an equal, even though she was a woman—all this caused her to soar to the top. Margarita Nelken did not have that kind of luck. Moreover, both when she wrote and when she spoke, if she had to attack, she attacked, and that caused her to acquire many enemies.[27]

What is important in Montseny's observation is that Nelken was considered "inappropriate," not only on the floor of Parliament or in her caustic journalism, but also in her private life. Too many factors caused men to think that Nelken did not conform to the rules defining what a woman should be, even an exceptional woman.

As we will see throughout this study, the sexual habits of women—both visible and invisible—who had any political leanings were closely scrutinized. Even though Dolores Ibárruri overstepped boundaries in her private life, she was indeed protected by the party. Nelken arrived too late to be coddled and pampered. She was considered an attractive woman—and she had assimilated that fact, which undoubtedly made her male colleagues uncomfortable. Ibárruri, and even Montseny, deemphasized their sexuality and focused on their maternal qualities, which made them much more acceptable in the context of traditional Spanish society.

By today's standards, Nelken does not appear to be a radical feminist, but in the Spain of the 1930s she was viewed as such. She had already made a stir among conservatives when *La condición social de la mujer* came out in the second decade of the century. Except for her original stand against women's suffrage, she did promote the cause of women and lived her free lifestyle "as a man." Amaro de Rosal, who had been a member of the executive committee of the Federation of Trade Unions of the Socialist party and who also abandoned the Socialists to join the Communists, was well acquainted with Nelken. He describes her as "passionate," "well endowed," "elegant," and "savvy." He emphasizes her polemic nature, both politically and socially. De Rosal remarks that, given her elevated economic position, some found it strange that she would be a Socialist. But he is very explicit that Nelken's political coteries and her diverse and constant male companions raised many an eyebrow. De Rosal claims that Nelken had a "free social life for the times," implying that her behavior was, in effect, scandalous for the Spain of the 1930s.[28]

Nelken remains one of the most provocative and enigmatic personalities of the 1930s, yet her life and work have not been studied in depth. She left Spain at the end of the war and became a Mexican citizen, returning to her work as a art critic. Her son, like Dolores Ibárruri's, was killed fighting in World War II in Russia. She died in 1968.

Victoria Kent, a lawyer who had already made a name for herself in the courtroom, was the most popular of the three original Republican congresswomen. Probably this was so because she complied with the dictates of the male-dominated party, rigidly adhering to the party line on the suffrage issue and later participating minimally in other polemical matters. Also, once she was named director general of the Spanish prison system in 1931, she became absorbed in her work and left key political debates to her male colleagues. Kent was a "first" for many reasons, above all because she was the first Spanish woman to be given a post of great responsibility.

Kent radically changed the prison system, challenging all the traditions of Spanish criminology. She replaced the Catholic nuns, who had generally served in women's jails as guards (and would do so again after the war), with trained lay officials. In addition, Kent proposed many ways of humanizing the penal system; she even created an institution for the instruction of female prison guards called the Feminine Corps of Prisons. She was keenly interested in the lamentable conditions of the penal system, for until that time prisons had not functioned as correctional institutions but rather as places where inmates were indelibly marked as criminals. As recently as 1986, Victoria Kent spoke of her work with pride. She emphasized the fact that under certain conditions she permitted prisoners to leave jail, with the promise that they would return in an allotted time. Kent claimed that all returned of their own free will.[29]

She also established the later-to-be-notorious Ventas prison for women. Equipped to house some five hundred prisoners—though Kent notes that there were only seventy-five individual rooms[30] she furnished the institution with modern appliances and even established a library, facilities unheard of in those times. Unwittingly, this model prison was later to become a house of horrors for some ten thousand to fourteen thousand women captured by the Franco forces after the civil war. This fact is one of the major ironies of contemporary Spanish history, although it is little known in Spain.

In spite of Kent's humanistic labor and her revolutionary reforms, her work became very unpopular with the Republican government. Azaña, who conceded that Kent was the "least offensive" of the female deputies, nevertheless was condescending in evaluating her.

> In the Council of Ministers, we have at least been "successful" in "executing" Victoria Kent, director general of prisons. Victoria is generally a simple and kind person, and the only pleasant one of the three parliamentary ladies. I think she is also the only discreet one. But she has failed in her post as director general. She is too humanitarian and has not had, in compensation, the talent for governing. The state of the prisons is alarming. There is no discipline. The prisoners escape at will.[31]

Included in the statements that accompany Azaña's indictment are remarks which illustrate that there were other problems. In less than one year and with minimal funds, the Council of Ministers had expected Kent to reverse the deplorable situation of the Spanish penal system. As we shall observe in Chapter 6, eight years later Spain was to become a hotbed of prisons. In 1939 all available convents, schools, and other large buildings were converted into penal institutions for political prisoners who had fought against Franco. Humanizing jails was no longer an issue. Quantity was to overshadow any thought of quality.

As mentioned, Kent felt that women were not sufficiently prepared to vote. Yet she was interested in the education of women and worked with María del Maeztu at the Residence for Young Ladies. Kent, even more than the other visible women of the Republic and the war, seemed to view herself as separate from her gender because of her exceptionality. In 1934 she joined the Communist-Socialist National Committee of Antifascist Women[32] and during the war worked closely with the Republican government in creating centers for refugee children. She was reelected to Parliament in 1936 but did not actively participate. Like other Republican government officials, Kent fled Spain in 1939. She lived in hiding in Paris during the Nazi occupation, pursued by the Gestapo and the Franco police, episodes described in her autobiographical novel, *Cuatro años en París (1940–1944)*. Kent lived in New York from 1954 until her death in 1987. With her friend and companion, Louise Crane, she founded the journal *Ibérica, por la libertad,* an important anti-Franco publication that she edited until the end of the regime in 1975.

Kent was ahead of her time, in that many of the reforms she effected have been instituted in other countries during the last few decades. She was a discreet, brilliant woman, who never gave up hope that the Franco regime would be crushed. Like many other exceptional women of the first half of the century in Spain, Victoria Kent seemed equipped to deal with the patriarchy in which she was immersed—but her colleagues were not ready for her. Kent's power, like Campoamor's and Nelken's, was limited by the fact that she was a woman. She was considered a "virile" woman, yet she was much more docile than the others. Unlike Montseny's bitter recollections about the past, Kent in her later years remembered the Republic with nostalgia, recalling her accomplishments rather than her failures.[33]

Other women elected to Parliament during the Republic deserve to be discussed here, but they have virtually disappeared into oblivion. An example is the lawyer Julia Alvarez Resano, who was elected to Parliament in 1936 by the Socialist party. The only testimony to her work that I have found is buried in the National Historical Archive in Salamanca, files that the insurgents collected during the war, which later aided them in the pursuit of their enemies. Alvarez Resano was very active before the war, lecturing and holding political meetings, and during the war years was involved in pedagogical issues. She was a defense lawyer for the Spanish Federation of Land Workers. Her name is rarely mentioned, yet her file is one of the largest at the Salamanca archive. De Rosal claims that she worked in the resistance in France and helped publish a Socialist newspaper until it was necessary for her to flee. He says that she went into exile in Mexico after the war.[34]

Several other women are of interest, perhaps more for cultural than for political reasons, although little is known of them. These are the women who were visible in their times, but became invisible once the war ended. They were well-educated, middle-class women who were generally concerned with women's rights.

Matilde de la Torre, for example, was elected to office in 1933 and again in the third election during the Republic, in the fateful year of 1936. A novelist and folklorist, she wrote insightful notes on the Spanish legislature, as we have observed in her remarks about Nelken. She also wrote a book of memoirs, which provides interesting details about her activities in Asturias. In 1984 one

[handwritten margin note: educated women in exile in time of Franco]

of de la Torre's relatives published a small, virtually unknown book on her life and work.[35] De la Torre, like several other activist women who were exiled, died in poverty in Mexico in 1946.

María Lejárraga, who worked directly with de la Torre after the Revolution of Asturias, exudes admiration for the congresswoman who represented Asturias:

> I have never known a more fearless spirit coupled with the most attractive feminine softness, more efficiency coupled with kindness, more virile[36] impulses inside such a fragile and sick body. She was nearsighted almost to the point of blindness; in spite of that, few people will have read and studied more than she. Her erudition, helped by her prodigious memory, was of the sort that startled. How many times have I said to her as an affectionate joke: "What luck to be your friend! Being near you, I don't need reference books." She truly knew ancient Greek and Latin, she handled French and Italian, understood English, and her written and spoken Castilian was purely classic, passionate and witty at the same time.[37]

In a long footnote to these remarks, Lejárraga tells us indignantly of de la Torre's fate, which was, ironically, very similar to what would be her own.

> Matilde de la Torre died three years ago in exile, in Cuernavaca [Mexico]. Spain with her death has suffered an irreparable loss . . . and remains unaware of it. Because of the misfortune of being a woman—in Spain, to be a woman still constitutes notorious inferiority—her eminent personality never achieved the fame that any male with half her talents would have received. . . . It can unambiguously be said that she gave her life for the cause; for her, in spite of her fragility, there was never any work, no matter how difficult, that seemed impossible. The illness that took her to her grave was pulmonary tuberculosis, the effect of a badly cured pleurisy contracted on a campaign trip through Extremadura. She died alone, poor, since all her worldly goods were confiscated at the end of the civil war, attended only by a tiny group of coreligionists, exiled like her.[38]

Given her progressive feminist attitude, perhaps the most interesting female member of Parliament was María Lejárraga herself. Known as María Martínez Sierra, she chose to give her husband the entire credit for their collaborations in theater, film, and essays. Although Lejárraga was at the forefront of the cultural scene, only in recent years has it become evident that she was actually the author of most of their plays and essays.[39] This fact explains why maternal themes dominate "their" plays and why "they" wrote an impressive number of essays about women, the poor, and the need for a revolution for women and the disadvantaged.

Curiously, although Lejárraga championed women's rights, she spent much of her life working to secure her husband's fame and fortune by writing his plays for him, even after he abandoned her in 1922 for his lead actress, Catalina Bárcena, and left Spain for Hollywood. Lejárraga explains in *Gregorio y yo* that she deliberately became "invisible," that is to say, she would not take credit for her writing. When she published her first book, her parents showed so little interest in her accomplishment that she swore to herself that they would never see her name on the cover of another. This curious, self-effacing decision was coupled with another factor: "Being a school teacher . . . having a public position, I did not want to mar the cleanliness of my name with the dubious reputation that in those times fell like a disgrace on all 'literary' women."[40]

By 1911 Gregorio's fame was secure, and in 1916 he started his own theater company at the famous Eslava Theater—in his name only. Once Gregorio began to dedicate more of his time to his actress, María wrote "their" plays more and more independently. After Gregorio left her, the year Bárcena had his child, she became a feminist political figure, giving lectures at the prestigious Ateneo in Madrid. It appears that when María was forced to trade in her role as wife and mother,[41] she displayed more openly her true colors as a feminist.

Lejárraga was active in many feminist activist groups that surfaced in the 1920s and 1930s. She was secretary of the Spanish branch of the International Alliance for Suffrage for Women and in 1930 became the first president of the Women's Alliance for Civic Education. She was elected to Parliament in 1933 as a Socialist representative for Granada, but resigned in 1934 after the demoralizing atrocities committed against the rebels in Asturias. When the civil war broke out, she was sent to Switzerland as commercial attaché of the Republican government. She lived first in France in 1938, later in New York, Hollywood, and Mexico, then settled in Buenos Aires in 1953. Lejárraga died there in 1974, poor and forgotten in a rest home, not unlike her friend de la Torre.

Lejárraga was one of the few modern feminists in Spain and championed the rights of women in most of her work. But she never published a book with her own first name until after Gregorio died in 1947. As Alda Blanco points out, in her waning years she reverted to using her maiden name in her letters.[42] Lejárraga's decision to make herself invisible in her writing is indeed a strange phenomenon, one that caused her to be ignored for many years as one of the most important feminist writers of twentieth-century Spain.

Other self-sacrificing "muses" include the wife of the Nobel poet Juan Ramón Jiménez, Zenobia Camprubí, who was active in the Lyceum Club and during the war, and María Teresa León, wife of Rafael Alberti. María Luz Morales is another anomaly in Spanish history. Although she took over the direction of Barcelona's most important newspaper in 1936 and was imprisoned in 1940 by the regime, she is rarely mentioned. The participation of another Socialist elected to Parliament during the Republic, Veneranda García, is nowhere discussed. As Jonathan Spence, the historian of China, says in his preface to *The Death of Woman Wang*, "It is always hard to conjure up from the past the lives of the poor and the forgotten."[43] In the case of these women who had been well known and not poor, it is extremely surprising that they became as invisible as the impoverished women who filled Franco's prisons.

Could the work of these exceptional women have been more fruitful? It is a difficult question, for their careers were limited not only by their female condition but by a war that precluded any possibility of continuing their work in Spain. Both powerful and powerless, they were aided by their air of exceptionality, yet truncated by it. Many of the comments of their male contemporaries labeled them as "aberrant" creatures. Ironic remarks circulated about their sexual habits and preferences if they were not married or had separated from their husbands or did not have children. It was thought that a woman who was capable of competing in an all-male sphere could not possess the normal biological and psychological makeup of a female. Just as radical social and economic changes could not be carried to term during the brief Second Republic, the resistance to women as power figures could not be easily reversed.

As Geraldine Scanlon points out, the marital status of several of these women provoked much speculation. In the same way that critical eyes were cast upon Nelken for her free lifestyle, there was similar censure of the women who were not married or who were very private about their personal lives. Scanlon remarks, "It was lamented that Spanish women were represented by two women [Kent, Campoamor] 'of the exceptional type' . . . because of their celibate condition at an age when the normal thing was for women to be mothers." This situation, it was thought, caused a "certain social abnormality."[44]

These are judgments made by men in a male world, men who wished to ascribe the same traditional roles to these women that they ascribed to their wives, mothers, and daughters. These exceptional women's lives were measured by their conformity, docility, abnegation, and maternal qualities. As we shall observe in Chapter 3, even Dolores Ibárruri and Federica Montseny—who were considered exceptions to this rule, perhaps because of their unique social, political, and economic status—also were judged by historians in ways that did not deviate much from the judgments of the other visible women.

María Lejárraga, founding president of the Feminine Association of Civic
Education, June 1933. *A.G.A. M.C.S.E. Fondo Fotográfico María Martínez Sierra*

Congresswoman Matilde de la Torre (*left*) and María Lejárraga (Martinez Sierra),
October 30, 1935. *A.G.A. M.C.S.E. Fondo Fotográfico María Martínez Sierra*

Margarita Nelken. *A.G.A. M.C.S.E. Fondo Fotográfico Margarita Nelken*

Margarita Nelken surrounded by other Socialist party members. *A.G.A. M.C.S.E. Fondo Fotográfico Margarita Nelken*

María Campo Alange. *A.G.A. M.C.S.E. Fondo Fotográfico María Campo Alange*

María Teresa León receiving a literary prize from Ramón Menéndez Pidal and
F. Rodríguez. *A.G.A. M.C.S.E. Fondo Fotográfico María Teresa León*

Victoria Kent and Margarita Nelken. *A.G.A. M.C.S.E. Fondo Fotográfico
Victoria Kent*

Victoria Kent, director general of prisons. *A.G.A. M.C.S.E. Fondo Fotográfico Victoria Kent*

Clara Campoamor, donating a flag to the Radical Youth Group at the Palace Hotel in Madrid. *A.G.A. M.C.S.E. Fondo Fotográfico Clara Campoamor*

Clara Campoamor at banquet in her honor when she was named Director
General of Welfare. *A.G.A. M.C.S.E. Fondo Fotográfico Clara Campoamor*

Clara Campoamor in lawyer's garb.

Chapter 3   Two Female Leaders of Revolutionary Spain

The most exceptional woman during the Republic and the Spanish civil war was undoubtedly Dolores Ibárruri, known worldwide as La Pasionaria. She emerged as the great maternal figure, a sort of "earth mother of war," who carried the official Communist party message to the masses, to spur the troops on to victory.

Born in 1895 into a modest family of eleven children in the Basque mining country, she had scant formal education—but a far better one than most of her countrywomen, since she managed to stay in school until she was fifteen. She aspired to become a teacher but, like many other women in this poverty-striken region, she had to begin working when financial woes overwhelmed her family. In 1915 she married a militant Socialist miner, Julián Ruíz; four of their six children died in infancy. Her remarks about the life of a married woman, in the rhetoric typical of a political speech writer, are brutally realistic. This extract is from her memory text, *They Shall Not Pass:*

> When my first child (a girl) was born, I had already suffered a year of
> such bitterness that only love for my baby kept me alive. I was terrified,
> not only by the odious present but also by the dismal, pain-filled future
> that loomed before me, as day by day I observed the lives of the miners'
> wives. . . . Out of my own experience I learned the hard truth of the pop-
> ular saying . . . "Mother, what is marriage? Daughter, marriage is weaving,
> giving birth, weeping." Weeping over our hurts and our impotence;
> weeping for our innocent children, to whom we could offer nothing but
> tear-stained caresses; weeping for our dismal lives, without horizons,
> without hope; bitter weeping, with a curse in our hearts and on our lips.
> A woman's curse? A mother's curse? What is so surprising about that,
> since our lives were worse than that of the most accursed?[1]

When she was in her early twenties, in spite of family obligations, Ibárruri began to read Marxist literature. She tells us: "For me it was a window opening on life. My ideas and sentiments began to change and take concrete form, although there was much I did not yet understand. . . . The struggle for a Socialist society . . . began to give content and substance to my life."[2]

Spurred by the Russian Revolution of 1917, Ibárruri joined the Socialist movement and made bombs with her comrades in preparation for a national strike. At that time the Spanish Socialists and Communists were at loggerheads, but the working class was becoming increasingly attracted to the Russian model of Marxism. The result was that in 1919 her group became part of the National Committee of Supporters of the Communist International. In 1920 she was launched on her career as a Communist leader: she was elected to the first provincial committee of the Basque Communist party and became a delegate to its first congress. In 1930 she attended the party's conference in Bilbao. In 1931 she moved to Madrid, was named secretary of the women's section of the national party, and became an editor of the Communist newspaper *Mundo obrero*. Juggling the double life of a prominent activist and a wife and mother was extremely difficult. Ibárruri separated from her husband and rarely spoke of him again.

Dolores' haunting, throaty voice was heard throughout Spain in the 1930s. Ibárruri explains her beginnings as an orator: "It was during the election campaign in 1931, which culminated in the overthrow of the monarchy, that I first began to speak at public meetings—not without a certain reluctance. It seemed to me that speaking to the masses was enormously difficult and carried with it a heavy responsibility."[3] In 1933 she was a delegate to the meeting of the Communist International and in 1935 became a member of the executive committee of the Seventh World Comintern Congress.

Ibárruri was the first woman to lobby in Parliament against the repression in Asturias; her defiance shook the establishment. Over the next five years she was in various prisons in Spain, once for ten months. She was even imprisoned for smuggling children of persecuted miners after the Revolution of October. With the short-lived victory of the Popular Front in 1936, she was elected to represent that party in Parliament. Then the war broke out, and she was everywhere: at the front lines, in the rear guard, with the International Brigades and in Parliament (however briefly). Pasionaria became a household term for the Left and stands next to Emma Goldman and Indira Gandhi as the most mythologized female figures of the twentieth century.

Pasionaria represents the dichotomy of the female Hispanic archetype. She has been labeled with unusual diversity by her admirers: as virgin, saint, mother, role model; as virile, courageous, self-sacrificing. She has been given all the qualities Spanish men have traditionally attributed to women whom they see in a positive light. In the eyes of her detractors, mostly Franco sympathizers, she was a "redeemed whore," a violent, fearsome woman. Describing in her memoirs a visit with some prisoners taken by the Republican forces, she emphasizes this image:

> They spoke of La Pasionaria with horror, of the crimes she had committed, of her cruelty with prisoners, especially with monks and nuns, of the songs about her on Radio Saragossa. After listening to them quietly, I asked:
> "What do you think La Pasionaria looks like?"
> "Well, we really don't know. But they say she's more like a beast than a woman."
> "Something like me?" I asked, smiling.
> "How can you say such a thing? You're a Spanish woman. They say Pasionaria isn't Spanish, that she looks like a man."[4]

It is evident from this and other published remarks that Ibárruri was envisioned by her enemies as an aberrant being. The historian Hugh Thomas remarks that there was a rumor that she had cut "a priest's throat with her teeth."[5] Curiously, both her supporters and her detractors attributed masculine characteristics to Ibárruri, one side seeing her so-called virility as positive and the other, as some unnatural, evil quality. Teresa Loring, a nurse for the insurgent forces, like most of the women of the Right saw female activism as a threat to patriarchal order. She reflects the feeling of reactionary women and men that activist women were profoundly evil. Speaking of Ibárruri, Loring told me: "Pasionaria was called that because she was passionate. I saw her kill someone and then defecate on them. When women wish to be cruel, they are more cruel than men."[6]

The real Dolores Ibárruri was totally enshrouded by these myths, during the war and also afterward, when she lived in Moscow and was protected by the Kremlin. Today there are attempts to break through the long years of hagiography and mudslinging. Joan Estruch attempts to do just that by demonstrating, first of all, that Ibárruri's husband was responsible for transforming her into the famed Pasionaria, and that once he did, she abandoned him for power. Estruch suggests that this was an unforgivable crime for a woman to commit; he falls into the trap of judging her according to tradition, rather than advancing any innovative or unprejudiced interpretation of her destiny. Further on, he notes that Ibárruri had a relationship with a "man twenty years her junior." Estruch concludes that Dolores utilized all of her political power to keep her young friend, Francisco Antón, from going to the front lines and afterward succeeded in securing him a position in the Soviet Union to be at her side. Estruch, therefore, does little more than dwell on what he considers the censurable behavior of a married woman who took a lover.[7]

Other historians fret over Ibárruri's companion. Her own party, it appears, tried to hush up her human "weakness" of having a male companion and desiring to have a personal life. As Franz Borkenau points out in his first-hand observations of the war, "The masses worship her not for her intellect, but as a sort of saint who is to lead them in the days of trial and temptation."[8] If Dolores' saintliness is, according to male societal rules, marred by her emotional needs, we do not find this factor affecting the women who saw her as a role model.

Ibárruri was, obviously, neither totally saint nor totally sinner. Nor was she a feminist. If we attempt to misrepresent her as such, we commit the same errors of history as those who have tried to analyze her within the framework of the male politician who rises to power. Yet Pasionaria's politicization did emanate from her consciousness of the repressive situation of women. The vehemence with which she bitterly assesses the plight of women makes the origin of her motivation clear: "Woman's goal, her only aspiration, had to be matrimony and continuation of the joyless, dismal, pain-ridden thralldom that was our mother's lot; we were supposed to dedicate ourselves wholly to giving birth, to raising our children, and to serving our husbands, who for the most part treated us with complete disregard."[9] She goes on to describe her rebellion in the face of this apparently hopeless situation.

> Was life worth living? My companions in misery and I often asked this question as we discussed our situation, our wretchedness. They spoke with resignation; after all, what could we women do? I rebelled against the idea of the inevitability of such lives as ours; I rebelled against the idea that we were condemned to drag the shackles of poverty and submission through the centuries like beasts of burden—slapped, beaten, ground down by the men chosen to be our life companions.[10]

Rebellion is the key to Ibárruri's motivation; she sums up her rebellion emphatically:

> That was the life of our parents, and that was our life. It was like a deep pit without horizons, where the light of the sun never reached, illuminated at times only by the bloody glare of the struggles that burst out in flames of violence when the capacity to bear brutal treatment had reached the limits of human endurance.

During my adolescence I was filled with a bitter, instinctive resentment which made me lash out against everything and everybody (at home I was considered incorrigible), a feeling of rebellion that later became conscious indignation.[11]

These statements about Pasionaria's political evolution point up the fact that her awakening to consciousness was indeed a reaction against male repression. They also suggest that, even though her husband may first have imbued her with Marxist ideology, precisely what maximized her politicization was her rebellion against a family life of poverty and self-sacrifice. Originally, there was something of a feminist element in her attitude. Yet when she became a vehicle for the Communist party, her total dedication to the party line required her to maintain an image in keeping with a profoundly male-oriented organization.

Essentially, as Mary Nash and others have pointed out,[12] there seems to be no place for feminism in Spain; even today, the word "feminism" is anathema; those who "practice" it are generally scorned and shunned. In those days of revolution and reaction, women of the Left were made to think that feminism was bourgeois and irrelevant. In addition, they were so steeped in religious and social tradition, which dictated male superiority, that campaigning for women's rights rarely entered their minds.

The most valuable quality of women on both the Left and the Right, according to all treatises on the subject, was *abnegation:* self-sacrifice, self-denial, giving up oneself, whether for the revolution, for the family, for the church, or for some other cause. In summary, selflessness was the prescription for females in Spain. Ibárruri pleads for abnegation—as does, unwittingly, her reactionary counterpart, Pilar Primo de Rivera (1912–1990), head of the Feminine Section. When Dolores Ibárruri was questioned about feminism a few years ago, she stated: "In general, I am not a feminist. I like women to participate in battles under the same conditions and with the same rights as men. To create a feminist movement out of the struggle of classes seems a little absurd, because the revindication of women is to be found within the fight for democracy."[13]

Marie Marmo Mullaney, analyzing the afeminism of Ibárruri and other activists, concludes, "In reality, for a woman to have adopted a more radical or aggressive line on this issue would have endangered her own acceptance, position and impact within the movement that always insisted that the woman question was one of class and economics and not gender itself."[14] We are reminded of Campoamor's ostracism from Parliament between 1931 and 1933. In Pasionaria's case, Mullaney's further remarks are particulary relevant: "Having broken from a stereotypical female role in their own lives, these revolutionary women feared perhaps that their future success would be threatened or endangered through their identification with the group from which they had managed to escape. Any reminder of their origins in a traditional apolitical or 'our' group might disturb, irritate or worry them, causing them to deny or minimize any alliance or allegiance."[15]

Dolores Ibárruri was scrupulously faithful to the party line from her earliest commitment to it,[16] a fact that became evident as I observed her seated, erect and composed, at her desk at party headquarters in Madrid. She visited there every day until her death in 1989, as though waiting for fresh instructions from the long defunct Comintern; she sat stoically—ailing and nearly blind, only vaguely aware of the present, immersed in a heroic and remote past. Juana Doña, in an autobiographical novel based on her experiences as a young Communist activitist[17] inspired by Pasionaria, explains: "Dolores was a symbol even before the war, but during the war she became the archetype because she was a woman. Dolores was exclusively a party woman. Yet she was a role model; to be like her was our goal. The feminists reproach her for not being a feminist, but I think they are unjust. In those days no one had a feminist consciousness, and Dolores' visibility didn't permit her to have one either."[18] Carmen Camaño, who was also an activist in the Communist party during the war and knew Dolores well, attributes Pasionaria's position to the machismo of her party, though she insists that this was and still is true as well of other political parties in Spain.[19]

Obviously, Ibárruri earned the respect of her male colleagues by playing the role of the superexceptional female, who had the savvy to deal with every situation and the perspicacity to take the right stance on each one, whether fierceness, joviality, or cool distance. No one has more astutely or more expressively—with the wry impartiality of a journalist—described Pasionaria's political talents than her colleague in the Republican Parliament, Matilde de la Torre. One particularly revealing passage provides some insight into Pasionaria's presence, which was obviously enhanced by the total support she had from her party and by the fact that she unfailingly obeyed its dictates:

Pasionaria's smile is contagious. She has silver and bronze notes in her somewhat hoarse voice, like a bell cracked from overuse. Many people approach Dolores to say hello—people who, when she is out of earshot, scathingly criticize her "propaganda." . . . These people, nevertheless, surround Pasionaria; they flatter her, they laugh when she laughs, without even knowing if the little devils within this feminine spirit are not laughing at the joke that she manages with childish simplicity. And when she becomes serious, adopting that peculiar tone of the doctoral wizard, these gentlemen also become serious and they show their approval.

And I dare say all this, and I beg the pardon of the illustrious political men whom I have seen act in this manner, because it is necessary that someone come forth and tell the truth (at least the apparent truth) among the many petty anticommunist comedies played out behind her back.

On the other hand, Pasionaria's noble figure and physical presence add to her very respectable parliamentary and political stature.[20]

These observations point to the power Dolores had over her male colleagues, given her physical[21] and psychological presence, her sense of humor, and her capacity for utilizing her talents; they also emphasize the political intrigues and hypocrisy surrounding her persona.

Her other female colleague, Lejárraga, comparing de la Torre to Ibárruri, points out:

Pasionaria is, as a personality and a speaker, diametrically opposed to Matilde de la Torre. Daughter of the common people, her education and instruction never went beyond the elementary, but you could not find a better "instrument" of propaganda for the masses. A worker, the wife of a miner, she has the clout and the figure of a queen: her grave and low voice, well modulated, is inevitably emotional and it draws people. The most simple commonplaces seem new and original when she pronounces them. Her noble and theatrical command emphasizes the commonplace slogans like lightning on a stormy night. She says what they tell her to say. Since she is bound by blind enthusiasm for Communist discipline, she cannot permit herself one iota of personal opinion or a comma outside of party orthodoxy, but she says it in such a way and with such real and apparent conviction that there is no simple soul who can be kept from being influenced; and even we skeptics who think we know where she fails in her affirmations, cry upon hearing the voice that affirms.[22]

Ibárruri was undoubtedly the most visible and provocative figure in her party, and it is logical that she would be treated with an ambiguous combination of fear and reverence. A singular presence in Spain, she was capable of moving Republican soldiers to tears. More important, as the war progressed and the Left lost momentum, she was highly successful in convincing the troops that in spite of their materially inferior situation they could win the war. She inspired wives and mothers to accept the mutilation and death of their men with abnegation.[23] During the war she became the most significant role model for women of the Left—especially those who were Communists or Socialists.

Federica Montseny (1905–1994), Ibárruri's counterpart as a major leader of the Anarchist movement, cut a more intellectual figure than Pasionaria. Yet she never attained the same grandiose proportions among the mythologized figures of the war.

A creative writer in her youth, Montseny was the daughter of two major Anarchist intellectuals, Teresa Mañé and Joan Montseny.[24] Together with her parents, between 1923 and 1938 Federica renewed the publication of *Revista blanca*—with constant harassment from the government—as a "cottage industry," while they survived financially by running a farm. Mañé and Montseny also briefly published a weekly newspaper entitled *El Luchador*. Montseny thus grew up in a family where social ideology and political thought were daily fare and where there was little fear in the face of government sanctions. She studied at home with her parents and has been faithful to their Anarchist ideals throughout her life.

Montseny began her career as a novelist and wrote some fifty novels and novellas, many of which advance Anarchist theory and plots. Some were published at their rural home on the outskirts of Barcelona. Federica gave up her literary career to dedicate herself to politics and political journalism.[25] Along with other Anarchists who envisioned a social revolution, Montseny took part in the founding of the Federación Anarquista Ibérica in 1927, known as the FAI.[26] In 1930 Montseny and Germinal Esgleas, also an Anarchist activist, began a liaison that produced three children and has lasted throughout her long career. In 1936 she became the first female cabinet minister in Spain's history[27] and attained an unbelievable goal for women: the right to abortion. That right was, of course, rescinded in 1939 at the onset of the Franco regime and continues to be a hotly disputed, unresolved issue in Spain today.[28]

Montseny was continually concerned with the woman question, although, ironically, she too has consistently rejected any notion of feminism. As she explains in a book of interviews with Carmen Alcalde, "We have never been feminists[29] because we feel that a woman should have the same rights as a man and that like a man, she possesses the same qualities and the same defects."[30]

Yet Montseny, conscious of the fact that Spanish women have been denied a place in politics and in history, invariably contradicts her antifeminist rationale. For example:

Although there is an unhealthy tendency to forget it, there were, there are, women in the CNT [Confederación Nacional de Trabajo] . . . exceptional women because of their organizational capacity, their dynamism, their personal worth. History will not record their names. . . . We have never been, we are not, we will not be, feminists. We think that the emancipation of women is intimately tied to the true emancipation of men. That's why it is enough to just call ourselves Anarchists. But it has seemed to us that, above all in Spain, our movement suffered from an excess of masculinity; men, in general, do not like women to represent them.[31]

Montseny's stance often appears quixotic. Her concern and work for the advancement of women is in essence feminist, though like the vast majority of Spaniards even today—both male and female—she finds the word "feminism" to be offensive. All the same, she blatantly denounces the unfair situation of women within her own party.

Unlike Dolores Ibárruri, Montseny has not been simply a vehicle for the party line. She addresses women as a group, in which she normally acknowledges her membership much more explicitly than Dolores. Anne Jenkins describes Federica's attitude about Spanish women: "Montseny abhors their lack of education and lack of opportunity for expression, the distortion of women's 'natural' identity, and their miserable situation, that they lack not only economic and intellectual means, but also the emotional strength and self-assurance they need to extricate themselves."[32]

Montseny was the only female leader of the 1930s to address questions of sexuality and reproduction frankly. Idealistic and contradictory on questions of love and sex and maternity and sex, she made the only real attempts to liberate women from the bondage of patriarchy. Her optimism during the war about these topics often made her the object of severe criticism. In a notorious interview with the journalist H. E. Kaminski during the war, Montseny reflected on the flash of freedom that women in Catalonia were enjoying at that time. In response to a question about the problems of women in that region, she said: "They don't exist. There are women in the government, in all the administrative branches, in all professions; many are even in the militia. They can live their lives as they like. It all depends on them. . . . Since the start of the war, women have conquered equality everywhere, above all in their sexual relations in Catalonia, just as in other countries."[33]

Yet from all indications, Anarchist men, in spite of their espousal of free love and equality, did not seem substantially different in their treatment of women from others at the time, as Gabriel Jackson remarks. "The anarchists preached the equality of the sexes, but continued to feel that human dignity required separate dining rooms for men and women workers. Despite outward appearances, they were often more conservative in their social instincts than the *bourgeoisie.*"[34] This is a baffling statement indeed, considering the expectation that women's liberation would be achieved within the Anarchist scenario. The situation is reflected in much of the literature written by female Anarchists of the times. Because of this fact, the most feminist group in Spain prior to the 1970s, the Anarchist Mujeres Libres was founded. The organization will be discussed in Chapter 5.

As noted in her interviews with Alcalde, published in 1983, Montseny's optimism during the war years later turned into bitter indictments of the machismo of Spanish politics. Montseny points out that of all the women active in her party, only she had any real power.[35] She describes the life and work of several outstanding women of the twenties and thirties who made decisive contributions to the Anarchist cause, but nevertheless fell into oblivion. These include Teresa Claramunt, one of the important women of the CNT and a friend of Federica's mother, Teresa Mañé (who she also feels has unjustifiably disappeared from the annals of history); the worker Rosario Dulcet, who inspired thousands of other workers to fight for victory during the war; and Josefa Cacicedo, a journalist active in the Basque country.[36]

Montseny was the only truly visible Anarchist woman, the only "exceptional" woman in her party, according to the canon texts. She was never by any means the mythical figure that Pasionaria was, and Montseny is clearly bitter about her contemporary. "History is written on the basis of tendentious information . . . and sometimes according to graphic documents that are available and that can be used for a film or for a TV report. In this regard, the communists will always be superior to us because we never 'pose' before history; we are too occupied in the defense of revolution and making it a reality."[37]

Montseny clearly received much less attention than Ibárruri in spite of her unprecedented accomplishments and her extremely important negotiations during the war. Her journalistic work, which she continued during her exile in France after the war, often addressed the status of women and her actions were constantly directed toward improving their situation. If we cannot describe her as a feminist, we must reckon with her attempts to change the fate of women and her success during those years. In essence, she did a great service to women, even though it was temporary. But her squeamishness vis-à-vis feminism—which she considered "fascist"—and her idealistic optimism in thinking that the male-dominated CNT would respond to the needs of women have provoked accusations against her by feminists.

The fact that Montseny saw maternity as woman's "artistic" expression has led critics to believe that she did not wish to change the role of women in society substantially. She appears to be confused about how far she was willing to go, perhaps because she was so immersed in her quixotic stance on Anarchism as a result of her family background. Yet, Shirley Fredricks points out, "Montseny insisted that liberated women were essential to the progressive improvement of society and to a successful future for humanity. Federica Montseny's greatest emotional commitment throughout her life went into this struggle for the emancipation of all women."[38] Martha Ackelsberg, however, claims: "Paralleling the arguments of Emma Goldman, she [Montseny] insisted on the internal nature of the struggle: only when women came to respect themselves would they be able to effectively demand respect from men. She agreed with other Anarchist writers, both male and female, that the appropriate goal was not equality with men under the present system, but a restructuring of society that would liberate all."[39]

Of major concern to Federica Montseny was the attainment of an intelligent, sophisticated, and responsible understanding between men and women that could lead to the liberation of women; at least, such is the posture she assumes in her articles and novels. Nonetheless, on many occasions she concedes that women are not equipped to deal with freedom. In practice Montseny was optimistic about women, but in theory quite pessimistic, a position taken by many "exceptional" women" such as Kent and Nelken in their stance on women's suffrage. This paradox is ever present, but it is perhaps most noticeable among the Anarchists.

At any rate, Montseny was one of the strongest and most outspoken female leaders in Spain. It is fortunate that we possess not only her creative writing, but also her autobiographical texts and the material she published in journals and newspapers.[40] Of all the visible women of the Republic and the war, she was the most conscious of what Lerner has called "the single most important force compelling humans to record the past and preserve it"—the desire for immortality.[41]

Part Two *W*ar as Memory

Chapter 4   Toward a Theory of Memory Texts

Recounting memories is a slippery task. Questions of truth versus fiction are based on the fickle nature of memory, the passage of time, the need for self-justification, self-compassion, and self-aggrandizement, and so on. These issues have been analyzed and dissected repeatedly in relation to the so-called auto-biographical genre, a notion on which few critics and historians agree. The first scholars who began to view autobiography as a genre were preoccupied with the element of truth; both historians and literary critics were engaged in the attempt to discover the level of historical veracity of the text. Autobiography had been defined as an exegetic, apologistic, printed discourse of the Western white male—the universal "I"—who, as Bella Brodzki and Celeste Schenck have explained, "placed himself at the center of his own cosmology."[1]

Sidonie Smith explains the androcentrism of autobiography in her most recent book on the topic: "Western autobiographical practices flourished be-cause there seemed to be a self to represent, a unique and unified story to tell that bore common ground with the reader, a mimetic medium for self-representation that guaranteed the epistemological correspondence between narrative and lived life, a self-consciousness capable of discovering, uncovering, recapturing that hard core at the center."[2] This statement assumes that auto-biographers knew they had an audience, that the "genre" was essentially ap-ostrophic in nature—and often apologetic as in Saint Augustine's confessions or the pseudoautobiographies of the Spanish picaresque.[3]

But many autobiographers also advanced "a theory of their lives" that dem-onstrated flawless achievements and importance in history, thereby attempting to provoke the reader into unquestioned admiration. This is the universal, in-dividualistic "I" of autobiographical discourse whose subject, George Gusdorf tells us in 1956, "takes delight in thus drawing his own image" because he "believes himself worthy of a special interest. Each of us tends to think of himself as the center of a living space."[4] Autobiographical criticism of this nature reveals that such writing occurs only in developed countries and is an instrument of instruction and exegesis for the members of colonized societies. It is the work of white Christian colonial males of good standing. As Gusdorf says, "Autobiography is not to be found outside of our cultural area; one would say that it expresses a concern peculiar to Western man; a concern that has been of good use in his systematic conquest of the universe and that he has communicated to men of other cultures."[5]

Later came a dismantling of the critical framework of the truth seekers. By deemphasizing the interest in the strict truth of autobiographical discourse, literary critics laid claim to it and converted it into the problem child of literature. Roy Pascal saw it as "a wrestling with truth" and began to analyze the question of form.[6] Philippe Lejeune introduced another problem when he published *L'Autobiographie en France*. In addition to the mental and emotional unreliability of the subject and the form of "his work," Lejeune raised the question of the reader, thus obscuring further autobiography's already murky waters.[7] The ontological self became a determining factor in autobiographical discourse; the subject became suspect because of tautological and psychological factors. The autobiographical subject was placed under a microscope and "his" memory cells, literally and figuratively, became the object of discussion.[8]

In nearly all of these deliberations, the question of gender was not addressed until French feminist psychoanalytic theory began to talk about the self in relation to "the other," especially in relation to the female body. The works of Kristeva, Cixous, Wittig, and Irigaray appeared, and epistemological debate ensued among scholars such as Derrida, Lacan, Deleuze, and Foucault.[9] In the United States, after a lengthy siege by first Roland Barthes and then the deconstructionists, who had ceremoniously but irrevocably "buried the author,"[10] the feminist movement began to take up the issue of gender in all forms of literature. Yet, as Linda J. Nicholson has pointed out:

> From the late 1960s to the mid-1980s, feminist theory exhibited a recurrent pattern: Its analysis tended to reflect the viewpoints of white, middle-class women of North America and Western Europe. . . . Not only did feminist scholars replicate the problematic universalizing tendencies of academic scholarship in general but, even more strikingly, they tended to repeat the specific types of questionable universalizing moves found in the particular school of thought to which their work was most closely allied.[11]

While resurrecting the author and focusing on the female subject, American feminist critics disinterred other bodies, thereby opening the floodgates on the dammed waters of race, class, ethnicity, and sexual preference. The "I" became many different "I"s; we could no longer identify the self without the individual's cultural, experiential, and historical accoutrements. The vindication of the subject and the renewed interest in referentiality brought with it not only a diacritical approach to autobiography, but also caused many of the feminist academics to see legitimacy in the insertion of their own selves into their critical texts.[12]

Estelle Jelinek was the first to produce a book (in 1980) that dealt exclusively with the theme of women's autobiography.[13] The critic Domna Stanton began her disappointing pilgrimage in search of critical theory on female autobiography in the early eighties. Inspired by Virginia Woolf's disillusionment with the female subject, which had provoked her to write *A Room of One's Own,* Stanton comments that Jelinek was the sole pioneer in this endeavor, and that three years after Jelinek's book was published it was still alone on the shelf.[14] Stanton was to name female autobiography "autogynography"; she became one of the next pioneers of the genre that had been the patrimony of the Western white man. And as American feminist autobiographical theory began to consider the "subaltern" voice,[15] or, in Sidonie Smith and Julia Watson's terms, the "colonial subject,"[16] the range of autobiographical possibilities began to multiply.

In framing the body of voices of Spanish women who speak in this text, I find that the notion of colonial subject is useful, if thorny. We are listening to white European women who were colonized, economically and politically, by their own white European countrymen. Their colonization did not come about through violence and force *explicitly* until after the civil war. We could say that their colonization was brought about by systematic church-state repression through the centuries, without respite. Until the 1930s and again after the war, they had a mentality so infused with a multilayered colonizing patriarchy that it is miraculous that they have spoken at all.[17] They were women, therefore less important than men; they were generally without personal financial recourse, therefore less worthy than the rich. And they were Catholic and Spanish, therefore doubly or triply subjugated—to men (husband, father, brothers)/ god (priest)/civil authority (after the war, Franco's "Gestapo-like" police). Smith and Watson say of the equivocal idea of colonization: "One cannot easily sever, separate out, or subsume under one another the strands of multiple determinations. For instance, colonial regimes needed and global economies continue to need 'classes' as well as 'races' in order to achieve their goals. And class identifications call particular women to specific psychological and cultural itineraries that may collide and/or converge with itineraries of race and nation."[18]

Yet I cannot adhere strictly to a theoretical framework for what I call the memory texts of the women from the Spanish civil war.[19] Shari Benstock, a major critic of women's autobiography, in speaking of religiously applying a specific idea of genre to a written text, comments:

> The question of genre has implications for notions of culture. Either genre definitions deny that there is any culture other than white-male-Western-bourgeois; or cultural complexity throws into relief the impossibility of such a definition. But if genre tries to incorporate all the multiplicities of cultural difference, then what kinds of assumptions can it make, what norms can it postulate? . . . Perhaps we should look beyond cultural explanations—beyond the cultural custodianship that is the heavy mantle of academic citizenship—to see culture in the ways we have recently learned to see texts, as "woven things." Woven, intertwined, a working together of parts without privileging one over the other (no "center," no "margin"), individual strains and colors still available within the larger pattern.[20]

The Spanish memory texts of war and its consequences are women-woven texts, fused together to form a historical quilt.

Caren Kaplan describes the relevance and convenience of remaining outside the literary critic's convention of academic labels. She says: "Out-law genres[21] renegotiate the relationship between personal identity and the world, between personal and social history. Here, narrative inventions are tied to a struggle for cultural survival rather than purely aesthetic experimentation or individual expression." Kaplan contends "that resistance is a mode of historical necessity, that Western feminism must participate in this moment, and that the critical practice of outlaw genres challenges the hierarchical structures of patriarchy, capitalism, and colonial discourse."[22] For Kaplan and for the women of this text, narrative is political protest; the voices here converge—as indeed "woven things" do—as though they were part of a protest rally from the past.

On the question of genre, especially whether or not oral and written testimonies can be viewed together,[23] the issue of class intervenes in an essential way in the memory texts: in most cases, the transcribed testimonies are those of women who barely have writing skills, let alone literary talent. The more "traditional" autobiographical texts have usually been written by upper-class women, though of course there are exceptions. In fact, the exception is the rule. Some of these texts will follow a pattern, others will not. We are dealing with an exceptional period in Spain, a hiatus for women who had been imprisoned in their silence. They broke the rules of patriarchy, for which they were severely punished after the war, and they broke the rules of silence by writing or speaking. These Spanish women are "outlaws" both in their lives and in their memory texts.

The question of truth—that is to say, historical accuracy—therefore becomes irrelevant;[24] what is important here is the "virtual reality,"[25] the emotive scenarios created by the women who have conjured up their lives from that stormy period. After all, we are dealing with war in all its apocalyptic nature. Robert Jay Lifton, who has studied the psychological effects of war and devastation[26], feels that memory becomes utterly selective because of "psychic closing off."[27] And this is civil strife, in which we are contending with the impact of war on former friends, neighbors, relatives, and compatriots, and also with the repression that is dispensed by the victors.

Among the works of the women who will be the subject of this section of the text, we find many "urgent voices of collective testimony." This is especially true of the prison texts written by (or transcribed from the testimonies of) women who were unable to flee Spain after the war or were sent back from exile in France. Many of their texts were not written or published until after the death of Franco in 1975, which raises diachronic and synchronic issues. The tone of urgency stems from the silence imposed on them by the regime, which in turn was so systematic that the women acquired a sense of self-censorship that silenced them doubly. Almost invariably, they display a need to denounce the injustice perpetrated not only against them, but also against many other people, especially other women. Herein lies the power and the empowerment of the memory texts: the political exigency of protest, a unified, primordial scream of solidarity.[28]

Women who had defended the Republic suffered a double tragedy at the end of the war: the disappearance of a short-lived democracy in which many had invested their hopes for social equality, and the destruction of further economic, social, and political advancement for women. Their double or triple oppression leads me to classify them among the "colonized subjects" of autobiography.

Most of these women do not express any feminist consciousness,[29] though they do provide information that permits us to envision their "flash of freedom." In general, these women have a strong need to break through the silence that engulfed so many from 1939 on. They need to tell their stories, especially their rebellion against a rigid social structure, their frustration as citizens who came to recognize that they had been kept from being part of the public sector, and the loss of liberty that engulfed them at the end of the war.

These are the underlying issues of most of the written testimonies. Yet we must analyze both their expressed intention and the format they employ to truly understand their "outlaw" (and "outlawed" before 1975) memory texts. The common denominator of their expressed intentions is a moral one: to protest the plight of Republican Spain primarily from a feminine perspective. The format of the works varies markedly, given their diverse experiences, their level of literacy, and their social and political indoctrination. They fit into the pattern Barbara Harlow describes: "These memoirs are to be distinguished too from conventional autobiography inasmuch as the narratives are actively engaged in a redefinition of the self and the individual in terms of a collective enterprise and struggle. The prison memoirs of political detainees are not written for the sake of a 'book of one's own;' rather they are collective documents, testimonies written by individuals who wish to remember their communal struggle."[30]

These unique testimonial writings emerge from a country in which there appears to have been little tradition of autobiography, especially among women.[31] Spanish autobiographical writing until recently was largely ignored. Though some theoretical texts have been published and several conferences on the subject have taken place, there is no theory of individual or collective memory about the Spanish civil war; this is true in spite of the fact that we now have a large body of memory texts by both men and women. The project of writing this book has not only had a sleuthing aspect, but has had pioneering proportions. The silence imposed on women made it very difficult to unearth their texts or acquire their testimonials.

In reviewing works by men about the war,[32] I find that their vantage point is very different from that of women. Their experiences and life views are distinctive, and there is a vast gulf in Spain between what was considered acceptable for men and what was considered acceptable for women. As Estelle Jelinek has indicated, females emphasize not so much their political and historical connections, but rather their personal relationships with others. Many of their works differ from those with a traditional first-person narrative about the author and the surroundings. Spanish women through the centuries had lived in the shadows of men and had been oriented toward helping and sharing; they were imbued with the idea of abnegation, not trained to see themselves as the main "characters" of their lives and work. This "collective testimonial" phenomenon becomes obvious in many of the works to be discussed here.

My purpose, then, is to analyze above all *how* women told their stories of war and repression, prison and exile, and *what* they told, in order to understand what was of utmost importance to them within the context of the trauma and devastation that the Spanish civil war caused. Given the diversity of these outlawed memory texts, the overall impressionistic value of the work, that is to say, the intuitive, emotional substance gleaned from the books, overrides judgments on whether they contain the absolute truth or a version of their lives made up of the embroiled schema of past recollections. The memory texts are treated here as oral history, which attempts to piece together a portrait of women's roles and perceptions during the greatest political upheaval in Spanish history.

We find the qualities that the feminist critics lay out regarding autobiographical-type texts to exist to different degrees in nearly all the works written by women about this period, including the apologistic *They Shall Not Pass* by Ibárruri. Pasionaria's need to vindicate herself before the public and to justify the acts of the Communist party during the war are obvious, but she also uses her pen to describe the destiny and plight of other Spaniards, especially women (as we have observed in Chapter 3). Constancia de la Mora, a press censor during the war and a Communist activist, sees herself as the protagonist of *In Place of Splendor*. Though she is less conscious of the notion of collectivity than other writers in the sections of her book that deal with the war itself, de la Mora does emphasize the role of women in Spanish society before and during the war.

The accounts of Ibárruri and de la Mora are not stories of quiet reflection. They are political autobiographies in which the authors seek to justify their acts as protagonists of Communist party activities. They also seek to project themselves as heroines for the future. During the war both were very visible women, who felt their writings could change the course of history and perhaps vindicate them. They have largely remained within the framework of the Western autobiography; yet, as has been observed in their portraits of the early twentieth century, they do provide intimate sketches of oppressed females in Spain. They, therefore, serve a somewhat feminist agenda: the need for rebellion against both the oppression of women and the oppression of Spaniards at large. They take on the double task of resistance literature, though they do insert themselves as the main subjects of their texts.

Both Ibárruri and de la Mora present us with various peculiarities of format and intention. In the case of *They Shall Not Pass*, the voice is more self-righteous than many others. Of course, Ibárruri was one of the major spokespersons for, first, the Spanish Communist party and, second, women in their condition of double oppression. Though Pasionaria claims that she wrote the book primarily for her grandchildren,[33] her outcry is so declamatory that this assertion could hardly sustain itself. Ibárruri claims to strive for truth in her work. Yet she is obviously a victim of the legend created around her, and her autobiography is no doubt affected by that legend.

Despite Pasionaria's insistent rhetoric about class issues, we must keep in mind that she was a propagandistic vehicle for the party. She wrote her book while living in Moscow after the war, thanks to the generosity of the Soviet Union. The tone is highly propagandistic; here, for instance, is a passage where she speaks for the masses:

> Over a country of chains, over the Spain of prisons, of torture, of summary executions, had come the light of new faith and hope. The light that inspires the epic resistance of our people against perfidious aggression; the light that guides humanity toward the future; the light that radiates from the depths of suffering of a nation and breaks through the thick walls of prisons, saying to all the world with the ringing voice of an immortal people: Spain lives! Spain fights! Spain is![34]

The major part of the book is written in the first person. Yet there are nonpropagandistic passages that appear to be strictly "historical" in nature. In those fragments Ibárruri outlines the salient political episodes of the early twentieth century in Spain. Occasionally she adopts a tone of intimacy; for example, when she speaks of her children and her need to sacrifice her family life for the party: "My own life and liberty were all very well, but did I have a right to sacrifice my children, depriving them of a secure and warm home, of the mother's care and affection that they needed so much? In my life as a Communist, this has been one of the most painful aspects of the struggle, although I have seldom spoken of it, thinking that the best way to teach is by example, even if I had to shed tears of blood."[35] In this rare show of emotion, we still find the author to be didactic and apologistic, proving herself to be a model Communist.

An interesting aspect of *They Shall Not Pass* is its genesis. Ibárruri has insisted that she wrote this book free from outside influences,[36] yet it seems more than likely that there was some creative intervention by the party. If nothing else, it seems logical that it would have wished to see the manuscript before publication to suggest changes. This factor would have necessarily influenced the style, tone, and thematic material. It is clear that her underlying intention is justification of her actions during the war. Also, the fact that *They Shall Not Pass* was written nearly a quarter of a century after the end of the war suggests that the author sought to create a revised past and present, thereby projecting a future image of herself. Ibárruri not only redefines her self-identity, she also re-creates a self of which the party approves.[37] Certainly, this autobiography is invaluable as a document about women and the class problem in Spain, if we keep in mind that the expressed intention—individual "truth," akin to the "urgent solitary voice of testimony"—is mediated by a design factor inspired in Pasionaria's politics.

Similarly, Constancia de la Mora's *In Place of Splendor* is an apology for her politics during the war.[38] She, too, demonstrates her rebellion in the context of her class and the repression she experienced as a woman. Her autobiography, though, is less apologistic than Ibárruri's, since her role was not as crucial as Pasionaria's. (She in fact disappeared from political life after the war and spent her remaining years in exile in Mexico, though no one to date has published an account of her life and death there.) De la Mora, too, uses examples from her own life to describe the role of women before and during the war. *In Place of Splendor* proposes also to be a political and historical analysis of Spain that outlines the causes of revolution and war. She is so conscious of the historical aspect of her autobiography that she includes an index of names and topics.

Because de la Mora is not speaking as an official voice of Soviet Communism, but rather as a Spanish Communist activist, her work tends to have a more individualistic, personal tone than Ibárruri's. She describes her marriage to and scandalous divorce from a parasitical husband who married her for money; she discusses her family's social position and her subsequent marriage to the Communist aviator Ignacio Hidalgo de Cisneros. De la Mora dares to give us facts about her personal life, whereas Ibárruri says nothing about her separation from her husband or her liaison with a young Communist, clearly because of her need to maintain her saintly political image.

In spite of de la Mora's more intimate details, her voice too is stoic. She never permits her emotions to overwhelm her. When she talks of her work with orphaned children, de la Mora tells us discreetly: "I could not prevent the tears from coming to my eyes. I had never seen a more pitiful sight than our first group of children. But it was no time to become sentimental. If we were to calm all those children and cope with their fits of hysterics, we had to appear natural, to give them the impression that what was happening was nothing abnormal."[39]

Given their role as public and political women, both de la Mora and Ibárruri tend to mitigate the dramatic nature of their testimonies; yet often their voices as mothers and wives confirm Carol Gilligan's theory that "women not only define themselves in a context of human relationships but also judge themselves in terms of their ability to care."[40] Also important about de la Mora's book is that she wrote it in English, published it in the United States, and, as has been suggested by acquaintances, had help from her American journalist friends. In addition, she wrote the book as the war ended. Unlike Ibárruri, de la Mora's conception of her life and her wartime experiences emanates from a fresh vision in which she lucidly pinpoints the problems that led to the civil war. Referring to the beginning of the unrest during the Republic, she brilliantly describes the chasm that was opening up in Spain:

> From that day, Spain was openly divided in two. The cleavage split families, brothers and sisters, fathers and sons, mothers and daughters, and even husbands and wives. Politics could no longer be a subject for polite dinner-table conversation. People lived as Monarchists or Republicans, reactionaries or progressives. Men decided for freedom or against it. Most of Spain, the peasants, the workers, part of the small middle class, stood for the Republic. And all of rich and privileged Spain, the big industrialists, the landowners, the titled nobility, the church dignitaries, stood against it.[41]

De la Mora fits her personal and political life into a larger context, a collective one that elucidates the fate of her country and its citizens. This double-voiced autobiography—historical as well as personal—permits us to view the life of the upper-class woman, in direct contrast to what we observe in Ibárruri's description of the indigent class. Yet their autobiographies converge precisely at the juncture of their intention: to insert themselves into the history of Spain and to denounce the repression of its citizens, and specifically its women. They purport to tell the truth about themselves and Spain. Never do they confess to the arbitrary nature of memory or its deceitful selectivity, and they seem to be unconcerned with (or unconscious of) the fictive element involved in telling one's own story or of the political bias that motivates them.

This lack of critical distance is true of most of the accounts of the war written by Spaniards. Their immersion in a tragedy of such magnitude, in which their own people massacred one another, made critical distance impossible. Perhaps this is a form of "psychic closing off." In fact, the only mildly "objective" accounts of the Spanish civil war were written by foreign witnesses. Any objectivity is at best theoretical, given the importance of this war for World War II and the passions that ignited it.

Interestingly, some writers do not even conceive of the mnemonic nature of their works. María Lejárraga, for instance, at the end of her autobiographical

Una mujer por caminos de España, which describes her activism in the 1930s, categorically denies that her work is an autobiography. She says it is

> a brief account of impressions that are merely pictorial, gathered during a few years—1931 to 1938—in which the change of posture of my country, a change which began with radiant hope and ended in black tragedy, led me to deviate from the path of my individual existence and·insert it totally and voluntarily into the torrent of our misfortune.
>
> There is not, I repeat, autobiography in these pages. They are precisely the opposite of an autobiography, given that in them, just as in the years that inspired them, I went from being the protagonist of my own life to being a spectator of others' lives. Writing these pages I suppress all traces of comedy or personal drama in order to throw all my energy, desire, longing, potential, fulfillment, hope, and desperation into the dreadful heap . . . that represents my mind, when right now I barely have the valor to think of it—the contemporary history that was my Spain.[42]

It is curious that Lejárraga does not consider this book autobiographical, merely because it is more a political memoir than a personal one. Yet what is essential is her intent in writing the book. She clearly wishes to tell us about Spain's tragedy, like de la Mora and Ibárruri, from her point of view as a Socialist and a political woman who traveled around the country giving campaign speeches. Lejárraga is telling us obliquely, by denying the existence of a personal voice, that she is an "urgent voice of collective testimony." What is important here is Lejárraga's consciousness as an intellectual, a political being, and an accomplished writer. Her obligation is to tell the stories of others who could not write or protest, rather than her own. She is not the center of her text; she is a medium of communication for the colonial subjects of her writing. Lejárraga produces an "outlaw" text in which she has placed herself—"a woman"—in the position of both writer (of memory text) and reader (interpreter) of the text and the social problems that she encounters "on the roads of Spain."

Dolores Medio, a teacher and novelist who in most of her works reflects the social climate of Spain during and after the war, published several volumes of autobiographical prose after the death of Franco. In *Atrapados en la ratonera: Memorias de una novelista,* she describes how she grew up in the Asturian city Oviedo surrounded by women while providing, like de la Mora, a detailed and researched history of the war. Yet this is a more personal account of Medio's coming to age because of the war. It is a *Bildungsroman,* in which the author's notion of selfhood is contingent on a "bigger reality." Medio wrote as a novelist, not as a colonial subject; she permits us to envision the opposing ideologies of her own generation and her mother's. She is constantly torn between her intellectual and rational vision and her loyalty to her self-sacrificing mother. Her father was deceased and she lived with a traditional mother, an aunt, and a younger sister. Both Medio and her sister were "exceptional" young women with careers, who were uninterested in clothes and gadding about. Medio, in fact, had a Communist activist lover, who was married and was later to cause her many hardships (she was pursued by the police because of this affiliation).

She describes, with a mixture of comicality and tragedy, the fateful Sunday—20 July 1936—when Oviedo was to be taken by the rebels, who had begun their siege in Morocco on 17 July and moved north the next day. Her mother decided to make her and her sister look like presentable, "marriageable" girls. Dressed in their finest, they were sent off to the movies and for the customary Sunday walk, so that they could be scrutinized by the local eligible bachelors.

> Sunday morning passed in tranquility, in an anguishing or a hopeful tranquility, depending on how you looked at it. After the midday meal, Mother insisted that we go to the movies and for a walk like other girls, instead of remaining locked in the house. She and Aunt Lola went to their rosary and vigilance, their daily spiritual food. We were worried and had no desire to go anywhere, but we finally went to the movies so that Mother wouldn't be upset—so as not to deprive her of what gave her the most satisfaction. . . . Because of that act, we were turned into two weird, anachronistic figures, moving—seemingly with a strange unconsciousness—on the surface of a tense atmosphere, almost suffocating, on the verge of blowing up around us like a grenade.
>
> What we did do, on turning the corner of our street and making sure Mother couldn't see us anymore, was take off the straw hats and dangle them from our arms, as though they were the flower baskets of two girls returning from the village. That was better. It made it different. Anyway, we suspected that afternoon, with our brand-new silk poplin dresses and our lovely straw hats—which we would never wear again—that we were burying an entire period of our lives.[43]

Medio describes the difficulty of finding food and potable water during the shelling of her town, Oviedo, in the northern province of Asturias. Once she did find food for her ailing mother and aged aunt, the problem of obtaining fuel rendered their survival even more problematic. Medio describes how she had to fight with her conscience about which objects in the house she could burn in order to boil water. Her intense repulsion for her mother's thick, ornate furniture, which reminded her of her strict and stifling upbringing, made her feel both gleeful and guilty as she contemplated its destruction. Yet when they decided that the first things to be burned would be the "heavy, ugly and styleless" nightstands, she was torn by the feeling that she was destroying part of her life: "Then something surprising occurred to me. As I was chopping those old nightstands, which I hated, I suddenly felt that I was mutilating myself, that I was tearing a part of my past from my life, something that still was part of me, like a sick limb that has to be amputated, but that it hurts to give up."[44]

Medio had broken all the conventions of the strictly provincial life in Asturias, which her intellectual self found to be ludicrous and uncomfortable. Yet the break with the past, which coincided with the apocalyptic war in Asturias and the end of innocence, proved to be painful. She was heroic in her own right, torn between respect for the blind Catholic faith and stoicism of her mother—who later died of starvation in order that her daughters might eat— and contempt and frustration for that blind acceptance of the oppressive Spanish monolith that had ruled through the centuries.

Medio's work is unique in that it shows the ambivalence of a Republican living in a Nationalist zone, surrounded by family and neighbors who support the Nationalists. She describes the need for silence and introversion alongside the desperate need to survive psychologically and ideologically while living in enemy territory. Medio's work is an anomaly—a story of exile within one's own town and country. In many ways, her testimony is not unlike the exile texts of Victoria Kent and Federica Montseny, who had to disguise their identities to survive in Nazi-dominated France, as we shall see. But Medio contrasts the boring intimacy of her home with a grim portrait of war and persecution.

The strength of these female voices and many others is that they speak both as individuals who have lost their dignity, privacy, democracy, freedom, and country and as part of a collective consciousness. They all speak—some more clearly than others—as women who have experienced war and its aftermath. Their voices form a chorus that is unique: no other historical, sociological, or literary source has provided us with such insights into the lives of Spanish women and the impact of the Spanish civil war. Female memory texts dealing with the early twentieth century in Spain, the war, and its consequences are undoubtedly the most important way to reverse the phantom role of women in the annals of contemporary Spanish history. From a literary critic's standpoint, they also provide a unique opportunity for reconceptualizing and reappraising the definition of genre when dealing with the immense lacuna between Western man's autobiographical practice and the outlaw voices of collective testimony.

Chapter 5   Women Remembering War

The violence perpetrated during the Second Spanish Republic continued to escalate as the "two Spains" wearied of each other's attempts to undermine their distinct political agendas. The Revolution of October had had grave consequences for the Spanish Left and for the state of morale in general; the Left could not forget that it was the Republican government of Alejandro Lerroux that sent Franco and the ghoulish Arab troops into Asturias to rape and massacre its countryfolk. The factionalization of Spain in those years presents a very complex picture.

The same year that Hitler came to power, in 1933, the Spanish organization Falange was founded by José Antonio Primo de Rivera. By 1934 Primo de Rivera was discussing Nazi ideology in Berlin. The Spanish Monarchists began negotiating with Mussolini on arms, even as Hitler was drawing up plans to stockpile oil in Spain. According to Robert Whealey, in 1935 Mussolini started giving Primo de Rivera a monthly allowance, which continued into 1936.[1] It is obvious that even though a class war was brewing among Spaniards, the international implications were far-reaching. Spanish, German, and Italian goals were beginning to converge as Hitler's plans to take over Europe congealed.

Catholic, Falange, and other Fascist youth organizations were cropping up as quickly as Marxist and Anarchists groups emerged. Land reform was a shambles. Repression against the CNT and the FAI intensified, while the Communist party gained strength. As Gabriel Jackson says, "What all these groups . . . had in common was their disgust with the parliamentary Republic, their combative ardor, their press and leaflet propaganda, and their assumption that a fundamental test of force was coming between the Right and the Left."[2] Of course, the young people were themselves the cogwheels in the process toward widespread confrontation.[3] The rightist organization Spanish Action, led by José Calvo Sotelo (who felt that CEDA was too "liberal"), strove for an authoritarian monarchy that bordered on an elite Fascism. On the other side, the Left had already recognized the spread of Fascism in Europe, and both the Anarchists and Marxists had begun to organize against it.[4]

Hoping to draw the polarized factions to the Center by promising a revitalized platform, the government staged new elections in February of 1936. The Catholics prayed for a victory for Gil Robles and CEDA;[5] but the coalition of Catholics, Fascists, and Monarchists did not see victory. The Center did not fare well either. The Popular Front—composed of Socialists, Center-Left Republicans, Anarchists, Communists, and the Catalan Esquerra—was voted into power, winning 257 of of the 473 seats in Parliament. Manuel Azaña replaced Alcalá Zamora as president.

The Left was euphoric, inspired by promises of land reform and amnesty for those still in prison since the revolt of October 1934. The wealthy and the church were in a state of extreme tension, and the military immediately began to plot an overthrow of the Popular Front government. The prevailing confusion and anarchy motivated the Left and Right youth groups to further mobilize into Falange, Socialist, and Communist organizations.[6] Strikes, riots, arson, street fighting, sniper attacks, and outright murder were rampant.

Azaña immediately moved the most subversive generals out of Madrid. The monarchist Manuel Goded was assigned to Barcelona. Emilio Mola, a leader in the Moroccan strife, went to Pamplona in the Basque country. José Sanjurjo, whose aborted coup of 1932 had sent him to exile in Portugal, was approached to lead the revolt again; but after a planning meeting in March 1936, which included Generals Galarza, Franco, and Mola, it was decided to give Mola the insurrectionist command.[7] Mola and other Right leaders were still vacillating as late as May, given the disagreement among Monarchists, Falangists, and the military. But on the night of July 12, leftist policemen and Socialist gunmen arrested Calvo Sotelo and murdered him shortly afterward. Although it is fairly certain that the military would have carried out the insurrection as planned, this unprecedented act of violence by government police against a well-respected rightist leader was to provide a justification for catapulting Spain into a three-year war of fratricide.[8] In response to the murder of Calvo Sotelo, an Assault Guard lieutenant, José Castillo, was murdered by his own colleagues.

Franco flew to Morocco on 17 July, and Hitler and Mussolini assisted him in flying his African Foreign Legion and native troops there.[9] Franco was accustomed to dealing with Moroccan troops, violent warriors who were known for their blind obedience. The other generals, too, moved swiftly with their troops.[10] In Madrid and Barcelona, bastions of the Republic, the Nationalists (military insurgents) were thwarted by the Loyalists (Republican and leftist soldiers).[11] In Seville, the Arab troops were instructed to slaughter those in the countryside who did not obey the call of the rebel forces. Nine thousand women, children, and men were massacred, primarily with knives.[12] Between 17 July and 20 July Spanish Morocco, the Andalusian cities of Seville, Cordoba, and Granada, the northern cities of La Coruña, Santander, Oviedo, Burgos, Valladolid, Salamanca, and Zaragoza, all fell.

In the more prosperous north (Salamanca and Burgos), where the Franco sympathizers outnumbered the so-called Reds, the uprising was less bloody. In the Basque country an immediate takeover had been impossible because it was staunchly anti-insurrectionist. Franco's takeover there implied centralized government and the disappearance of autonomy, as it would for the Catalonians. The organized and armed leftist groups in Madrid, Barcelona, Bilbao, and Valencia gave the insurgents no chance for conquest. The Anarchist strongholds and other cities where major workers' organizations had been established could do little to avoid the military takeover. Though only two major cities—Seville and Zaragoza—fell in that early sweep through Spain, the first campaign by insurgents was decidedly successful. A third of the country was in military hands by the end of July. And by this time the military had been fortified with German and Italian soldiers, bombers, and arms.

Although Franco would be unable to overcome Madrid and Barcelona in 1936, by September half of the country was in the hands of the insurgents. Franco became head of state on 1 October and set up his government in Burgos.[13]

Lawless executions that would go on throughout the war began to occur nightly. All of the accumulated rancor on both sides spewed forth: the Right shot intellectuals, teacher, doctors, proletariat leaders; the Left killed the señoritos, leaders of the Right, and some priests. Unfortunately for the Republic, the French had proposed a nonintervention pact, which was signed on 8 August 1936. The only country—other than Germany and Italy—that violated the pact was Russia.[14] But there was a heroic show of support for the Republic—in response to a worldwide call to Communists by the Comintern—in the form of the first volunteers of the International Brigades, who arrived in Spain in early October.[15] The stage was now set, and all the international players were in place.

The air assault on Madrid began on 29 October, and the Republican government moved its seat to Valencia on 6 November. In 1937, the destruction of the Basque town Guernica was carried out by the German Condor legion; Hitler was using Spain to test the newest bombing technology. In November 1938, when all was lost, the remaining International Brigade troops left Spain. Barcelona resisted until January 1939, when the mass exodus into France began. Madrid gave up in early March; Franco's troops entered on 28 March 1939. Hitler had already made his first move that March, when he invaded Czechoslovakia.

In 1939, the first battle against Fascism was lost on Spanish soil; the country became a moral and material wasteland and the revolutionary movement was destroyed. Franco's Holy Crusade was a success, and no one who stayed in Spain after the war was permitted to forget it for some thirty-five years. At the end of the war, according to Stanley Payne, nearly 300,000 people were dead. About 120,000 Spaniards and 25,500 foreigners died in combat; there were 15,000 civilian deaths, and 108,000 murders and executions. Payne claims that 165,000 persons died from illness during the war. Many other executions and deaths from malnutrition and disease would follow in the first decades of the Franco regime. Payne calculates that, of those who fled Spain at the end of the war, 162,000 remained in permanent exile.[16]

Information about women during the war is scant, as we have observed. Interestingly, there are fewer memory texts by women about the war years than about their lives before the war and afterward, in prison or exile. All of them refer to the war at some point in their narratives, but it is usually not the main focus. Perhaps the "psychic closing-off" phenomenon did not permit in-depth descriptions of personal war experiences, or perhaps the need to conceal their activism during the war caused them to censor the memory of their participation. It is also possible that depicting the war's consequences, which affected the lives of Spaniards for so many decades, seemed of more importance than describing the war itself. In addition, many of the women who wrote their memoirs or gave testimony did not actively participate in war activities and were therefore not equipped to discuss anything but its personal impact on their lives. Or they might not have felt that there was reason to write about the war; some believed that the stuff of war is death, not mourning or home-front activities.[17] Writing about war apparently is gendered; in the case of the Spanish civil war, it was the Hemingways, the Orwells, the Malrauxs, and the Koestlers who had societal permission to document the tragedies.

Constancia de la Mora, chief censor for the Foreign Press Bureau and wife of the famous Communist aviator Ignacio Hidalgo de Cisneros,[18] is one of the few women who explicitly describes, in her double-voiced autobiography, her personal and political reactions to the war, especially in her chapter entitled "Widows of Heroes Rather Than Wives of Cowards." Her work with orphaned children makes her focus constantly that of a mother, mainly concerned for other women and their children. For instance, when she and Concha Prieto, daughter of the moderate Socialist leader Indalecio Prieto, are sent to care for children in the south, she tells us:

> I had little news from Ignacio and Concha was too busy to hear very often from her father, the Minister of Air and Marine, but gradually we began to live with the tense military moment. In Madrid, General Franco's troops moved implacably forward. Bombardment followed bombardment. And all over Spain bombs dropped on Spanish women and children.
>
> And then, in the middle of October, I had a great shock. Concha got a peremptory note from her father. The military situation was tense. He could not work in peace with his daughters in Spain—in danger. They must leave. I could hardly believe my ears. The women of Madrid were fighting beside their men, building barricades, cooking food while the guns roared. We were comparatively safe, doing work, however unromantic, that was absolutely necessary. Why should the Minister of Air and Marine consider his daughters above the women of Madrid?[19]

De la Mora is not only emphasizing women's participation and bravery in Madrid, but also protesting the attitude of the politician who does not wish his daughters to be in the same sort of danger as are the millions of other women who are not in a privileged situation.[20]

The first assault on Madrid (18–20 July) was met with staunch resistance in the Republican capital, as it was in Barcelona, the second most important city in Spain. The first attack on the Catalonian city (19–20 July) is described by the activist Soledad Real, who tells how the young revolutionaries spontaneously challenged the rebel troops of General Manuel Goded.

> We organized in my barrio, Barceloneta, a cultural/sports club called Avanti. It's a workers' district of longshoremen, metal workers, ship salvagers, and fishermen. There were no battles right there. Rather, we organized a resistance group to close off the barrio, with all the stuff sitting on the dock like cotton, things that had been shipped in. But a moment came when there were so many wounded people that we had to open up the barrio to take advantage of the clinics there. Our group did that work with Esquerra Republicana, Estat Catala,[21] Communists, and Socialists.
>
> Some of the girls got together and decided to go around asking for sheets and cloth; we washed them and cut them into strips. We shouted through the streets: "Give us sheets for the wounded!" What impressed me from the very beginning was the call to arms. This was very emo-

tional because we followed it by radio—those who were politically conscious knew about the Popular Front (Republican government) and those of the Right—we followed its course from Morocco. In Barcelona we have always celebrated the 19th instead of the 18th.

The important thing to me was calling the people to arms. It was grandiose—inspiring the pueblo to unite against something that was going to annihilate what we had achieved. For me, the memory of that is incalculable. For as long as I live, that memory will make me tremble.[22]

When Franco arrived in Morocco to greet the insurgent officers and to dispose of the Loyalist officers, Virgilio Leret Ruiz, a Socialist captain of the Spanish air force, was among those present. Carlota O'Neill was a young Communist journalist who published a women's magazine entitled Nosotras, which was affiliated with the party. In the summer of 1936 O'Neill took her two young daughters to Melilla to spend the summer with their father, Captain Leret. Her autobiography describes a happy family jaunt through an old Arab cemetery and those first moments of the insurrection.

At first there was the scream of a faraway siren, like a cry torn from the heart; it was a chilling and ear-piercing scream, as if the air had been ripped like the tassels from a cloth. An apocalyptic scream that told us to get ready. And the words just hung from our lips. We looked back, seeking the reason [for the siren] at the base, while the siren called and called with its fiery attack. From afar, a group of men were coming toward us at furious speed. Virgilio went out to meet them while he told us, "Let's get back to the boat." The men, as they came closer, waving their hands in the air, screamed emotionally, like shipwrecked men. And they were. All of us were, right then. They were screaming for Virgilio, for the Virgilio they considered superhuman; yet he was only a man, like them.

Virgilio went running to them; they spoke so we couldn't hear them. Later he took us in his arms and put us back in the rowboat. I asked, "What is going on?" But he wouldn't answer me. He was rowing furiously. Mariela and Loti were staring at us very seriously, with a foreboding look. We climbed into the boat. Virgilio ran down to the cabin, grabbed his revolver, and put on the cap to his uniform; he was moving quickly, quickly, without hesitation. He returned to the bridge and went back down the gangway to the rowboat again, climbed on, and pulled the oars in the direction of the base. The girls were in shock, below deck, with Librada [the maid]. I followed him with my eyes to the bridge, the gangway, without speaking. And I let him leave. He wouldn't look at me; I don't think he even realized I was there.

From the other side of the big highway, above, the shots began in the hollow where we were. They were the first shots that would later start a worldwide fire. Virgilio rowed and rowed; he kept getting farther away from me. And I stared at him and thought, "I want to see him well, stare at his face, because I won't ever see him again." And we hadn't even kissed! The last one! A bullet flew by me; I hardly even noticed, I just kept staring. And Virgilio woke up. And he realized I was standing there and I saw fear in his eyes. "Go, go below." I listened without hearing him, but he reacted. He stopped rowing and stood up. Another bullet whizzed past my head. I must have been a good target, and those soldiers coming down the highway must have thought I had a machine gun. Virgilio screamed: "Carlota. Go below." And I couldn't answer him; I couldn't speak. I couldn't move. And then he said, "Do it for your daughters!" Then I woke up too. Those were his last words. His last motto. His testament. I looked at him for the last time, and slowly I started on my life mission.[23]

She was never to see her husband again; he was summarily executed shortly afterward. O'Neill spent the three years of war in prison, separated from her daughters.

The terrorist campaign in Seville was extended to the villages—Dos Hermanas, for instance, where Spain's prime minister, Felipe González, was born. One woman, Ana María Martín Rubio, still expressed the terror she had experienced during the war when I spoke to her in 1986. It seems that each time Martín Rubio opened the door of her home during the war, she would see the bloody bodies of friends and neighbors strewn outside. Like most other poor women in the Andalusian villages, before the war she had worked at secondary farm labor—olive, cork, and tobacco processing—for a few pennies for a sixteen-hour day. When a union was established, salaries went up slightly. (Martín Rubio's boyfriend was very upset that she joined.) But when Quiepo's troops entered Seville, unionized women were threatened with death unless they went home. The psychological effects of Nationalist terror were deep and lasting; Martín Rubio claims she did not venture into the center of town from 1939 until 1975, when Franco died.[24]

Dulce del Moral was one of the few women of the Left whom I encountered who wished to talk about her war experiences in Seville. A member of the United Socialist Youth organization, she spent eight years in prison after the war because of it. She said: "The eighteenth of July came around; I was ironing when I heard the news. I wanted to escape, but my husband wouldn't do it. The people immediately went out to barricade the streets. I survived by pure luck, but many of my young friends were dead in the streets. People were being turned in left and right; even the Catholic nuns aided in the witchhunt against leftist activists."[25]

Del Moral stated that women fought alongside men in solidarity, but like others in the highly male oriented region of Andalusia, she could not think of any women who stood out as war heroines. They are excluded from all studies of the war in Seville and other parts of Andalusia. Angelina Puig i Valls's essay on the women activists of the Andalusian region of Granada corroborates the fact that women were erased from history because they had crossed the border of female propriety into the public arena designated for men.

Even today the image of activists as "dishonest" women prevails. When the author asked a woman why the activities of the organization called Antifascist Women in her small town were never discussed, she responded that the women were "not clean" and that "they had made men crazy."[26] As we shall observe repeatedly, the inferences were sexual. The discrediting of activists was still a sport in the 1980s!

A number of religious women who had witnessed the first days of the uprising still lived in Seville in 1986. But even after I obtained written permission from a church administrator to visit several convents to talk to the nuns, they refused to speak to me about the war. When I talked to the mother superior of one convent on the phone, she said laconically: "Why not read the history books? It's all there." Another said she did not wish to remember the war and remarked, "It's enough that God remembers the war." I was never allowed past the convent doors.

These remarks suggest a heavy weight of guilt that these women have buried deep within their cloistered walls. In a land where for many years, people informed on their relatives and neighbors, causing death and prison sentences, it is not surprising that the clerics, heavily involved in the persecution of anti-Franco activists, do not wish to discuss their participation or their knowledge of church dealings. Interesting, though, is the fear on the part of the nuns, whose role in the witchhunts has always been considered minimal—though del Moral is not of that opinion. The nuns were the female activists' jailers, so the guilt may stem from their prison experiences. Other than their work in the prisons, the role of the female clergy in the war has not been discussed or documented.

Extremadura, a province in the poorest region of Spain, experienced one

of the most bloody uprisings of the war. In the city of Mérida I sought information about Anita López, a pharmacist who had organized the defense committee against the invasion of General Juan Yague in August 1936.[27] While her
name is still known to some people in Mérida, I was unable to obtain any
information about her activity during the war.

The most terrible massacres, other than those of Seville and Córdoba on
18 July, occurred in August, in Mérida and Badajoz (also in Extremadura).
Badajoz may have been worse, for leftists were gathered into the bullring and
killed en masse. Even today, few people are willing to discuss the nightmare
of those first days of the takeover. One woman told me how some of the men
witnessing the mayhem, including her husband, went into hiding in neighboring
Portugal. The Salazar regime, however, returned any exiles they found, so their
fate was scarcely more fortuitous.

The story of Madrid during the war, especially in the first months, is one
of the most remarkable tales of resistance by a group of citizens, especially
women, in modern history. Ibárruri's famous slogan, "No pasarán" (They shall
not pass), was heard all over Spain, above all when in November 1936 the
Nationalists attempted to take Madrid. Nieves Torres, then a teenager, was in
the Pasionaria sewing workshop[28] that dedicated itself to the production of
clothing for the troops. She describes that pivotal moment in the war.

> That winter of 1936 was one of the coldest we had ever experienced. We
> had to queue up in the streets all the time to acquire what little food was
> rationed out. That seventh of November, everyone thought it was the end
> for Madrid. All we could think about was that the Fascists were going to
> enter the city. If only we had been able to predict it! We had no food,
> no wood to burn, no matches, nothing. What a disaster! Then Dolores
> shouted, "No pasarán!" She told it to the soldiers, to the rear guard, to
> everyone. And they all rose up and said: "No, no, no pasarán. We must
> defend Madrid tooth and nail!" We all accepted the challenge. The men
> who hadn't already gone to the front went off to fight. We women accel-
> erated production—knitting, sewing, everything we could. Some went to
> the front as soldiers, above all, as nurses. Women went into factories and
> workshops, taking the men's places at their jobs; not just in secondary
> jobs, but also as "foremen" and directors of factories. Fortunately, "they"
> didn't pass.[29]

Torres' enthusiastic description of how the women responded to the call
to arms is corroborated by Julio Alvarez del Vayo, foreign minister of the Republic during the war, in an unprecedented feminist homage.

But it was the Spanish woman who best proved her worth during the war. An absurd tradition had kept her on the fringe of national life and and had confined her to the limited fringe of domestic work. . . . But by 1936 a change had begun to take place. The women had been deeply shocked by the savage reprisals following the October movement, and they registered their protest by voting for the Popular Front. . . . The women were attracted to politics chiefly by the powerful movement of the Young Socialists, which prepared them for the moment when their remarkable qualities could be placed entirely at the service of the people. That moment arrived on July 18. It was the Spanish woman who dominated the magnificent mobilization of the people against the rebels, and it was she who for two and a half years kept the flame of resistance burning.[30]

Del Vayo goes on to talk of the bravery and stoicism of the women and ends his dramatic tribute with the following paragraph: "But it was not merely in her capacity for emotion and sacrifice that the Spanish woman rose to the full height of her powers. For the first time in the history of Spain she undertook work of the greatest responsibility both in the government and the civil service, thus giving the lie to those who had so long and so stupidly considered her as inferior to man in dealing with problems affecting the general well-being of the country."[31]

If the main term ascribed to women's lives throughout the centuries is *abnegation*, rebellion against social injustice is what made these women seek the "flash of freedom" they experienced during the decade of the 1930s. Abnegation, the most valuable quality women could possess before the war, is replaced by bravery, though unacknowledged, during and after the war. Women represented more than half the Spanish population in the 1930s; there were some twelve million women and eleven million men, making it particularly startling that there is so little mention of them in historical texts about the war. Young Spanish women of the working class, who had been kept under strict familial supervision and had been generally discouraged from learning anything but household duties, witnessed a revolutionary change in their possible destinies at the onset of the war.

Maruja Cuesta, who spent fifteen years in Franco's prisons for her activism during the war, describes her specific flash of freedom. Frustrated because her parents could not afford to pay room and board for her to study in Madrid, even after her teacher had offered to sponsor her, she says:

People finished school very young then, at about twelve. This law of impotence that made it impossible for me to study made me rebellious. The war broke out in June, and that's when I saw the sky open up for me. I would have liked to be a teacher or a lawyer, for example. The war limited many of the dreams of our youth, but at the same time all wars have a positive side, of course. I saw my chance, and it was to work for the "cause" on the Republican side.

I never would have dreamed of being a Fascist, even if I went to jail for fifteen years. I joined the Socialist Youth Group (JSU), a young people's organization. I was about sixteen then. I was very active. In the war young people became very committed. They created the farmers' centers; they fought against illiteracy, which was very high then.

I had studied typing. They called me to become part of the staff in the offices of my village. There, because of my activity in the JSU, I became the general secretary. And from there, they put me in a training school, against my parents' wishes, because I knew I could get an education there. They taught everything—not just politics, they also prepared us well culturally. In the JSU, we taught each other what we knew. It was a three-month course.

But the war came and we started an intense activity, traveling to villages to mobilize the farming youth. In the village where I lived, they created sewing and other workshops to help the militiamen in the mountains. Two voluntary divisions were formed by very young kids, boys and girls. Many women took over factory jobs from the very beginning. Many organizations were created, like Muchachas. Women were in workshops, offices, war factories, on the production line, on the streets collecting money. Women played a key role in the war. They were even in the trenches. In the hospitals, nurses and female doctors.[32]

Asturias suffered a demoralizing defeat early in the war because General Antonio Aranda, who had sworn allegiance to the Republic, turned traitor and took over the region for the insurgent forces. Matilde de la Torre describes the women who had gone to work in the factories in Asturias, where she was politically active during the war. The plight of many of these women was particularly dramatic, since they were working in the weapons and dynamite factories.

There are some six girls. All of them young, all beautiful. No one raises her head to look at us. They are working. They are working in the management of death. And not a slow, dark death, of toxic gases and gunpowder cotton. No, no. These girls are working in the management of a deadly clamorous substance. If it blew up right now, as it could . . . all of these girls, and us, and whoever else is around, and those outside, and the walls and the roofs and the houses near and far . . . all of them would fly through the air converted into minimal particles, into deadly bullets, and the only thing left of this building would be an immense hole, and the birds would die, hit by the deadly blast.[33]

After they finished there, they would go back to their normal "female" tasks: preparing the food for their men at the local fronts and carrying it to them, all in a state of extreme and constant tension, fearing that they would arrive to find their men fallen in battle. In her quirky, lyrical, yet laconically journalistic style, de la Torre praises these women for their ability to carry out such dangerous tasks and simultaneously be mothers and wives. She is in awe of their versatility and bravery and ends this chapter about the women of Asturias by suggesting that they do not pretend to be the flashy milicianas who get their pictures in the paper.

Those girls who arrive at the frontline trenches. And without a fuss, without photos, or lipstick, or cute overalls [the outfit of the miliciana], dole out food and . . . and, while the men eat, they grab the guns and sit in the earth's bowels, before the machine guns, as though they were sitting before a sewing machine.
They shoot . . .
They shoot plenty, calmly, continually. . . . And it's been like this in Asturias for nearly eight months. . . . On the Asturian fronts, many girls have died, machine-gunned down. Not because they are tomboys or heroines of this truculent drama, but because they are used to this atmosphere. Because they are the everyday heroines of the arms factories and they know how to manage mercury explosives.[34]

But women were also heroines even in the smallest tasks, such as food shopping in the midst of constant shelling. Dolores Medio tells us that "the need to go out into the streets to look for food obliged us to defy all dangers."[35]

Soledad Real describes the heroism of women working in the Barcelona arms factories:

They had to work without masks, which were necessary because of the poisonous materials they produced. Also, they had the right to a glass of milk a day in order to detoxify themselves. But instead of drinking it, they saved it for the children in kindergarten. (The men, metalworkers, nevertheless refused to work if their meal conditions weren't improved. Men get angry when I refer to this particular case, but I've seen all this.)

No one can tell me it isn't true. I experienced all this. I went into an arms factory and saw the women with the whites of their eyes the color of eggyolks—and their skin was a disgusting yellow too. I was perplexed until I saw the posters around saying, "Milk to save the children!" and others explaining, "Comrades, we have no masks, but our comrades need arms!" Women have always been required by custom and education to practice abnegation. It was so exaggerated that I think when you compare this with the heroism of facing the enemy, the latter is diminished.[36]

Many women worked in less dramatic scenarios, as de la Mora describes. In the south, thousands took over the farms to provide food for their families. Other dramatic roles played by women—such as spying on the enemy—have been suggested, but there is no documented information. There are big gaps when we try to study women's activities in the war, but there are also some very revealing passages in the many autobiographies and testimonies.

Other authors attempt to explain that though women normally become visible in the public sector during war, their gender relations and "feminine" identity do not change significantly in the long run. "To explain the 'lag' in the development of women's consciousness, we must take a broad view, looking not just at wartime changes themselves, but also at how they were discursively encoded, and how women, like men, drew on existing cultural resources to make sense of their experiences."[37]

Of course, at the end of the war Spanish women were stripped of any notions of feminist consciousness, if they had had them earlier. But the fact is that the patriarchal encoding of women in Spain—in spite of the anomalous narrative by del Vayo—confined them within a gender-based discourse that could not change their destinies. In *Behind the Lines* we find the following remarks: "When the home front is mobilized, women may be allowed to move 'forward' in terms of employment or social policy. Yet the battlefront—pre-eminently a male domain—takes economic and cultural priority. Therefore, while women's objective situation does change, relationships of domination and subordination are retained through discourses that systematically designate un-equal gender relations."[38]

Ronald Fraser comments on the activity of women in Madrid: "Women were playing a large and important part in the Popular Front effort, working in factories, farms, hospitals, in industrial and rural collectives. The depths of the revolution were, at one level, nowhere better revealed than in the change of attitudes towards women in a traditionally male chauvinist society." Yet in remarks about women in Barcelona, he says: "Abortion was legalized under controlled conditions, centres opened for women, including prostitutes and unmarried mothers, birth control information disseminated and 'marriage by usage' instituted whereby cohabitation for ten months, or less if pregnancy occurred, was considered marriage. Despite these considerable gains, the revolution did not fundamentally alter the traditional roles or—but rarely—the customary inequalities of pay. Women continued to launder clothes, cook, keep house and look after children; they continued to get paid less than men."[39]

We shall observe throughout this text that Spanish women in the war apparently had a circular evolution: from repression to relative freedom and back to repression. Yet their discourse was always inscribed within the codes of the church and the state, and while they had a feeling of freedom during the war because they had been given more responsibility and some choice over their minds and bodies, new gender relations were not incorporated into Spanish society. The notions of equality disappeared quickly, as the Franco regime took over at the end of the war.

Take, for example, the case of the milicianas, the women who actually went to the battlefront. Although the miliciana phenomenon has never been adequately addressed, it is obvious that the issue of women at the front lines produced a great deal of consternation and controversy in Spain during the war. We have few statistics on the number of women who actually fought. Beevor states vaguely that "no figures are available, but there were probably fewer than 1,000 women at the front." He goes on to point out that "there were, however, several thousand under arms in the rear areas and a woman's battalion took part in the defence of Madrid. This move towards equal participation was severely curtailed under the increasingly authoritarian direction of the war effort as the military situation deteriorated. By 1938 women had returned to a strictly auxiliary role."[40] It was Dolores Ibárruri herself who was to recall women to the rear guard.

Remarks about the participation of the milicianas in the war have generally been negative, even among leftist women who wrote about the war. One autobiography, by a woman who had been a leftist militant and later championed Franco's cause, contains the following remark: "About the milicianas, of these poor women who in other days had offered their favors in the streets of Madrid at the early morning hours, it was said that they caused more discharges among the milicianos than the bullets of the Nationalist soldiers—and that's how it was, in fact, because of the lack of hygiene and the lack of any moral ideas among them."[41]

A Mexican Communist activist, Blanca Lydia Trejo, who visited Spain during the war, makes equally disparaging remarks despite her sympathy with the leftist cause: "The collaboration of women as milicianas has been a total failure." Trejo explains that although she felt that many of the women went off to war in a romantic, courageous spirit, they were vilified for doing something only men "should" do. But she remarks—and this has been confirmed by various testimonies of males[42]—that the men reacted like Spanish *caballeros*, coming to their rescue when they thought the women would be wounded or killed, and this caused more deaths. She also notes that venereal diseases were rampant.[43]

The journalist H. E. Kaminski provides a view of what the milicianos thought about their female comrades.

Another thing that shocks me and that one does not normally see so close to the enemy is that there are women. They wear pants just like the men. It is useless to mention that here vanity serves no purpose and that women do not use lipstick or powder. The majority wear short hair like the men, to the point that often it is difficult to distinguish them.

I do not think that any human beings are made for war, especially women. But the truth is that women carry out their duties with the same devotion as their masculine comrades. Many have distinguished themselves for their bravery.

In reference to their presence there, the opinions are divided. Some of those whom I speak to approve of it because, in the name of free will, they consider military service as an act of revolutionary will. "Everyone has the right to do what they wish with their lives. We would be bad revolutionaries if we wanted to prevent a woman from giving her life in the fight against Fascism," one of them told me.[44]

After the war, Franco propaganda denigrated the image of the miliciana to such an extent that no one spoke of them. There are only a few remarks about the milicianas in texts about the war[45] in spite of the curious fact that art posters and photographs portraying them abounded in newspapers during the war years. Obviously the novelty of female soldiers—unheard of until that time in Spain's history—motivated photographers and artists to capture their new visibility and overrepresent them in action, often in sexually provocative poses. Mary Nash makes the following observation:

In the early days of the war, the image of the miliciana was innovative and a break from the traditional behavior and conventional social roles of women. Nevertheless, a close analysis of this highly visible figure in the first weeks of the war demonstrates that in fact this new model of woman soldier was scarcely representative and does not appear to represent a new and genuine image of the feminine prototype, but rather a symbol of war and revolution. As such, it was not necessarily designed to become a real model for the collectivity of women. . . . The belligerent image of the miliciana was not directed to a feminine public, but instead tended to serve as a vehicle for a message directed toward men, to stimulate them to comply with their duty as soldiers in the antifascist struggle.[46]

De la Torre comments on her view of why the milicianas were so poorly regarded. She tells us that they dressed up for photographs in the typical revolutionary uniform (overalls), complete with makeup and often high-heeled shoes, so they were not taken very seriously. There were a few exceptions, such as the Catalonian Lina Odena and the Asturian Aida de la Fuente.[47] Both died at the front and became heroines of the cause. Nash remarks that "in general there were a few milicianas . . . who actually fought, while others were employed in auxiliary aid, health, supplies, kitchen, or laundry services. The typical profile of the miliciana was that of a young woman with political, familial, or affective ties to her militia companions."[48] This is more in keeping with the *soldadera* phenomenon of the Mexican revolution, in which women accompanied their men to the front.

"Rosie the Dynamiter" was a seventeen-year-old from the countryside near Madrid when she responded to the call to arms at the outbreak of the war.

It all began at night. Everyone was in bed. We heard some explosions and wondered "What's going on?" I was living here in Madrid with some relatives on Noviciado Street in the San Bernardo district, I did housework for them; they didn't pay me, but the arrangement was that they sent me to sewing school. I was from the country. I had come to Madrid two years before, all by myself. While I was in sewing school, some girls whom I had become friends with said, "So you work to pay for your living; well, we know a place where you can go to sewing school for free." And guess where it was? The Aida de la Fuente Group. I was there a few months, learning to make patterns. I also took classes, remedial classes, free for poor kids. It was sponsored by the JSU [the Socialist Youth Group]. While I was there studying, the war broke out and some of the guys arrived, desperately begging for volunteers because the Republic was in great danger, the military could take it away, they could make the constitution disappear. Well, I knew they were addressing the boys of our group, not the girls, but I sensed so much danger in what they were saying, so much need for help, that it occurred to me to ask in a soft voice:

"And the girls? Can we women go too?" A strong voice answered: "Well, of course." I said, "Well, put me on the list." I didn't say anything, not a word to my family. They were in the village. I was thinking about telling the relatives I lived with, but I thought: "Why? So they don't let me go?"[49]

Rosario was indeed an exceptional case, initially because she had come to Madrid alone—though of course she lived with relatives. Normally, only prostitutes and teachers relocated on their own in Spain in those days. A "decent" woman almost invariably lived with her parents. In addition, the fact that she volunteered for the trenches was unusual.

It is obvious, therefore, that the mythologized Lina Odena—who, the story goes, committed suicide when she was captured by the African legionnaires—and Aida de la Fuente were exceptional cases because they had been appropriated to inspire young women and men to work harder for the war. Others who survived the war did not fare as well and were not used as subjects of propaganda; rather, they were sexual objects who were told to take their proper places in the rear guard.

Mika Etchebéhère's memoirs of her activism in the war provide an anecdote about two milicianas that corroborates Nash's remarks. In a conversation between some male soldiers and a miliciana, we find what appears to be a realistic portrait of the plight of the female soldier.

"My name's Manuela. . . . I'm from the Pasionaria Column, but I'd rather be with you men. They never wanted to give us girls guns. We were only good for washing dishes and clothes. . . . My friend here, Nati, also wants to stay with you. She used to have long pigtails. Now she's cut them off. You know, if we get caught by the Fascists they'll shave our heads, so it's better to have short hair. So can we stay?" The response is negative because one of the soldiers comments that they don't know how to use a gun. Nati rapidly replies: "Yes we do, we can even dismantle it, grease it, everything. . . . We can also fill the cartridges with dynamite. But if you won't give us a gun, let us at least stay to cook and clean; this floor is very dirty."[50]

From 1986 to 1989, a series of conferences was held in Spain and abroad celebrating the fiftieth anniversary of the war. Several were dedicated to vindication of the female role in the war. The Ministry of Culture published the proceedings from the conference and for the first time the subject of the milicianas was openly dealt with. The historian Mary Nash sums up, in those proceedings, the reasons that prompted Spanish women to go to war: (1) youth-

ful enthusiasm, (2) rejection of a secondary role in the rear guard, (3) to accompany their men (in a few cases, mothers actually accompanied their sons!)[51]
and, (4) romantic adventure. Nash notes that, for the most part, the men expected the milicianas to do kitchen and laundry duty and to act as nurses.

Nash attributes the rumors about their prostitution at the front lines to a
sexologist who promoted this myth by writing that the women were wasting
"men's energies." Although Nash points out that there were some prostitutes
near the battlefield, such activity was short-lived. She claims that the Anarchist
hero Durruti actually executed several prostitutes who refused to leave his
camp.[52] Nash also remarks that there was a legitimate reason for their dismissal:
as the spontaneous troops of foot soldiers disappeared and traditional regiments
were created, the women no longer had a place at the front lines.

Rosie the Dynamiter winced many times in face of criticism of the milicianas for their "prostitution." During the October 1987 conference honoring
Spanish women of the war, several of the militiawomen protested that both the
Left and the Right denigrated their work and smeared their reputations without
cause, and that they expected to be vindicated from the calumny perpetrated
by the discourse of patriarchy.[53] Sensitive about the aspersions cast on women
at the front, Sánchez addresses the sexual interpretations that have been offered
by the Spanish public as well as by most male historians:

> Spaniards are very critical. They called the milicianas prostitutes and the
> milicianos thieves. And when the brigades arrived, they called them every
> name in the book. I don't understand it. Precisely the reason I came here
> today was to explain this to you. I never saw anything. First of all, one
> would have to be very stupid to go to the front lines to be a prostitute,
> where you can get your head blown off. . . . We women wore overalls like
> the men. They criticized us a lot for that: "How shameful for women to
> wear overalls!" When overalls cover you up more than anything! Women
> went to jail after the war for having worn overalls and for having carried
> a gun! You didn't have to have used it, just carried it, and worn overalls!
> If you go to war, naturally you have to be armed![54]

Later in my interview with her, Rosario admitted that it was likely that there
were some prostitutes at the front lines, an allegation that is reinforced by the
remarks about sexually transmitted disease. The machinations of the Franco
regime soiled the name of all women who participated in the war but the
reputation of the miliciana was destroyed most viciously, given her prominent
role in those belligerent times.

Gender roles did not change substantially after the war. The symbolic space
for women was still the kitchen, and their "uniform" an apron-covered hou-

sedress. The gender discourse of the Spanish war was embedded in the patriarchal talk about the female body: the woman as the angel of the hearth, the mother, the comforter, the womb, absent of mind and spirit. When she shed those symbols, she became filth, a carrier of dreaded diseases.

During the war the National Committee of Women against War and Fascism, created in 1933, was renamed Mujeres Antifascistas.[55] In August 1936 the ministries of war, industry, and commerce called for the creation of the Commission of Feminine Assistance; appointed by the national defense minister, Dr. Negrín, were Ibárruri, Victoria Kent, and other women who were very active during the war but have remained in the shadows of history. These include Encarnación Fuyola and the writer Isabel de Palencia. The commission was responsible for producing, acquiring, and distributing war supplies to the fronts, especially food, clothing and articles of hygiene. In October 1937 the second national conference of Antifascist Women was held, to assess their contributions to the war effort. Carmen González Martínez claims that "because of its activity, Antifascist Women was to become from 1936 to 1938 the great national organization of Spanish women."[56]

Antifascist Women divided into two groups, those who wished to go to the front and those who preferred working in the rear guard. In January of 1937, a group of girls—which grew out of the Socialist Youth Group (called JSU in Spain)—ranging in age from fourteen to twenty-five was also organized. The group, called the Unión de Muchachas, had some two thousand members in Madrid.[57] The major goal was to recruit these young women to employ them in workshops and factories. Furthermore—and this was true of all leftist women's organizations during the war—the group served as a vehicle for obtaining an education. For many of the members of Antifascist Women and groups like the Girls' Union were illiterate or had minimal skills. In those days girls who had six years of grade-school education were considered well educated. But their ability to read, write, and work with numbers was negligible. There was a concerted effort to emphasize the need for knowledge in order to change society and, in this case, the plight of women; indeed, education was one of the main goals of the Socialist and Communist organizations. Many women who participated in the courses, lectures, and classes offered them in the war years feel that it was within these organizations that they received their first authentic education. Even today these proletariat women, who are in their seventies and eighties, remember with nostalgia their awakening to what they call their "cultural formation."

The educational system of these groups was far from sophisticated. Women who had more than a six-year grade-school education were often called upon to give lectures in a field in which they were considered more prepared than others. Classes included the three Rs for those who were illiterate; there were also courses on cultural themes and some with a political orientation. Sewing classes were common, given the fact that a large number of women were working in the manufacture of supplies for the front, especially clothing. The girls even formed "brigades" to fight illiteracy.[58]

Both the Girls' Union and the Antifascist Women published magazines as a forum for their work, which also kept up the morale of the members. Ibárruri was mentioned constantly in these publications. When the Republic began to lose ground, both magazines folded for lack of funds and energy. Whereas the Girls' Union was confined to Madrid, Antifascist Women had units all over the country. Nash has identified 255 groups, and she claims that when the war broke out there were fifty thousand members.[59]

The main purpose of Antifascist Women was the education of women and their introduction into the workforce to take the place of the men who had gone to the front. Women worked in war industries, sewing shops, car repair shops; they took over jobs on trolleys, on subways, in hospitals. Women were given bureaucratic and clerical positions in offices. They collected clothing and scrap metal; they learned trades and became political administrators. Serving as a kind of quartermaster corps, the female population also was an important link between the rear guard and the front lines. Often traveling to the front, women sponsored social affairs for soldiers where possible. Those who did not go to the front performed the typical tasks: they wrote letters, sent packages, kept up spirits, and maintained solidarity between the vanguard and rear forces. They organized nurseries and dining rooms for children, refugees, and the needy; they visited hospitals, helping the wounded to get in touch with their families.

These women had problems in the public sector, mostly because they met with male resistance during those three years. Like nearly all political groups, they were told to win the war and put other social issues on the back burner. Some of the correspondence of Antifascist Women with the unions suggests that the male population was slow to facilitate jobs for women, since the men feared that after the war they would be left without employment.[60] Yet that was not to be the case. In 1939, with the Franco takeover, leftist women once again disappeared from public life and, in the best of cases, were sent back to their homes. In the worst cases, they were pursued, imprisoned, tortured, or executed for their political activities—or, often, for those of their men.

In general, Antifascist Women did not have a feminist focus. Rather, in nearly all instances, their thrust was to help the war cause, in keeping with

Pasionaria's dictum.[61] Fuyola, the secretary general of the National Committee, for example, in traditional fashion emphasized the rights of women as mothers. A few women within the group did reveal a feminist consciousness. Matilde Huici, another woman whose work has never been acknowledged and who, according to Ibárruri, was a major activist,[62] attempted to fight for genuine equal rights, which she felt were sorely lacking in Spain.[63]

Antifascist Women—and to some extent the Girls' Union—demonstrate, therefore, an awakening of Spanish women to their intellectual and physical capacities in the workplace. Perhaps even more important, women recognized their resourcefulness and resilience in the face of strife and opposition, qualities of which they had been unaware among their gender. There was a new sense of pride. One can perceive it in the voices of those women who tell their stories today, and it is perceptible in the tone of their memory texts. It is indeed a different voice from the one we encounter before the war, especially before the Republic, since those voices reverberated with silence and frustration.

One more group of mobilized women emerged from the ranks of the Anarchists. Unlike Antifascist Women, which had been indoctrinated to think in terms of the general cause but not women's cause, Mujeres Libres was a strongly feminist organization. Established in April 1936, was founded by female Anarchists, who clearly stated that their group and their magazine, *Mujeres libres*, were strictly for women and by women. As Martha Ackelsberg explains it, the group grew out of the frustration women felt because they were not treated by men as equals: "Those women who were active members of CNT unions or who participated in ateneos [cultural clubs] or in FIJL [the Anarchist youth organization] were always a minority. Their efforts to incorporate other women into the activist core never seemed to get very far, whether because of the sexism of the men, the diffidence of the women, or some combination of the two."[64]

The Free Women organization did not emphasize Anarchist political tenets, since it felt that this could alienate a good many women.[65] In a letter about the first issue of *Mujeres libres*, we read: "I was about to end my letter without telling you that the magazine has been a success! What a tremendous need these poor women had for someone to worry about them! If you could only see the letters we've received!"[66] The letter, from "Luci" to "Trini," was obviously written by Lucía Sánchez Saornil, cofounder of the group with Mercedes Comaposada and Amparo Poch y Gascón.[67]

Mary Nash has pointed out that "Free Women posed, for the first time in Spain, the problematics of women from a class perspective: that is to say, feminine liberation from the perspective of the emancipation of the working class.

which we could call 'proletarian feminism,' as opposed to feminist movements of bourgeois characteristics."[68] The first group of Free Women was organized in Madrid; associations quickly sprang up all over Spain, especially in the center of the country and in Catalonia, where the Anarchist movement was strongest. Altogether 153 groups were formed and some twenty thousand women were affiliated.[69] The goals of Free Women were directed, above all, toward the emancipation of women. One of the major objectives was the education of women through schools, institutes, random lectures, and courses.

The organizers were also very interested in helping women achieve control over their own bodies. "Most of the attention Mujeres Libres devoted to issues of sexuality focused on the relationship between economic and political exploitation and women's sexual subordination, a relationship made manifest in prostitution . . . which they saw as emblematic of human relations under capitalism."[70] One of the most ambitious projects was the creation of the Casal de la Dona Treballadora in Barcelona, which provided educational facilities for six hundred women. As one of the articles in the magazine comments, the first goal of Free Women was to "emancipate women from the triple slavery to which they have generally been subordinated and to which they continue to be subjected: the slavery of ignorance, the slavery of their sex, and the slavery of reproduction."[71]

Like all Anarchists, at the start of the civil war Free Women envisioned the possibility of a real revolution of the working classes. But unlike other groups that preferred to overlook the particular problems of women, it insisted on the importance of preparing women for the work force, but not just during the war; rather, it hoped for a solid education that would introduce women into the public sector in a permanent way. The group did, in fact, create a network that crystalized the empowerment of women for a brief period in Spanish history through education, their magazine, and social involvement.[72]

Sara Berenguer, in her memory text, outlines her life during the war and her activism in Free Women. Her book is another example of an outlaw text; not only does she describe her own life, but at the end of the book she provides biographical sketches of many of her Anarchist friends and fellow activists, including Emma Goldman.[73] She gives us her reasons for writing the book; in a somewhat convoluted style for which she apologizes beforehand,[74] Berenguer sums up the problems of Spanish women through the centuries:

> Female and male friends, you who are about to read of the experiences
> of three years of battle of an inexperienced young worker, surprised by a
> revolution which which came about because of a military uprising that

wanted to smash the vital fluid of a people, I want you to know that for me it was a time of enrichment, in spite of many difficulties which I debated with myself, between conscience and reason; my freedom and that of others; between the value of simplicity and obstinacy; the insufficiencies of some and our own ignorance—the ignorance we were plunged into because of the centuries of bourgeois domination, machismo, the monarchies and dictatorships, how much we women did not know, and the lack of social and cultural preparation.[75]

From all appearances, Berenguer is a particularly intelligent, outgoing, and brave woman even in the 1980s.[76] She describes her close relationship with her father, a miliciano, who guided her into activism until he died in the war.[77] She then traded her boyfriend for political activism. Berenguer also describes how one of the male activists, seeing how fearless she was with guns, offered to teach her to fly, and she became an aviator. Her interest in Free Women came about because she attended one of their meetings, and the men present laughed about the organization. She launched into a defense of Free Women and was promptly persuaded to become a delegate for the group. Berenguer eventually became the group's secretary of propaganda.

With lively strokes Berenguer provides a closeup of the young, vital, and attractive Anarchist; she permits us to examine the personal and political life of a female activist during the war. She is very frank about the contradictions of Anarchism regarding sex and love; for instance, although she is approached by male Anarchists who believe in free love, she tells us that she does not believe that promiscuity is a form of freedom. She describes the Anarchist weddings, the political struggles for power among the leftists, the men who pursue her, the sad farewell to the International Brigades, the final days in Barcelona. Berenguer also sets forth the platform and justification of Free Women, transforming those pages of the book into a manifesto of sorts.

When the insurgents are about to take Barcelona, Berenguer refuses to recognize the imminent danger and continues her work with Free Women. As her friends try to talk her into leaving the city, she cries out: "How could it be? How could we have to abandon Barcelona, our Barcelona we fought so hard for, sacrificing every waking hour, three years of our youth, without one holiday?"[78] In the biographical sketches at the end of her text, Berenguer pays homage to her comrades. Lola Iturbe, who also wrote a book about Spanish women activists,[79] is described in detail, as are Aurea Cuadrado, Libertad Ródenas, Pilar Grangel, and the founders of Free Women: among them Sánchez Saornil, Comaposada, and Poch y Gascón.

Although as a support group Free Women appears to have been quite strong, in general it was not taken very seriously by the male population. Montseny, from her pedestal as an "exceptional woman," points out the lack of support for Free Women, typically taking advantage of the chance to criticize the Marxists:

> While any action by Antifascist Women, the Girls' Union, etc., is
> launched and supported, we somehow forget what Free Women is. . . .
> We have not conquered the women. . . . Only now do we think about do-
> ing it, and it is sad that this work has to be carried out by a group of
> female comrades fighting tooth and nail against all odds and in the midst
> of all sorts of economic, even moral, difficulties—because they don't feel
> that they are supported by the unions and the movement.[80]

This testimony, in addition to revealing the lack of support for Free Women, also demonstrates that Montseny to some extent sympathized with the efforts of the group. According to Shirley Fredricks, because of her position as minister of health, Montseny "did much to promote the education, technical training, and employment of women by working closely with organizations such as Mujeres Libres."[81]

Unfortunately, the fragmentation among the Left during the war, which tended to weaken Republican efforts, is also reflected in the attitude of Free Women toward other groups, especially Antifascist Women. Dolores Ibárruri made numerous attempts to form a coalition, to unite efforts. Free Women envisioned this more as coercion, fearing that Antifascist Women's only goal was to absorb their group entirely. Free Women was without doubt one of the most remarkable women's organizations during the war because of its concerted effort—though thwarted by the lack of support and resources, and then by the Franco regime—to reverse the repressive role of women in society. Its educational goals and attempts to eradicate prostitution and promote sexual freedom attest that Free Women took the most feminist stance of any group in Spain before the 1970s.

Federica Montseny has been the most outspoken of the visible political women of the Republic in denouncing the anonymity with which women who participated in the war have been treated in the annals of history.

> The Communists and even the Libertarians have kept silent about us. It
> wasn't worthwhile to mention us. They condemned us to ostracism. They
> didn't even mention women who fought alongside them, or those who
> did not fight but freed them from anonymous battles, who were not any

less important. One has to realize what it has meant for Spain to have thousands of women whose men were killed or imprisoned and who have had to work to survive, support their children . . . whatever else, pursued, harassed, imprisoned. I could name innumerable cases of comrades who, for the simple reason that they were married to a dead or exiled militant, were jailed and spent ten, twelve, fifteen years in prison. No one talks about it, and this is an enormous injustice.[82]

Montseny urgently outlines the need for a new perspective on the Spanish civil war and provides a justification for writing the silenced stories of women's lives as they were affected by the politics of war and repression.

Women of the Right also participated, though except for a few nurses not at the front lines. They were generally from good families, and members of the bourgeoisie did not permit their daughters to disgrace them by working in the public sector. Yet some of these young women played an important role in the civil strife. They were active in the early 1930s, when the street warfare provoked by the Falangists began. María Teresa Gallego Méndez, in her book on the organization,[83] contends that "the Feminine Section of the Spanish Falange of the JONS[84] was created in 1934 to offer a cover for the violent activities of the Falange group. At that time, no other function for women had been visualized except that of attending to the needs derived from the clash between their men and the established law and order."[85] Pilar Primo de Rivera unwittingly corroborates this statement:

The Feminine Section movement was born within the Falange organization. It was very necessary, since the Falangists were strongly persecuted during the Republic. The boys were put in jail; the offices were closed. We busied ourselves with taking care of prisoners and their families, the dead Falangists, because many were killed in the streets. We collected money because the Falange was dirt poor. We disseminated information, whatever we could do. We were their auxiliaries. At first, we were incorporated into SEU,[86] because we were mostly students. But then José Antonio realized that we had enough vision and that the Feminine Section was something important, and he made us a separate group.[87]

Speaking of those early years when the Falangists were trying to prove that the Republic had failed by constantly provoking street violence, Primo de Rivera reveals later that the activities of her group had implicated them in the violence and subsequent war: "Sometimes in the street fighting, the girls hid the boys' guns in their clothing when it was necessary."[88]

She describes the founding of the Falange:

> It was everything to us. We went to the first meeting in the Comedia
> Theater in 1933, October 29th. That was when José Antonio introduced
> his ideas. There was no solution for Spain but that one. We were com-
> mitted from the very beginning. All the young people were. Young
> women and men alike, everyone became passionately committed. We
> knew it was the solution. We weren't thinking in terms of Right or Left.
> Spain was a disaster, and all it needed was a new solution.[89]

Primo de Rivera makes no excuses for her sympathy for Hitler and Nazi
Germany when she describes one of her trips to Germany. Her tale would be
amusing if it were not macabre.

> I was entrusted by the Caudillo [Franco called himself "the Chief"] to
> give Hitler a sword from Toledo in his name. When I gave him the
> sword, that was the first and last time I saw him. But that is where the
> rumor that I was going to marry him must have come from; or maybe it
> was because the historian and great friend of mine Giménez Caballero
> conceived this idea to unify Europe, which he even communicated indi-
> rectly to Hitler through Edith Faupel and Magda Goebbels, and also to
> the Caudillo and my Uncle Antón, so they would tell me—which I found
> out recently from Giménez Caballero himself, whom I thank for having
> so much confidence in me. But the truth is that I never heard about the
> project, nor would I have consented, among other reasons because I
> never felt that I could be the trustee of such an important mission—and
> besides, my private life was mine only.[90]

Women—from both sides—were considered "men's helpers," not protagonists of the war, but the vast majority of females from the conservative sector had
no direct participation. Statistics show that fifty-eight Falange women died carrying out war duties, a far cry from the number of women of the Republic and the
Left who lost their lives.[91] Primo de Rivera discusses their rear-guard activities:

> Women's participation in the war was very important because all the
> tasks of helping and social services were done by women. In the battles,
> women didn't intervene. There were some nurses at the front, but no fe-
> male soldiers. That was for the boys. . . . We've never been feminists.
> We've done everything together with the men, helping them with every-
> thing, the propaganda, money questions. And we saw them as professors,
> advisers. . . . War was for men, and women were for helping men.[92]

The headquarters for the female counterpart of the Nationalists was first established in the conservative university city of Valladolid. A Falange women's organization called Winter Help was created (inspired by the Nazi *Winterhilfe*),[93] under the guidance of the Feminine Section.[94] The group—which Hugh Thomas has called the "most remarkable Falangist institution" to evolve during the war[95]—took care of children, pregnant mothers and the destitute; it also helped with production of supplies for the soldiers. Pilar Primo de Rivera in 1938 took her national delegation of the Sección Femenina to Burgos, the headquarters of Franco's government.

The memory texts written by women of the Right often dwell on negative physical aspects of female Leftist activists. For example, Ana-María Foronda, describes the first days of the war in Madrid. Foronda, whose husband had a clinic, obviously was wealthy. Her home was raided by leftists and she was detained. (Later her house was restored to her.) She depicts all leftists as filthy, ignorant, and violent. Describing a confrontation in which women were involved, she says: "The women, those ugly, disgusting beasts. Is there, was there, one pretty one among them? They are cursed witches that exasperate one's nerves with screams: 'Rip out their tongues! Chop the hearts of the Fascists in half!' "[96] Another text by a woman of the Right describes a miliciana: "That so-called militiawoman was a mulatta, with thick lips and a pug nose; she was utterly repulsive."[97]

In the narrative of a wealthy young woman who was imprisoned by the leftists in Madrid in 1936, we find a description of the "Red" criminals who were her cellmates: "One was a miliciana and she had murdered her colonel; another had killed a Communist to steal from him; another had killed her husband. There was even a cannibal."[98]

Of course, this is the usual encoding of women in patriarcal terms—the female body as filth and the activist female as violent and brutish. But these are not only gender statements; they are also class statements: the population that waged war against the Republic was, as we have seen, primarily from the upper classes. The uneducated and the poor—the "unclean masses"—were objects of repulsion for the Right, as we observe time and time again in the literature on the war.

The Feminine Section represents a paradigmatic case for understanding the patriarchal process. In Gerda Lerner's terms:

Women themselves became a resource, acquired by men much as the land was acquired by men. Women were exchanged or bought in marriages for the benefit of their families; later, they were conquered or bought into slavery, where their sexual services were part of their labor and where their children were the property of their masters. In every known society it was women of conquered tribes who were first enslaved, whereas men were killed. . . . Thus, the enslavement of women, combining both racism and sexism, preceded the formation of classes and class oppression. Class differences were, at their very beginnings, expressed and constituted in terms of patriarchal relations. Class is not a separate construct from gender; rather, class is expressed in generic terms.[99]

Lerner goes on to describe how privileged women cooperated in this endeavor through "reciprocal agreement . . . in exchange for your sexual, economic, political, and intellectual subordination to men, you may share the power of men of your class to exploit men and women of the lower class."[100]

Ironically, like the activist women of the Republic, women of the Feminine Section have had little visibility in the annals of history. Unlike Montseny, though, Primo de Rivera does not denounce the phantasmagorical state of her organization and the way it was ignored by the males. Rather, she applauds men for subordinating the women of the Feminine Section. In a speech given in May 1939 to celebrate the victory of Franco, when she and ten thousand members of the Feminine Section greeted him in the city of Medina del Campo, she promises to carry on the tradition of the subjugation of women:

We are here solely to celebrate your victory and to honor your soldiers. Because the only mission women have as their patriotic task is the home. That is why, with the arrival of peace, we will increase the labor initiated in our formatory schools, to make life for men so pleasant that within their homes they will find all that they lacked before, and therefore in their spare time they will not have to look for satisfaction in the taverns or in the casinos.

We will teach women to take care of the home, because it is a shame that so many children who are God's servants and future Spanish soldiers die. We will also teach them how to arrange the house and to know crafts and music. We will teach women the way of life that José Antonio wanted for all Spaniards, so in that way, when they have children, they will mold them in the love of God and the ways of life of the Falange.[101]

The conception of self among the women of the Left is at all times diametrically opposed to that of the women of the Right. Even those women who did not recognize the bonds of patriarchy during the war, but who fought for the Republican cause, have expressed in testimonies or memory texts their desire for empowerment and for improvement of their lot. The Republic's desire for separation of church and state, for agrarian reform, and for a generally more equitable life for Spaniards, was impossible. And the Feminine Section was to become the vehicle for destroying any sense of empowerment among the majority of Spanish women.

Part Three   *P*rison as Memory

"La Pasionaria." *A.G.A. Fondo Fotográfico "Archivo Rojo" Photo no.* 54576

Bombing victims. *A.G.A. Fondo Fotográfico "Archivo Rojo" Photo no.* 54328

Bombing victim. A.G.A. *Fondo Fotográfico "Archivo Rojo" Photo no. 54393*

Woman replacing men in the fields. *A.G.A. Fondo Fotográfico "Archivo Rojo"*
Photo no. 55573

Women working for the war cause in Valencia. *A.G.A. Fondo Fotográfico*
"Archivo Rojo" Photo no. 56051

"Antoñita" on her tractor in the fields. A.G.A. *Fondo Fotográfico "Archivo Rojo" Photo no. 55634*

Women working in the arms factory in 1937. *A.G.A. Fondo Fotográfico "Archivo Rojo" Photo no. 55760*

Parade of Antifascist Militia men and women. *A.G.A. M.C.S.E. Fondo Fotográfico*

Isabel de Palencia on the Queen Mary enlisting support for the Madrid offensive, October 1936, United States. *A.G.A. M.C.S.E. Fondo Fotográfico Isabel de Palencia.*

Pilar Jaraiz Franco with her child in a Republican prison in 1937. A note on the back of the photo says that she is: "recognizing the good treatment she received in prison." *A.G.A. M.C.S.E. Fondo Fotográfico Pilar Jaraiz Franco*

"La Pasionaria" with the "Steel" Battalion. *A.G.A. Fondo Fotográfico "Archivo Rojo" Photo no. 55549*

Federica Montseny with other Spanish ministers in April 1937. *A.G.A. M.C.S.E. Fondo Fotográfico Federica Montseny*

Federica Montseny giving her speech in March 1937. *A.G.A. M.C.S.E. Fondo Fotográfico Federica Montseny*

Rosario Sánchez (hiding her missing hand under a coat), 1937. Also pictured are
(*middle*) Valentín González, alias "El Campesino," famous Communist general of
the 46th Division known for his prowess as a guerilla leader; (*left*) Francisco
Galán, another popular Communist leader who was later made a colonel and the
military governor of Cartagena. Next to Sánchez is the commanding chief of the
101st Brigade of El Campesino. Sánchez writes on the back of the photo: "I am
Rosario Sánchez Mora, "La chacha" (The little girl), my war name and the one
that the poet Miguel Hernández used in his poem written about me called
"Rosario Dinamitera." The officers are discussing whether Sánchez should hide
her injury or show it proudly. *Personal collection of Rosario Sánchez*

Young women collecting money for the men of the Soviet supply ship Komsomol, February 1937. Sunk earlier that year by the Italians, the ship had brought arms and tanks to the Republic in 1936. *A.G.A. M.C.S.E. Fondo Fotográfico*

Miliciana on guard duty. *A.G.A. M.C.S.E. Fondo Fotográfico "Archivo Rojo" Photo no. 55567*

Miliciana with her child before she leaves for the battlefront. *A.G.A. M.C.S.E. Fondo Fotográfico "Archivo Rojo" Photo no. 55566*

Woman volunteering for active duty. *A.G.A. M.C.S.E. Fondo Fotográfico "Archivo Rojo" Photo no.* 53273

Milicianas preparing a meal. *A.G.A. M.C.S.E. Fondo Fotográfico "Archivo Rojo" Photo no.* 55673

Woman being recruited for the militia. *A.G.A. M.C.S.E. Fondo Fotográfico "Archivo Rojo" Photo no. 53950*

Parade for the Antifascist Militia women. *A.G.A. M.C.S.E. Fondo Fotográfico*

Chapter 6 The Lost Women of Spanish Prisons

En Madrid, no hay alegría,
en Madrid no hay ilusión
que sus mejores mujeres
las tienen en la prisión.

(In Madrid, there is no gaiety / In
Madrid nothing goes well / 'Cause her very
best women / She's got them in jail.)

Marisa Bravo, unpublished memoirs

Prison signifies silence, obedience, repression, and rules designed to punish and humiliate.[1] By taking away the freedom to do as one wishes, to come and go at will, we assume that criminals will change, will recognize that the violation of societal rules makes it impossible to choose what they wish to do with their lives.

What about political prisoners? They generally do not feel that they have committed a crime against society. If they are not terrorists, their only crime is often ideological deviation. Can they be "reformed"? Can they be brainwashed into believing that they have committed an infraction against society? Political prisoners are aware of the fact that what is in question is merely an ideal, an abstraction that has nothing to do with crimes such as robbery or murder. They are the least convinced of their culpability. In fact, they often feel exactly the opposite: they are vehemently convinced of their innocence. They feel liberated from guilt. There is little hope for reform in the case of such prisoners. The only potential means of changing them is brainwashing or other mental and physical torture.

Many male political prisoners of the Spanish civil war did feel guilt. Typically, they had fought in the war and participated in its arbitrary brutalities.

They were disgusted at having violated the rules of humanity, which are invariably thrown aside in wartime, especially during a civil war. On both sides, Spain was weighed down by the guilt of war crimes. Yet most of the women imprisoned after the Spanish civil war had a very different experience. They could not conceive of the guilt which was imposed upon them. Some milicianas and other female activists were responsible for loss of life. But the majority of the women had been imprisoned by association with others, primarily their men; they had aided family and friends in distress, with no political agenda.[2]

Many women's testimonies describe helping husbands or brothers to escape from their villages. For example, María Castanera was accused of aiding her brothers; she was detained, then released, and later found in a ditch near the highway with a bullet through her neck and her hands cut off. Some women who were charged were pathetically innocent; their crimes were as heinous as having sewn a Republican flag.[3] Teachers, almost invariably sympathetic to the Republic, were imprisoned for actions such as removing the crucifix from their classrooms (as they had been instructed to do when the Republic took over). Many women were imprisoned for activities that were deemed for men only, such as carrying a gun or wearing overalls. Others went to jail for having participated in a leftist organization, working in the rear guard to win the war and to achieve the revolution they saw as necessary to create social justice in Spain. Here is the testimony of an unnamed woman in one of Tomasa Cuevas' volumes:

> The young girls and some veteran activists in political and union organizations could consider their detention from a broader perspective, but the women who had been detained because the regime couldn't find their husbands, or sons, or because they had insulted the Fascists, or screamed at the planes that were bombing, or had voted for the Popular Front, or had done the militia's laundry (for which they received quite long sentences), who had been beaten and abused upon detention—for all those women the individual drama produced irrational and inconceivable suffering.[4]

Often women were denounced for inexplicable reasons, a result of the inquisitorial fanaticism that reigned in Spain in varying degrees during the entire regime. As the same woman emphasizes, "It was enough that anyone— any neighbor or coworker, any widow or relative of someone killed by the 'Reds'—walked into a police station, the civil guard barracks, or a Falange office, vaguely denouncing the ideas or actions of someone, for that person to be detained, mistreated, and sent to rot in prison."[5]

What we find in the written and oral testimonies of most activist women is a conviction that they had done something positive and nothing at all to deserve imprisonment. The majority of the activist women who wrote about their prison experiences, or have discussed them openly, went back to militancy—either underground during the regime or publicly once the regime ended in 1975. These voices of "collective testimony" are emphatic that the world should know about the crimes committed against them, and the injustices of the Franco regime.

It is difficult to determine the number of people who were imprisoned for political reasons during and after the war, or the number of those who were executed. The best estimates we have toward the very end of the war, around 1 April 1939, are as follows: the people imprisoned in the Nationalist zone had reached some 100,000, and within a few months the numbers doubled. Estimates of the number of people executed between 1939 and 1944 vary from 200,000 to 400,000.[6]

The statistics on women are particularly difficult to determine because of the lack of research on the topic. The Vital Statistics Office in Madrid verifies that 23,232 Spanish women were in prison in 1939;[7] given that crime rates had traditionally been very low, and among women almost nonexistent, we can venture that the vast majority of those women were political prisoners and that only a few were prostitutes. The female prison most documented and described is Madrid's Ventas jail. Yet statistics on the prisoners even there vary by the thousands. The *Libro blanco sobre las cárceles franquistas* mentions 10,000 women at one time;[8] other sources speak of up to 14,000.

Women had spent three years managing Spain virtually on their own. Even though many remained in their homes and did not work in factories or belong to political organizations, they still ran the household singlehandedly, caring for children and the elderly, and many became the breadwinners for their families. The still-primitive conditions in much of Spain—the lack of refrigeration and indoor plumbing, for instance—made even the simplest tasks difficult and time-consuming.

In normal times, a working-class woman's life—Spain was then primarily an agrarian country—was consumed in the daily work of taking care of the family and the household and also raising animals and gathering food. During the war all of these tasks became infinitely more difficult. In urban areas women had to stand in food lines, fighting a perennial battle among impatient, hungry people who were all attempting to survive on a day-to-day basis. And they often had to do so while avoiding bullets and bombs. Even the women who did not take to the streets to campaign and organize, or did not take men's jobs in industry and transportation, could no longer be invisible. Women had to make their own decisions about nearly everything, a situation unthinkable in prewar Spain. Women had to become political beings to some degree. They had to learn how to deal with strangers, to overcome the psychological shackles that submission and abnegation had taught them through the centuries.

After a life of repression, the flash of freedom during the Republic and the war experienced by many of the women who did take jobs in the public sector represented a veritable release from the bondage of societal strictures and gave them a new sense of pride. In 1939 all of that suddenly and radically changed. The Feminine Section took on the task of monitoring the reinstatement of women as mothers and figures of religious piety. The phallocentrism of Mussolini's fascist Italy during the 1920s and 1930s took root. Mussolini had said, "He who is not a father is not a man."[9] Fascist machismo became the overriding philosophy of Franco's Spain.

As we have seen, the regime's female mouthpiece, Pilar Primo de Rivera, laid out the prime dictates that reigned during the forty-year dictatorship: obedience to church, to state, and especially to men. The Civil Law Code of 1889 was reaffirmed. This doctrine emphasized the psychological and intellectual incapacity of women and their absolute inability to make independent decisions, rendering them inevitable wards of fathers, husbands, or brothers. For women, the code implied not only total subservience to the two dominant institutions, church and state, but also emphasized that women were to be, once again, self-sacrificing to husbands and children—primarily, as we have seen, to male children, the "future soldiers." Women became responsible for the new order that was to take hold in Spain. They were to make their men happy, since they had "obviously" failed them before.

The campaign after the war for order and obedience and female subservience was highly successful. Educational subjection and religious repression were not the only ways that Spanish women were guided back to the straight and narrow path. Spain was still eminently rural and illiterate, and the radio became a key vehicle for retooling Spanish society in the "way of life of the Falange."[10] Control of the female mind was achieved through all the media and in this way, control of the female body was restored. Abortion, of course, was banned, as was divorce. Women again became the exclusive property of their husbands, to be used as men saw fit.[11]

Along with political repression, sexual repression reached new heights; the tradition of the Spanish Inquisition was still embedded in Spain's culture. The church, with the assiduous aid of the Feminine Section and the censor's office, managed to create a rigid and arbitrary infrastructure of repression that legitimized female subjugation and carried it to ludicrous extremes.[12] Not only were Spanish women removed from the workforce, but men were rewarded for keeping their women at home and having large families; it was not unusual for women to bear ten or twelve children. Of course, exceptional women were generally thwarted in their efforts to acquire prominent professional government positions. All single women (with few exceptions) were required to join the Feminine Section; they were drafted, as men were, to perform "social services" for six months.[13] Intellectual oppression in the early twentieth century was reasserted at the end of the war.

> Reading was for the Feminine Section of very little importance. Its manual for little girls[14] recommended that they "never be stuffed with books," since there was nothing more detestable than an intellectual woman. A well-known Falangist woman, upon campaigning for social—never political—education for women, added that it was necessary that such education be concealed as much as possible. A woman could have some knowledge, on condition that she hid it so that she wouldn't seem pedantic.[15]

This statement corroborates the remarks made by women who in autobiographical texts focused on their intellectual development in turn-of-the-century Spain. Reading was thought to rob women of either their faith or their innocence, and, therefore their virtue; the same fate was feared from apparently even more sinful activities: dancing, dating, moviegoing—the list goes on and on. We need only consult the religious pamphlets of the time, which show, for example, a dancing couple in which the partner is depicted as a devil.

Because it was once again confirmed by male writers and politicians that women were mentally and biologically inferior, Spaniards were discouraged from sending their female children to school. The literacy level among women declined in the 1940s.[16] The timid advances of the 1930s were carefully erased from Spanish society, only to be insidiously replaced by the age-old attitudes that saw women as inferiors. The first issue of the magazine *Medina* in 1941 sums it up: "We love the women who await us—passive, sweet, behind a curtain, near their tasks and prayers."[17]

The confinement of those women who were imprisoned after the war meant a return to submission, in a more nightmarish form of repression than they could have dreamed possible. The years of silence and suffering are depicted by a handful of these women—if not always with elegance, with eloquence and conviction. Theirs is a brave effort to break through the years of silence, to tell the stories of mute suffering. These memory texts and testimonies form a chorus of voices chanting their protest against imprisonment because of a cherished ideal and then the scorning, punishment, and shunning after their ordeal was over. Their memories are nostalgia for their freedom during the Republic and the war, and despair at their confinement in the asphyxiating atmosphere of the inquisitorial Franco regime.

The plight of these women can be equated to that of women of the sixteenth and seventeenth centuries—"young, lost women who walk through the streets offending our Lord."[18] The offense of these "delinquents" was felt not only by the church, also by His Majesty the King, and both institutions were encouraged to purge the streets of their presence. It is obvious that some of the "lost women" were prostitutes, but included in this group were other pariahs: beatas[19] go-betweens, soothsayers, vendors, beggars, saints, and sinners, with voices that purported to come from the heavens from the underworld.

All were accused of transgression—often, in fact, they were condemned by the Inquisition—since they had escaped from the shackles imposed on women by husbands, fathers, confessors, or other male figures of authority. Many were women who had been abandoned and were without economic recourse apart from their own devices. They were considered to have mysterious, demonic, or erotic powers over men, or a mystical voice that challenged the authority of the all-male establishment. But they were lumped together as lost women and often incarcerated as a group, receiving the same treatment and branded with the same stigma as all other female transgressors in a masculine world. It is evident from the oral testimonies and the memory texts that after the war the female prisoners were to receive the same treatment as the lost women of centuries before. The basic sentiments had not changed: these women had transgressed, and they were to be punished as "Red whores."

Prison life was distinctly different for women than for men. It was customary to punish them by shaving their heads and parading them through the streets to expose them to jeers and insults, after forcing them to ingest large quantities of cod-liver oil. This was also true of innocent women who were not imprisoned, but who were held up as examples because the male members of their families were in prison for "war crimes." Gabriel Jackson describes this phenomenon in 1939:

> During August and September, dozens of priests suspected of being Basque Nationalists were arrested in the Insurgent zone and many Basque political leaders were imprisoned, if not shot. In Vitoria their wives and daughters had their hair cut off as a sign of shame. A short tuft was left on top—enough to be tied with the ribbon of the colors of

the old monarchist flag. The women were marched to mass on Sunday morning by Falange and Requeté guards, and afterward they were paraded through the streets of the city.[20]

Of the thousands of women who passed through Spanish prisons, many remained there for years. Others were shot without trial, and many died from the effects of torture or illness contracted because of the lamentable conditions. The newly established prisons for women were located all over Spain; among those mentioned most often are the jails in Madrid (three prisons), Zaragoza, Gerona, Alcalá de Henares, Saturrarán, Aranjuez, Barcelona, Palma de Mallorca, Málaga, Valencia, Amorebieta, Oviedo, Tarragona, Larrinaga, Córdoba, Avila, Teruel, and Jaen. It was customary for prisoners to be herded into trains and dragged from one jail to another around the country, usually to avoid the establishment of solid political organizations in the prisons—though, as we shall observe, these did almost invariably, form, especially where there were large groups of Communist activists.

Ironically, most people in Spain today seem to think that women were spared incarceration and/or execution. If we read the majority of the accounts of the war, there is little or no mention of female prisoners. During the Franco regime, it was obviously not possible to publish any literature in Spain about these captives, and the majority of the foreign writers were males who wrote only of males. A few autobiographical works by women circulated outside Spain in the early Franco years, such as those by de la Mora, and Palencia. They went largely unnoticed and, of course, did not appear in Spain. No testimonies of resistance against the insurgents were published within the country until after the death of Franco.

Since the late 1970s, a number of memory texts and testimonial works have appeared that shed new light on the topic of women in prison. Their limited number results from the fact that few of the women had sufficient skills to write about their memories of incarceration. I interviewed a number of activists who laughed with embarrassment when I asked why they had not written their autobiographies. Petra Cuevas put it succinctly: "But my dear, I am barely literate!"[21] Others, educated women, felt they did not possess the talent to write a book that would be worthwhile as literature. Carmen Camaño, for example, a university student before the war who spent time in Franco's jails, responded to the question in this fashion: "I haven't written my memoirs because I don't have any literary capacity. One more book of memoirs means nothing. I'm not capable of writing something of literary value. I have a sense of criticism."[22] Camaño's response has a certain logic, although certainly, because of her education and background, her written testimonies would have been extremely valuable.

There are other reasons for this silence. Franco's propaganda discredited female leftist activists so thoroughly, equating their political activity to frivolous and lascivious sexual promiscuity or innocuous intrigue, that they themselves seem to have been somewhat brainwashed. One thinks of Marisa Bravo, who kept her memoirs hidden because her activism and the trials and tribulations it caused were considered taboo subjects within her family.

Often, after spending several years in prison, the women imposed a silence on themselves that was to last until recent years. Fear of repression against anti-Franco Spaniards and their families motivated everyone from the resistance to hide the truth; but for women, the tension was doubly problematic. If being a leftist meant that you were a disgraced "Red," being a female leftist meant that you were a "Red whore." As Camaño describes it:

> After the war, a female prisoner was referred to as "that one" or "that tart." Ruiz Giménez[23] defended me when I was accused of clandestine work and asked the judge to be more respectful of someone who had studied with him at the university. But the Franco regime had to react to the fact that women had changed their mentalities. It had to discredit the people who had a political ideology with regard to their role in society. So the way they did it was to devalue leftist women. . . . The proof is in the small towns; repression against women was tremendous. Women could be isolated in a small nucleus, whereas in Madrid they could go unnoticed. Remember that "honor" is still of importance with regard to women, so they attacked from that angle. The first thing the police did when a woman entered jail was to try to take advantage of her. If that was impossible—beatings, head shaving, cod-liver oil; if she was easy, she was discredited for the rest of her life. Anyone who wasn't the Virgin Mary type was a tart. This all was propagated by the Feminine Section.[24]

José Antonio had already characterized the leftist woman in 1936 at the onset of the war. In a speech about the revolutionary movement that had sprung up all over Spain, the leader of the Falange tells us that such a movement

> belittles honor, upon encouraging the collective prostitution of the young female workers in those picnics where immodesty is cultivated; it undermines the family, which is supplanted in Russia by free love, by using the collective dining halls, through facilitating divorce and abortion (haven't

you heard the Spanish girls these days—"Children, yes; husbands, no!) and repudiating honor.[25]

The term "honor" is used twice in this short fragment. The only consideration was the good name of the masculine population, and Primo de Rivera knew that "honor" was still a very grave topic in a country where calling a man a cuckold could be a life-or-death matter. José Antonio was already envisioning the freedom that women were to experience with the onset of the war. As Teresa Pàmies explained, the war was a "revolutionary explosion that gave us absolute freedom."[26] Primo de Rivera reflects a preoccupation with what Robert Jay Lifton describes as a "pyrrhic victory" and what it could mean for Spanish society. Camaño's reference to the regime's reaction to the autonomous woman who emerged from the war brings to mind Lifton's work, his study of the psychological impact of war and devastation.

> Historical change creates a disparity in psychological balance between the sexes in which feminine achievement becomes something of a pyrrhic victory, accompanied as it is by impaired capacity of both men and women to relate to one another. Yet precisely this combination of disappointment in male partners and expanding criteria for self-realization gives women particular capacity for new kinds of accomplishment, for the development of new forms of knowing. Men may feel themselves doubly threatened: not only dislocated and possibly emasculated, but also "seen through" in their weaknesses more clearly than ever before by women whom they can no longer dominate and to whom they feel distinctly inferior.[27]

Lifton's assessment of this unbalancing of the double standard is certainly corroborated in the way leftist women were treated by the regime's sympathizers, both male and female.

Chapter 7   The Intent and Format of the Prison Texts

Let us look now at the genesis of the autobiographical works of female activists whose outlaw texts describe the painful consequences of resistance in prison. Angeles García-Madrid had an intensely moral purpose in the autobiography she wrote and published after the death of Franco:[1] "I never thought about writing this book. But these are things which must be made known."[2]

García-Madrid's autobiographical protagonist, "Angeles," is one of the clearest examples of what I call the "urgent solitary voice of collective testimony."[3] She speaks very little of herself and focuses instead on her cell companions. In this work, *Réquiem,* as in many of the other texts, the individual self as subject is transformed into the collective self as subject, by virtue of proximity to and solidarity with the author's cellmates.

Angeles García-Madrid spent three years in Spanish prisons; she gives testimony to the numerous victims of torture, illness, verbal abuse, rape, hunger, and insanity with whom she shared cells during that time. She also describes the execution of a number of her cellmates. Her story, like other prison accounts, is a blood-chilling tale of the persecution of women who had committed the "crime" of becoming activists during the civil war. She speaks from the point of view of a working woman from the rank and file, and is very explicit in her focus. She notes in her preliminary remarks: "It is important to know that these women, victims of an adverse and senseless situation, are absolutely simple folk and normal people. They are not famous leaders or great activists. They are simply a group of women who fought at all costs to defend their own dignity as human beings—some with more consciousness of the cause than others; the majority, only because of their natural instinct."[4]

García-Madrid's desire to tell the tragic stories of her cellmates is coupled with her own need to denounce those who caused their misfortune. As a self-taught writer—with several volumes of poetry to her credit—García-Madrid was clearly utilizing her talents to tell the stories of thousands of other women who were incapable of committing their tales to paper. The primary importance of this author's testimony, like a number of other books composed by relatively uneducated women, lies in its capacity to portray events that would otherwise remain in oblivion.

Juana Doña, in *Desde la noche y la niebla,* has the distinct purpose of outlining the flash of freedom women experienced because of the war. She demonstrates that the civil war did indeed act as a catalyst for Spanish women in the twentieth century: "The necessities of war have incited the immense majority of these women to live an active life. This fact has made them radical activists; in these three years they have learned so much, waking from their lethargy and seeing themselves as new beings."[5] Some of the same elements as in *Réquiem* mediate in the writing of Doña's "novel-testimony," where she tells the story of "Leonor" (who is really Doña) and her prisonmates. Doña chose the format of a novel, changing the names and some of the events, as she explains in the introduction to the 1978 edition.

> When I wrote this story in 1967, my years in prison were still fresh in my memory: the remembrance of those I saw taken out to be shot, the others who died at my side, those who survived all the hardships, and the bitterness of thinking about the women who were still in prison suffering what I had left behind.
>
> Because of this, I had no desire other than to give living testimony to my surroundings, but I was bound by the confines of clandestinity and I could not use authentic names. . . . So I decided to do it in novel form with false names. But I want it to be known that not one of the stories told here is the product of my imagination. And I want to clarify at the same time that this is not an authentically autobiographical novel.[6]

Underlying this expressed intention of format and content is another, less apparent motive, which Doña suggested in an interview. When asked why she used a novelistic form for *Desde la noche y la niebla,* she replied: "I don't know. Perhaps I haven't rationalized it. I think I started that way and it was easier, more accessible. It was. Of all the books written about women in Spain, this one has been the most widely read. And the best-known abroad."[7] So Doña was clearly in pursuit of a wide readership when she used this approach. She suggests the importance of the self as subject in her book, which is less visible in other memory texts. In addition, she found it a personally safer way to break through the silence about women activists and their treatment during the Franco regime. Yet Doña's book elucidates more clearly than any other the fact that the role of Spanish women in the war has not yet been fully articulated.

She sees her goal as "giving testimony to the suffering of thousands of women who were persecuted, tortured, and executed for defending the general rights of our oppressed people, but who never questioned their own oppression."[8]

Doña's novel-testimony might have been influenced by her desire to hide names and especially by her literary pretensions. Hers is a "creative reality" that permits us to envision the transformation from freedom to silence. Similarly, García-Madrid's *Réquiem* expresses the sense of the loss of "liberty" through the novelization of her experiences. She agonizes over the desire to be objective in her portrayal of events, as she tells us when she analyzes the way prison guards treated the inmates: "I would not be objective in this story if I did not say that, on some occasions, the soldiers demonstrated with their behavior that they did not agree with the atrocities and injustices that their bosses carried out."[9] It took García-Madrid two years to write *Réquiem,* she explains, "because there were moments that made me feel as though I were choking. It was like opening up an old wound and, of course, to remember I had to open up the wound in the most profound fashion. It was very painful."[10]

García-Madrid has stated that she uses the third person in her narrative to distance herself from the horrors of prison and death. She was already distanced in time; she wrote the book some forty years after her three-year sojourn in prison. So we can assume that she was well equipped to provide an "objective" version of her own and other women's experiences in prison. Still, her autobiographical work is not necessarily totally accurate in its accounts. Its interest, in any event, lies in the oscillatory nature of the desperation and solidarity we find throughout the text and the way women dealt with these phenomena. Judgments about autheticity must be set aside to grasp the inner meaning of how a text can present what is somehow indescribable: incarceration, torture, illness, desperation, and death.

Other prison memoirs utilize the first-person form. Some seem to focus on their own desperation more than that of their cellmates; this is especially true of the works of Angeles Malonda[11] and Carlota O'Neill, both of whom wrote their memoirs while their prison experiences were fresh in their minds. They are also similar in that—unlike Doña and García-Madrid, both of the working class—they were from the middle class and were well educated. Malonda had not been a militant, but was imprisoned because she had helped her husband (they were pharmacists) in his Socialist activism. O'Neill, as mentioned, published her magazine for women under the auspices of the Communist party and, according to her niece, Lidia Falcón, was also a member of the party.[12] O'Neill spent the entire war in prison, was courtmartialed and sentenced to death, though in 1940 she was released. She wrote her book four times, explaining the quadruple genesis in the prologue:

Dear Reader:

I think I have written this book more than twice. I had it hidden there in Spain, underground, wrapped in oilcloth; it was also hidden once in an unlit oven, but its destiny was fire. That's where it ended up, thrown in by my trembling hands and my daughters', when the Falange was trying to get into our house.

Time passed and I again began to feel the need to reconstruct it. It was like a command that kept me restless and obsessed. And I wrote it again, sure that I would not have to hide it, because the Allied troops were rounding up the Nazis. I wrote it, and upon finishing it, I had to hide it again. . . . Those who knew me said, "It's like a lighted bomb that you carry around in your hands!" And they urged me to destroy it. When America was nothing but a premonition for us, this book again became a threat. But before I destroyed it, I took notes to continue later. And I stuck a few sheets in my suitcase in hieroglyphics that could be understood only by me. They said, "Notes for a detective novel and other adventures." Everything on those pages was pure nonsense, so that no one could decipher it if I died before I got there, not even my own daughters.

In Venezuela I wrote it again in the first year of my arrival. I did it tired, and the book turned out tired and tiring; when I went to correct it, I found everything badly expressed. So I set out to write it again. And I hope that the version I now offer you is the last. Not because it is perfect—well, nothing I've done is perfect—but rather because, like Don Quixote when he tried on his helmet the second time, I will not get into self-criticism and I will leave it as it is, putting myself in your hands, indifferent or friendly reader.[13]

O'Neill herself comments on the focus of the first version. It was written in rhetorical style, full of adjectives describing the violence and destruction of those first days. Since she was a writer, she differs in her style from those who were writing for political and personal reasons without having polished writing skills. Obviously her final version, written years later and far away from Spain, was vastly different from the first. Yet her original shock and vehemence at the injustice of prison are intact in the last writing.

Another curious factor mediating the style of O'Neill's memoirs is her use of the first person. Initially, O'Neill deals with her own tragedy—the destruction of her family, the loss of her husband, her sentencing, her imprisonment and separation from her daughters—and she uses exclusively the first person singular. Yet shortly after her arrival, as she watches hundreds of women entering what she labels the "choir of desolation," she begins to identify with them and commences using the second person plural. She becomes part of the collective subject of the text. O'Neill identifies so strongly with her cellmates that when she is finally absolved of her imaginary war crimes, she finds it difficult to leave, genuinely fearing the outside world and preferring to remain with her "family" as she calls it. We shall examine other examples of this phenomenon later.

Marisa Bravo recounts her story of freedom and activism before and during the war, her subsequent odyssey through Spanish prisons, and her bout with insanity as an exile in France after her children had been taken from her because of her "delinquency." Bravo writes, she says, for "all the women who will never have the opportunity to sing this song" (found at the beginning of Chapter 6). She is a survivor; she is the "urgent solitary voice of collective testimony." In fact, she remarks at one point in her incomplete manuscript, "I have so much to say about that horrible period that I am terrified that the ugly witch called death will overtake me before I am finished"—a prophesy that apparently came true.

The voice of Tomasa Cuevas is a remarkable voice, one that has defied all the constraints—political, financial, and verbal—of a barely educated, working-class woman who was at odds with the regime from her teenage years until its demise. She used her own savings to publish, in large part, her three volumes of transcribed testimonies of women in prison. She has confessed that she would be incapable of writing a book of memoirs, yet she found a way to present her testimony and that of many others: she taped her own story, then traveled around Spain over a period of several years to find her former cellmates in order to tape their testimonies. Her work, more clearly than any of the others, elucidates the "voice of collective testimony."

In these volumes Cuevas has collected the oral testimonies of her prison companions, with the intent of bringing to light the lives and destinies of thousands of women who survived Franco's jails. She explains that she would not have taken on this long and arduous task if it were only to tell her own story, "one among so many thousands."[14] The multiplicity of viewpoints and topics discussed with regard to the emotional and psychological, physical and material conditions of prison life often converge and coincide, providing some proof of the validity of the testimonies. Cuevas firmly believes that these women have remained too long in the shadows. They "are part of the history of our

Spain. They have worked for freedom and democracy. They have suffered interrogation, torture, prison. I don't think that this should be hidden any longer. On the contrary, it is necessary that people know about it."[15]

Cuevas has consistently challenged Spanish women to tell their stories. "I would ask all women who have suffered repression, who have passed through prisons, who have fought, that they write or speak into a tape recorder. It would be a great contribution, of great benefit to Spanish historians, to know what so many don't know: the suffering, the bravery, and the tenacity with which Spanish women tried to achieve freedom and democracy for our country."[16] Cuevas refuses to accept the death of collective memory; she uses her texts as a means of resistance to the loss of that memory.

Soledad Real says that her testimony, *Las cárceles de Soledad Real*, is dedicated to "all the women who, having lived a life like mine, have not wished to, have not known how to, or have not been able to speak."[17] García tells us that her goal was to personalize a history that was her own, which she sees as unreal, monumental, and dehumanized. "I had wanted to relive the history that had been mine or that of my generation and that of our parents, and that had been silenced, spirited away, or falsified and that once Franco had disappeared, we felt the need, since the heroes still lived, to hear it, feel it, and see it."[18] Real tells of her life and its vicissitudes in Spanish prisons. In spite of its nonliterary quality, Real's testimony, like that of Cuevas, gives us unprecedented information because it provides a female perspective on the tragedies of war. She also relates details of the prison system during the regime, which are of great interest in light of the lack of historical data on the conditions of incarceration of Spanish political prisoners.[19]

Several other volumes on imprisonment provide details of this nature. Mercedes Núñez' *Cárcel de Ventas* is a series of vignettes on life in prison—above all, the life of her cellmates. Núñez writes as though she were merely an observer of other people's tragedies, even though she was suffering the same fate in that nightmarish prison. Her book too falls in the category of the "urgent solitary voice." As Núñez explains, she wrote it because, as she left prison, her comrades begged her to. "Explain everything you have seen here to the people in the streets."[20] So it is really a series of anecdotes describing the bravery and tragedy of these women.

Nieves Castro's *Una vida para un ideal*, like Ibárruri's text, is an apology for her Communist militancy. The book focuses more on its writer than do some of the others: her imprisonment, the various escapes from jail, her life in Nazi prisons in France, and the end of the Franco regime. Yet, she tells us, "my objective in writing this is not to lament my sufferings, but rather to offer a picture of how great it is to live sustained by such humane ideas that form and moderate us to go in the best direction with a sense of purpose: the Communist way."[21]

Una vida para un ideal does not concentrate on the war or on the most repressive years of the regime (1939–1946); it spans all the decades of the regime and adds information that we do not find in the other books. Like Real's observations, Castro's are written from the perspective of a woman who has seen the death of Franco and the arrival of democracy with a more equitable situation for women in Spain. But Castro's text is somewhat more political and ideological. Like some of the memory texts of "visible" women, Castro's tends toward the rhetorical naiveté of political pamphleteering. For example, she says, "In the imagination of a Communist, the necessity to be involved in action wherever it is to be found, is always present; by overcoming all types of obstacles in order to place oneself at the service of the cause and serve it even in the smallest details at times ends up being great and worthwhile."[22]

Castro is the most exaggerated example of the activist who becomes mystically religious about the "cause." Like Ibárruri, she is even able to accept the fact that her children lived in an uncertain state when she was imprisoned: "This pain from such a brusque separation can only be endured when honor and the defense of a cause that is so human and so just—the Communist cause—come into play."[23]

Another curious, pamphlet-type outlaw text was published in London in 1939. *A Young Mother in Franco's Prisons: Señora Fidalgo's Story* was probably narrated to "the publishers" by Pilar Fidalgo and then transcribed, as is suggested in the introduction. "Señora Fidalgo tells in the pages which follow only what she herself has seen and what has been told her by eyewitnesses. Her account adds to what was already known of Franco's White Terror a new note of cruelty. It is the imprisonment and the martyrdom of mothers in the Spanish 'Nationalist' zone. The story is told in her own words."[24]

Fidalgo describes her own purpose at end of her testimony:

> In freedom I am still one of them, as I was when I was in prison, and to this day I share their sufferings. What else can I do for them but denounce the cruelty of their executioners?
>
> If the state of being human is made up of respect for right, of love for one's neighbour and of liberty, there are in the prisons of Franco thousands of beings whose sole hope is to be able one day to be called men again.[25]

Angeles Malonda, educated in the Association for the Diffusion of Scientific Studies and Research in Madrid, describes her years in prison after her husband was assassinated there and emphasizes the injustice of her case. Her format is one of short, anecdotal stories with specific themes, rather than a diary or autobiographical prose. Malonda is aware of the fragmentary and urgent nature of her work and exempts it from any literary aspirations.

The pages that you have read are not memoirs; they do not obey a plan nor do they have a preestablished finality. They are written "in the here and now" and on the spot; they paint an immediate reality, the state of mind of each moment. For that reason they do not constitute a homogeneous whole, but rather a succession of unquestionable facts and profound, sincere impressions of a spontaneiety unweakened by literary pretensions.[26]

Because of the emphasis on her affective state of mind, Malonda's is a more personal story. In addition, the temporal factor has an impact on her point of view: she wrote while still feeling the intensely painful emotions of the death of her husband and separation from her children—different emotions from those who wrote their memory texts many years later, who had decades to digest the psychological upheavals produced by the effects of unjustified incarceration, and who saw the gradual abatement of repression in Spain which began in the early 1960s. Even Malonda's introduction deals with her background and education, and her dedication is more personally directed than others: "To my grandchildren and to all the grandchildren of the world, with the desire and hope that they never have to be spectators of a war, much less of a civil war."[27]

In spite of the different foci and intentions of the memory texts and testimonies of women lost in Spanish prisons, they have a common explicit goal: to protest the systematic violation of their rights during the regime. Implicitly, they also wish to engage the reader in revising Spain's history by recording and revisiting the stories of their anguish and heroism.

The most pervasive theme in the texts and testimonials we are considering is the indomitable solidarity of the prison women, the single phenomenon that kept many women alive emotionally, psychologically, even physically. Juana Doña describes the unity among cellmates that helped them overcome mental and physical illness, the loss of loved ones, torture, and terror of the death penalty.

We have mentioned that the "protagonist" of *Desde la noche y la niebla* spent time on death row until her sentence was commuted to thirty years. She understands the importance of political solidarity perhaps better than any of the other prison autobiographers because of her long-term jail experience. Like her fellow writers, Doña tells the story of many cellmates; she invites her readers to intuit the lives of female political prisoners and sense the agony of living death. Yet underlying those stories of tragedy is an eloquent testimony of hope and a desire to survive in spite of the odds.

The same is true in Angeles García-Madrid's book, where we witness the fortitude and solidarity among imprisoned women.

> These women made it clear that they could totally ignore the "weakness" of their sex, go through a thousand calamities, and endure any tragedy without letting their executioners have the pleasure of seeing them subjugated by the jailers' whims. They were conscious of solidarity in everything, and they never allowed themselves to be demoralized . . . in spite of the fact that so very many lost their lives there, and many others were close to losing them.[1]

García-Madrid has described herself as a "tape recorder" of those years and laments the fact that many of the inmates she spoke to years later had erased the experiences in prison from their minds.[2] She decided that she would remember for them. García-Madrid, who was young and quite articulate, given her circumstances, was even commissioned by her jailers, the nuns, to write poetry. She became the recorder of the injustices committed against her fellow prisoners. "I suffered so much for my cellmates. I always felt everyone was suffering more than I was, that I could handle it. When they put me in the room with the dying women, I didn't think I was dying. I wrote poetry about them."[3]

The grim sides of solidarity—sharing sorrows and illnesses—are counteracted by the obstinate will to enjoy life in spite of the nightmares of prison. The young women in particular danced and sang and made attempts at theatrical performances. Paz Azati, one of the more eloquent voices of Cuevas' books, tells us that despite the disease and lack of food and water, the women rose above the humiliating filth and dehumanized conditions.

> We were full of bedbugs, and every day we bet on who had more of them and who killed more. I must say that Spanish women, in the midst of tragedy, in spite of the death, the firing squads, the beatings, the fleas, the bedbugs, hunger, and everything, had great spirit and nobody was ever able to dominate us. We even had enough of a sense of humor to do silly things at night.
>
> I remember that I had a fine memory then, and since I had read a great deal I recalled poetry and fragments of books and at night, wearing a nightgown one of the girls there had given me, which had been her grandmother's, I would stand up and recite bits and pieces of books. I looked like a ghost, and we would giggle a great deal. We had tragedy looming over us, but we were young and it was a time in which youth and the lust for life were more powerful than the entire tragedy.[4]

Women also set up classes and study groups. One inmate comments that the desire to learn to read and write, in addition to passing the time, was prompted also by practicality.

> One of the things we dedicated ourselves to with real enthusiasm, since we all followed the motto that we had to take advantage of the time, was studying. Everybody studied, and there was nobody who after six months in prison didn't know how to read and write.
>
> People were crazy to learn, because they had to write to their families. . . . Also, there was so much time and they wanted to read.[5]

Speaking undoubtedly for the Communist women, she emphasizes that the classes and seminars they organized helped women to maintain their dignity and to avoid "morbid" friendships in prison, meaning lesbian relationships.

Discipline and strength of character were key factors in the solidarity of the Communist women, and these traits are repeatedly discussed.

Soledad Real describes the group readings that took place in Ventas, where the solidarity was most active:

> I remember that in Ventas one of the things we did the most was collective reading of books. Intellectual women were being detained, and then foreign intellectuals came to see how they were being treated, to see if they were being abused. And they got them to send them all kinds of books, even books that had been prohibited in Spain, like the novels of Ramón Sender.[6] They would change the covers on the books, and at night they were read collectively. They'd say, "Tonight there's a reading." And everybody would rush off to the bathroom.[7]

Some women remember with nostalgia how the cellmates would group together based on their common criminal dossiers. Women who were in maximum-security cells were aided by the clandestine notes they received from other prisoners. They found many ways to pass the time—anything to forget that their trials were imminent; they assumed they would be condemned to death or to many years in prison, and that their youth would pass into middle age in the filthy prisons of the regime. Reflecting on the theme of solidarity, one inmate tells us:

> It's a noble sentiment in which personal sacrifice doesn't count. The essential thing was to rise above all the unpleasant things, the hard things, together in a collective way. That's how the link of camaraderie, which only takes place in the most horrible situations, flourishes. I have often reflected on those years now that I live in freedom, on the years that I was in captivity. And there are many months that I recall when I did not feel unfortunate.[8]

The majority of the available testimonies are those of women who were affiliated with the Communist party—which, most agree, had created a more profoundly established network of solidarity than other leftist or Republican groups. Their underground activities inside and outside prison became stronger when the Nazi defeat was imminent; they were convinced that Franco would fall with Hitler.[9]

While García-Madrid and Malonda (Socialist in background), do not speak of politics a great deal, political themes are obsessive among the Communists, as we have seen with Castro. Real tells us how morale was sustained among her cellmates:

The good side of prison was our moral strength with such a large group of people. Not all of us had our depressions and our moral crises at the same time; there was always someone who wasn't having one and could help you through yours. The best recourse, the real recourse, was always work. We'd propose, for example, a play. We'd rehearse, create a stage set and costumes, and that helped maintain the morale. I've had tremendous crises, the kind that make you want to die. Because it's logical that you would think about the fact that your youth was passing you by, that you were getting too old to have children. And this weighed on you a lot, especially in the second part, when we had been there for several years and we were convinced that it was going to be a long haul.[10]

The theme of life passing them by is often mentioned, though sometimes very subtly. This aspect of prison was obviously very difficult for women. Their reproductive systems were often damaged from abuse and lack of proper nutrition, and the aging process was accelerated through mistreatment. Furthermore, the extreme double standard in Spain at that time meant that women who came out of prison in their thirties—often after more than ten years—were considered old and no longer of childbearing age. And, of course, maternity was considered by the majority of Spanish women an essential part of their lives, an attitude that still prevails today.[11]

Their solidarity was politically constructive in the face of the brainwashing, torture, substandard conditions, and other dehumanizing tactics of the regime, but it was also directed against the prison authorities—the nuns, priests, and lay workers who tried to pressure the inmates into participating in religious functions and taking the sacraments. A religious order called Las Cruzadas had been founded by the Nationalists during the war. Its exclusive function was to take care of political prisoners. Specifically, its main objective during the entire regime was to reform "wayward" women (unwed mothers especially) for either political or sexual reasons. In this endeavor they collaborated with the Feminine Section. Núñez recounts one of the many methods used by the nuns to pressure political prisoners into returning to the church. A woman with a newborn child who had been condemned to death was told she could breastfeed her child if she made her confession to the priest. When she refused, her child was taken away and never heard of again.[12]

Numerous women with children were punished in this fashion. Their babies would be taken from them, or not given medical treatment when they were ill. Petra Cuevas—secretary of the Dressmakers Union in Madrid before the war—in *Cárcel de mujeres* speaks almost exclusively of the abuse the children suffered, mostly through negligence; the objective was invariably to punish the mothers. Cuevas had given birth to a child in prison, who was born with an infection because of the lack of hygiene; at the age of six months the child was dead, having been denied any medical care. Her obsession with imprisoned mothers with babies is evident throughout her testimonies.[13]

Cuevas is not the only one obsessed with the mothers in prison. Doña dramatically describes the painful experiences of women in prison who were pregnant or accompanied by their young children. Many children died from malnutrition, dysentery, and other diseases. Mothers were often too ill or abused to nurse their babies and watched helplessly as their children's lives slipped away. Nearly all of the testimonies emphasize the tragedy of mothers with children in prison. It is ironic that precisely what Franco held as the most priceless commodity in Spanish society after the war—the reproductive capability of its women, which could replenish Spain with able-bodied males—also represented the most tragic aspect of prison life for women.

Guiliana di Febo points out that the laws protecting mothers in the free world were also supposed to "favor" imprisoned mothers; they were to be freed from prison labor while they were breastfeeding, as long as they "were showing signs of repentance."[14] This edict produced a crisis for the politicized women who had to choose between spending time with their newborn and renouncing their ideological convictions, or forgoing the care of their children to maintain their religious boycott. The dilemma for women activists was always the clash between the political and the private.

A law passed in 1940 permitted children to be with their mothers until they were three. As Antonia García describes it during her stint in the Ventas prison, this regulation was not the least bit fortuitious:

The children were another of the great misfortunes in the prisons. The first moments were horrible. The friends and families outside couldn't help because they were in the same situation; inside we didn't have clothing, or water, or any sort of favorable conditions. When they placed them [the babies] in the cell with their mothers, there was a ringworm epidemic besides the fleas and bedbugs they already had. The children were dying, their little heads covered with scabs full of pus. The humidity and heat were horrendous in that cell. Dirty clothes were hanging because there was nowhere to wash them, and they got dry and filthier. Truly, I suffered more because of the children than because of the women who were condemned to death. The two things seemed tremendously brutal, but the situation of the children made me insane. Also they were dying, and dying in a state of atrocious suffering. I can still see their looks, their sunken eyes, hear their continuous cries, and smell their pestilent odor.[15]

This type of naturalistic description is found repeatedly throughout the written and oral testimonies. The death of babies caused by dysentery, food poisoning, rat bites,[16] malnutrition, and the like are pervasive themes as these women retrospectively tell or write of their experiences. All of the women agree—both those who had children and those who did not—that the worst fate was to have a child in prison.

Juana Doña is perhaps the most eloquent in describing mothers who were often too ill or too abused to nurse their babies:

What could those poor children hope for, with such emaciated mothers? They did everything possible to transmit life into their dying children; they hoped by sheer willpower that they could save them. They spent minutes and hours in hell when they realized that willpower was useless in the face of hunger and poverty. Why does it always have to be the mothers, the women, who get the worst of the deal?[17]

It seems that many of the women did not have husbands. The chaos and violence of war typically leaves many children without fathers. But the other aspect has to do with the drama so often portrayed in films about war: the syndrome of "eat, drink and be merry, for tomorrow we die." As Petra Cuevas unabashedly told me, she wanted to have a child out of wedlock when she was released from prison the first time. She was convinced that because of her clandestine activities on the outside she would be hauled back into prison, and that the time spent outside jail was her only opportunity to conceive a child. Cuevas felt there was a distinct possibility that she would grow old in prison.[18]

Other women whose children were in the outside world speak repeatedly of their obsession with separation from them and their feelings of guilt. When Angeles Malonda's two young daughters visit her, she expresses the anguish she feels when she is not permitted to touch them. In a passage from 1943—four years after her incarceration—she tells us:

Oh! Along with the joy of contemplating them my heart aches to think that their father will never be able to see them, that they are growing up without my caresses. They [the prison guards] won't even let me give them a kiss. I have begged, but they say that it's prohibited. In the name of what law are a mother's kisses prohibited? The children, poor things! they open their eyes wide in puzzlement. The adults are scandalized, but . . . how is this possible?[19]

Though the women tragically lament the death or incarceration of their husbands, they do not express the same pain as they do about their children. Obviously, Malonda's description of hearing the shots that killed her husband, who was in the same prison and working in the infirmary (they were both pharmacists), is heartrending. But as we observe with O'Neill, who also learned of her husband's death while she was in prison, the women's ability to survive is based on the need to raise their children.

The memory texts and testimonies tell the stories not only of imprisoned women and children but also of those who were outside the prison walls. In *Réquiem por la libertad,* García-Madrid demonstrates a keen sense of compassion for the women who were not behind bars but had a loved one in prison. These women, whom she calls "prisoners of the street," make her consciousness of the collective extend even beyond the parameters of her condition and that of her cellmates.

> As I speak of the spirit and the strength of these women, it is impossible to ignore those who suffered a similar prison outside the prison gates. The women who stood at the doors of the jails! The fiancée who spent years with a package in her hands, at the entrance to different prisons, putting up with the cold, rain, heat, and insults in exchange for seeing her loved one . . . the wives, sisters, daughters, but above all the mothers. The "free" mothers suffered as much or worse misery than the jailed ones. They bore so many insults and outrages, and so much pain, that perhaps they would have lived more peacefully inside the prison.[20]

García-Madrid also stresses that when women in prison heard their sentences—handed down, ironically, by the Palace of Justice—they suffered more for their families than for themselves, especially of course if they were sentenced to death. Malonda, in a tone of anguish and despair, speaks of the mothers who traveled hundreds of miles to visit their daughters "in disgrace," without even being able to kiss them: "Poor relatives of the prisoners! How much they suffer. 'Patience, patience,' they tell us, 'Don't suffer, everything will work out.' But you can feel how the words are drowned in lament. Those inside and those outside would like to encourage each other, and we tell each other merciful lies; but the truth is that we can't stand it anymore, we are on the verge of desperation."[21]

Malonda also speaks of the orphaned children who roamed Spain at the end of the war. On one occasion a group of fifty children, on their way to an orphanage, visited the prison and the inmates are permitted to spend the day with them. Malonda reflects on the devastations of war with regards to children:

The aftermath of war chooses the poor children as its innocent victims who are left abandoned, without homes. And those men who have caused the tragedy are those who are now bragging about helping them. The lack of civilization, the lack of culture, that makes men think they can solve problems by shooting, by hunting down other men, that which our children contemplate speechless, is the basis for the fact that these little creatures find themselves sent out into the world without any help in attaining the minimal rights that were given them at birth: parents, a home.[22]

Countless testimonies are about the women whose children are outside prison, as in Malonda's case, and whom they do not see for many years. Toward the end of the war, Carlota O'Neill realizes that her daughters will be raised by people with Fascist ideologies, since she is still in prison.

In January—it was 1939—Mrs. X sent me a letter telling me that someone from the paternal side of the family, who was in Fascist Spain, was going to Melilla to take charge of the girls. Bad news; it was the continuation of the Fascist ambience; the prolongation of the same one they had lived in since 1936. In the grade schools the picture of Franco, the Nazi salute, the hymns sung in the morning and in the afternoon; the Nazi-Fascist formation; the humiliation by the men who killed their father always present.

Again I felt constrained by the circle of fire, without the possibility of flight. Strangled by a sensation of anguish, impotence, vanquishment, and something more, like a flash of insanity; I let out screams that couldn't escape the wind, that stayed there, prisoners between the black rocks; shouts that were insults—tiny, impotent insults.[23]

The prison conditions that caused so much suffering and death among the children were of course shared by the women, although adult suffering is always thought of as far less dramatic. The women's descriptions of their arrival at the prisons and their transfers from one to another emphasize the cattle-car conditions; women and babies were packed into the closed cars with no food or toilets. The purpose of these constant transfers was to diminish political and psychological solidarity. García-Madrid describes one experience:

The train cars that awaited told us clearly that they had just been abandoned by other travelers, and not exactly human ones. The animal dung accumulated on the inside was accompanied by dry alfalfa leftovers with their usual disgusting odor. And there they were placing the women as if they were sheep, until there was not a space on the floor where another woman could sit. Then they closed the car door, the only ventilation being a crack produced by a badly fitted piece of wood. And they closed up the doors as if they were canning sardines.[24]

Yet those conditions did not differ greatly from what would become daily fare. Food was an obsession, because of its scarcity. The inmates were fed what we traditionally call "mess" (*rancho*), and descriptions of the various types of watery fare are innumerable. The quintessential plate of rancho was a bowl of brownish hot water that floated some lowly vegetable: a few lentils or peas, an onion, a brussels sprout. Invariably the soup was accompanied by a few pieces of dirt or stones, a bit of weed, some protein in the form of bugs or worms. Filthy and often fermented, the food caused constant dysentery at best, and food poisoning at worst (especially when the soup included rotten fish). One anecdote speaks humorously of the condition of the food:

> Something warm was nothing less than broth, made with peas, water, and salt; if it had a splash of oil, I never saw it. What it did have were little worms that came out of the peas, and we left them until the very end so we could eat them with a small chunk of bread because they were meat, the only meat, we ate. Sometimes we'd yell from one mat to the other:
> "Hey, how many did you get?"
> "Ah, I got five."
> "Well, I have three."
> "Shucks, what bad luck you have—I got seven."[25]

Some women passed the time sharing recipes, an ironic way to while away the day amid such hunger and deprivation. One inmate recounts:

> There were eleven of us, and if anyone got any money, we would buy a tiny tin of hake fish in oil. We would grab an infinitesimal piece of bread and the portion of hake that corresponded—one-eleventh—and rub it on the bread and taste it. Such was our hunger that we would fall into the strangest habit of writing down recipes. After eating, there in that room of sixty or more women, there was always someone who knew a typical recipe from their region. To be precise, I have in a notebook things like "Segovian pastries" and "Andalusian tarts."[26]

The majority of the stories about hunger are less than entertaining; yet some transgress the boundary of tragedy to become comically macabre. One inmate explains that another prisoner, who owned a restaurant, commented as follows:

"Listen, little one, if they give you the death sentence and really intend to kill you, if they take you to the military prison, don't worry—because you won't lack a thing in your last moments. I will tell my husband to send you the best from my restaurant every day. You can even ask for whatever you want."

I laughed, thinking: "With all the hunger that I am going through right now, dying full doesn't faze me. What I'd like is to stuff myself right now."[27]

What is most remarkable is that the women can tell the stories of deprivation with such glibness; their collective strength of character was indomitable.

Such unpalatable, indigestible, and unhealthy plates of liquid motivated the women to dream of "packages," humble baskets or bundles wrapped in newspaper that contained urgently needed supplies. Even if the packages consisted of only a can of sardines or a bar of soap (a rare commodity) there was always a celebration among the lucky person's group; the women who were fortunate enough to receive almost invariably shared their food, however meager. One woman speaks of dividing a boiled egg into sixteen pieces, and there were many such anecdotes.

Yet there were those who received healthy parcels of food. In the rare cases of a privileged woman such as María Luz Morales, who had taken over in 1936 as chief editor of the Barcelona newspaper *La vanguardia*, we find that she was spared the prison food. Each day, her family delivered hot meals, which she shared with others who were less fortunate.

Rats were a constant threat, especially while the inmates were sleeping, for the majority slept on floor mats. In *Réquiem por la libertad*, García-Madrid graphically describes the conditions. Talking about her determination to avoid the rats, she remarks: "She thought that . . . if they had walked all over her the night before and she still had her ears, she would not always be that lucky. She had to do something."[28] From another perspective, the rats were a diversion for some of the teenage girls who sought a respite from the tedium and depressing surroundings.

As always in prison, any distraction helped inmates to survive and to avoid thinking about their pending sentences. Perhaps the most extreme tale is that of Mercedes Núñez, who speaks of an inmate in solitary confinement awaiting the death penalty. The girl had been there for five and a half months during the coldest time of the year. She was without any kind of hygiene (except for a liter of water a day, which was also for drinking), in the midst of filthy clothes and unbearable odors, with no comb or anything with which to distract herself. She feared that she would lose her mind, until one day she found a nail.

That nail, bent, rusty, without a point, made me deliriously happy. It was as though I wasn't alone in the cell, you know? That nail saved me. For almost eight days I kept rubbing it against the cement until it was straight, shiny, and had a well-sharpened point. . . . I made a calendar on the wall, on which I marked the date and the day of the week. On top I put my name. I thought, "If I disappear, someone will know I passed through here." That idea consoled me a little. Also with my nail I did numbers to entertain myself. I drew geometric figures on the wall. Until one day . . . but you're going to laugh. . . . One day I drew the head of a child. I don't know how to draw, and anybody who would have seen it would have thought it no more than a simple scratch on the wall. But for me it was my son, the son I would like to have had; and I could see him, I could talk to him, and I even baptized him José Luis.[29]

The nameless protagonist of Núñez' vignette, entitled "The Nail," is the most exaggerated example of the will to attain psychological survival. The woman with the nail created her child through a symbol on the wall, and that artless graffiti kept her alive, in spite of knowing that she would probably die before a firing squad.

The prison authorities are remembered in great detail, especially the women who doled out the most inhumane treatment. Whenever their names are mentioned, some graphic term such as "poison" always describes them. Their crude threats of violence against the inmates are reminiscent of an army boot camp.

Illness—both mental and physical—is also a recurring subject in the testimonies and memory texts. There were occasional food strikes, for which the inmates were doubly penalized; not only were they punished by the authorities, but their bodies became weaker as a result and left their immune systems more vulnerable than ever. The diseases contracted by the women are unclear, even mysterious, since the inmates are unable to explain adequately either the malady or the cause. Soledad Real tells us that her ovaries detached themselves because of a "lack of fat" in her diet. She then describes an operation in which there is no anesthesia and no hygiene.[30] It is truly miraculous that women survived the lack of attention or the butchery when they were attended by the regime's physicians. A woman who was lucky enough to be so ill she had to be taken to a hospital felt she was living in luxury. O'Neill, rushed to a hospital because of what appeared to be pneumonia, describes her experience.

That was better than prison, and the air entered without the impediment of bars. There were two big windows without bars, open above the garden, on the second floor, and the green from the high leaves entered through the window. I had at last found nature. Everything was better than in jail. I had a bed just for me, an authentic bed with a mattress and bed linens, even a steel night table. Everything was white; everything was better.[31]

When Nieves Castro became ill with bronchitis and pleurisy, she was moved to a bed in her cell and visited by a doctor. However, the authorities refused to transfer her to the prison infirmary or treat her illness because she was under accusation by the military court. Finally she was taken to the infirmary, where she was cared for and survived.[32]

Malnutrition was rampant. Women speak repeatedly of the various epidermal eruptions that were caused by it; they frequently mention the disappearance of their menstrual period, sometimes for years, because of the lack of vitamins. Most obsessive is their need for "fat," ironic note in view of our obsession with cholesterol today. These women long for a bit of meat fat, or even a drop of oil in their soup.

Physical and mental disorders are repeatedly described. They were caused both by the conditions and by the physical and mental abuse to which the women were subjected. Psychosomatic illnesses were often brought on by the death of a loved one. Soledad Real describes her sudden illness when she hears that her young boyfriend has been killed. "I got so sick that I went to the doctor, who finally looked at me. He called three nurses and another doctor and said that I had a mass inside and that he couldn't distinguish my ovaries from my womb. I was covered once again with sores and eczema; they put bandages on me and the pus seeped out from under the bandages."[33] Rarely is a cure or even a diagnosis offered in the testimonies.

Often the women's mental derangement was a direct product of war: usually those affected were women who had watched their children die or witnessed the torture and death of other family members. Núñez tells of a woman who rocked her pewter plate to sleep at night and occasionally screamed out that they had killed her daughter. One woman broke down when her baby died in prison; she cared for the corpse until it was finally taken from her. Others were crazed from multiple rapes or constant torture. Some became ill because they lived in constant fear of death. Mental illness resulted primarily from the ever-present threat of death, the devastation of the war, the prison conditions, hunger, and, most important, the effects of torture. Physical torture took the usual forms—beatings, rapes, shock treatment—but some humiliations were uniquely macabre and reserved for women, such as forcing them to parade

around nude, or to stand or sit in grotesque positions in front of male inter-
rogators.

Mercedes Núñez, with her distant observational prose, speaks of the physical abuse of the Ventas inmates in a section called "The Modern Inquisition."

> It is not difficult to find an inmate in Ventas who has been mistreated
> and tortured; the difficult thing—if not the impossible thing—is to find
> one who has been able to escape without receiving even the ritual slaps.
> Sticks and electric currents are the two most common variants of tor-
> ture. In general, the torture has as its objective "to make the victims
> sing," trying with these methods to oblige them to denounce other anti-
> Francoites. But often the torture is simply gratuitous, the expression of a
> ferocious hatred and a sadism that borders on insanity.[34]

Núñez goes on to give examples. One woman's back was broken; she was
forced to climb onto a chair and then it was pulled away. Another woman's
genitals were cut; bleeding and maimed, she was made to walk—a source of
entertainment for the inquisitors because she "walked like a frog." Nuñez
speaks of an old woman who was made to ride a bicycle until she fell and broke
her arm, and of a young woman who was ignited with gasoline. She describes
the beating of a pregnant woman until she aborted, and the many cases of
electric shock administered to the genital area.[35]

Pilar Fidalgo, who from her exile in Paris had a special perspective on the
tortures inflicted on women, reports that "prisoners were considered by those
who conducted them [these scenes] as spoils of war, and excesses were as
terrible as they were common." Speaking of atrocities committed in her hometown by a respected lawyer and of others by an assassin named Mariscal, she
continues:

> These two murderers would make a fit study for psychiatrists.
> When we read the crimes of the monster of Düsseldorf with such in-
> dignation at the time, such disgust and shock, we were far from thinking
> that in our own country we should see even more terrible madmen
> emerge from among people whom we had considered normal. The fact is
> that there is no village, however tiny, in the rebel zone which has not its
> ten or twelve criminals at least equal to the Düsseldorf monster—and
> many who surpass him in horror.[36]

Fidalgo refers to crimes against both men and women, of course. The volume and the degree of atrocities against men are often greater, given their
superior importance in the war. Yet in a country where women were placed

on a pedestal and revered as virgins and mothers, or if they deviated even slightly were mocked as whores and lasciviously viewed as aberrant creatures, the grotesqueness becomes more pronounced, more twisted.

Women also were demoralized and humiliated by the epithets hurled at them during interrogations; most commonly, the police tried to frighten them by threatening sexual violence, which succeeded in making many of the women fanatically obsessed with such abuse. What was known outside was only that women were punished by the typical cod-liver oil, head shaving, and parades around the villages. The public knew only a small part of what went on inside the prisons.

Soledad Real describes one of these public episodes and the typical reaction. When Soledad is detained with a group of women and taken from the train in the city of Linares in the midst of a holiday celebration, the guards tell them they can walk to the prison and be humiliated or take taxis at their own expense. All the women opt for walking. The comments quickly begin:

> "Look, a group of black marketeers!" One of the women said, "Forget that, we are political prisoners." And a young Civil Guard said: "Listen, girl, you're very proud of being a political prisoner, but today is fiesta in Linares, and I'll let you participate. To get to the jail, we are going to walk past all the señoritos of Linares, and of course all the señoritos of Linares belong to the Falange, so don't flaunt the political prisoner thing." We went on the walk through Linares . . . and the señoritos were seated on the sides—what chairs! what tables! And one says, "Well, look at those prisoners!" And another says, "They must be whores." And one of the girls says: "Whores! Not whores, unless you think Communist women are whores, because we're Communists!"[37]

Not only is the equation "activist = whore" emphasized here, but also the fact that this was a class war. The idle señoritos with their opulent furnishings (probably at the casino, the normal meeting place of the wealthy men of the towns) gleefully jeer at the poor female prisoners. They are both "tainted" women and poor women; otherwise they would not be political prisoners who are paraded through the streets. The women have lost not only their cause but also their pyrrhic victory. Class and gender order had been restored, and these women would not be permitted to forget it until forty years later—though, as we can see, some have not wished to forget it.

In García-Madrid's *Réquiem por la libertad*, it becomes clear that for the secret police of the Franco regime, women who had defended the Republic were invariably considered Red whores. Scenes of both verbal and physical abuse are consistently linked to the equation "activist = whore." When the police were attempting to get more information from the women, scenes like the one described in *Réquiem* are typical. As García-Madrid is interrogated, the commissioner screams, "She thinks she's smart, but she's nothing but a Red whore!"[38] Customarily, these words prefaced an episode of physical abuse.

Doña denounces every aspect of prison life but becomes most vehement when she describes experiences specific to women. For instance, she insists that age did not determine who was raped; teenagers, adult women, and grandmothers alike were victims. She elaborates on the topic: "Rape was the daily fare; the abuse of power by men against women in those circumstances acquired dramatic proportions. The so-called Reds [women] were less than nothing to the macho Fascists. The rape of female prisoners had nothing to do with sexual desire; it was simply an act of power, humiliation, sadism."[39]

Castro was physically and psychologically abused during her years in prison. She does not explicitly describe the sexual abuse, but recognizes that she has blocked out these painful experiences:

> I spent many years without speaking of this terrible act, thinking that hardly anyone knew about it: first because I felt such shame when I was able to coldly examine the situation, and also because anytime I remembered, I got cold chills. Many years went by and I was never able to remember it calmly, in spite of how many times I told it; and today, after so many years, I find it difficult to recount it with the exact details that it deserves.[40]

Although sexual violence against women is often referred to—though rarely graphically described—sexuality in prison is only fleetingly commented on. The references are occasionally in a pitiable or comic tone, but mostly they are moralistic. Sex is a topic that traditionally was never mentioned in Spanish literature—fiction or nonfiction (although this has changed radically since the death of Franco). In addition, for the Communists sexual desire was considered the most insidious form of weakness, with homosexuality obviously considered one of the worst crimes against human integrity.

The only woman who even discusses her sexuality is Soledad Real—who has the most straightforward of the testimonies analyzed in this text—and her comments are extremely revealing. She says, as she reflects on the inflexibility of the Communists in those days: "If someone would have told me, for example, that the majority masturbated, I would have beaten that person up. Today I realize that it must have been true. But then I would have never admitted it. And possibly I have been one of the most tortured women in that sense because I wouldn't permit myself to do it." In discussing lesbianism, she says frankly:

As far as sexuality was concerned, our intransigence came from the very prejudices of our education and the times. Because today homosexuality is something that is justified, that is defended, but in those days we fought ferociously against it.

Among us, the comrade that fell into this lesbianism separated herself on her own; she knew she had to be one thing or the other, since among us this type of relationship was not permitted.[41]

Doña speaks laconically of homosexuality: "There were rare cases of lesbianism among the thousands and thousands of women who passed through the prisons for political crimes. Those rare cases were written in stone and became history: rejection, disgust, and isolation followed them wherever they went."[42]

O'Neill relates a case of lesbianism without the moralistic tone of the Communists, rather as one more story about prison life that is narrated lyrically and explained rationally:

They were two young girls; they weren't even twenty years old. They arrived terrified, their weak breasts trembling, their lips pale, their hair in disarray, signs of violence on their bodies, their clothing torn and full of dirt from some road, tottering, and with blood on their skirts.

They met in the Falange truck, at the hour of the roundup. They were raped. But then they didn't kill them, they brought them to prison. And they arrived, holding hands, hugging each other like two wounded female animals. They ate their mess out of the same container—there weren't enough to go around—they drank out of the same can, they isolated themselves from the others so they could whisper. They consoled and kissed each other and wiped each other's tears. At night they would go to sleep in the laundry room.

This love caused jeers and embarrassment among the mothers. And upon feeling persecuted, they loved each other more. The other young women gave them condemning, curious, perhaps envious, looks. For the lovers the horror was less than for the others. When one found out that the other's brother and father had been shot, the only consolation was in kisses. And they kissed full of tears; the orphan leaned her head on the breast of her lover. In ancient Greece, Sappho would have dedicated her best verses to them.[43]

Unlike the other inmates, especially the strict Communists, García-Madrid finds a lesbian prostitute to be merely amusing. Prostitution was a problem that political inmates confronted constantly, more often with concern and compas-

sion than with amusement or anger. Juana Doña alludes to the victimization
of hungry women after the war who had little choice but to turn to prostitution
for survival. She tells of their plight in the prison in Oropesa dedicated to their
reform.

> Eight days before, eight women arrived from the Oropesa camp, which
> housed thousands of prostitutes who hadn't attained the category of "ele-
> gant whores"—that mass of women who had to sell themselves at the
> end of the war for a "dish of lentils," who swaggered through the streets
> and gave themselves for two pesetas or a bottle of oil, those poor women
> who didn't have fire in their houses and prostituted themselves for a din-
> ner—those were the "prostitutes" of Oropesa.
>
> And Oropesa was famous for the life there. Run by nuns as hard as
> granite, the first thing they did to depersonalize them as women was
> chop off their hair. . . . They covered their bodies with stiff cloth robes
> that made them look like executioners, so that the forms of their bod-
> ies—the cause of their sins—wouldn't be noticeable. And to overcome
> their "laziness," they made them work ten to twelve hours hunched over
> in the garden or on their knees scrubbing floors, or made them primi-
> tively wash dozens of sheets with bleeding hands for the nuns and also
> for private homes. The meals were just enough to keep them working
> like slaves; the two hours of recreation were utilized for saying rosaries
> and litanies, always kneeling, as "penance for sins of the flesh." The pun-
> ishment had no limit or measure. Who cared if a whore died in solitary
> confinement or from exhaustion? Who was going to ask for explanations
> from those "little nuns" who were there out of love for humanity?[44]

O'Neill paints an equally lamentable picture of the plight of prostitutes,
though she focuses on those who were more "successful": the whores of the
Falangists.

> In the bordellos Falange military and civilians unloaded their lust through
> the torture they inflicted, the blood they spilt, all very violently, on the
> prostitutes, whom they stood in line nude and beat with their whips. One
> of them we had there showed us her chest with four deep scars, as
> though they were deep pockmarks, that were made by a judge. As she
> was dining with him in her room, he made her take off her clothes and
> he stuck his fork in her chest. Their drunkenness awoke subhuman in-
> stincts; the men who the next day were to preside over courtmartialing
> for hours, sought in the brothels not the lust that men don't dare to or

don't wish to ask of their wives, but something more complicated and prohibited. But it wasn't prohibited because no woman dared protest; the threat of being considered a red was too terrible.[45]

For the most part, the women were very careful not to stoop to anything considered degrading. For instance, water was scarce, so thirst took priority over hygiene. Although there were showers in some prisons, the queues were endless and exhausting for those who were too weak from hunger and illness to stand in line for hours. The stench, from both the women and the children, was unbearable. Núñez emphasizes that the lack of hygiene was used to humiliate and demoralize, with the objective of breaking down the will of these women. One activist woman warns others of falling into the trap: "They try to create here all the conditions possible to turn us into brutes. . . . And we, against all odds, must do everything humanly possible not to let that happen and keep watch on ourselves in the smallest details. A simple slip in language, in cleanliness, no matter how small, is important. It means a concession to the enemy."[46]

The Communist women were especially conscious of this plot. One remarks:

One of the things that we have always seen very clearly, and that we have tried to be efficient about, is that we only had one weapon, and that was dignity. We couldn't lose that and they couldn't take it away. No matter what punishment it cost us, we have always tried to maintain it and get them to respect it. There have been so many things that we defended as political prisoners, no matter what happened, and for that reason we had hunger strikes, revolts, and that's why we were punished.[47]

One of the most talked-about scandals resulting from the inmates' rebelliousness happened in 1949 when a Chilean woman visited the Segovia prison. She had been promised that she could speak freely with the prisoners. Yet a young woman who told her about the repression in the prisons and outside was shot to death the next day. In solidarity, the Communist, Socialist, and Anarchist inmates protested, screamed to the people in the streets, and went on a hunger strike. All were beaten severely, their clothing and belongings were taken away, and they spent six months in solitary confinement.[48] Repression was still severe, even though several years had passed since the regime had attempted to dissociate itself from its neo-Nazi past.[49]

Many of the women talk about suicide as the only alternative to freedom. Malonda speaks about it abstractly on one occasion: "The time comes when you are so exhausted, so overcome morally, that you would like to go up in smoke, disappear, fuse yourself with nothingness. You long for what is called fading into peace."[50] In a more desperate moment, when she has again been found guilty, Malonda reflects the sense of guilt that prisoners felt about putting their families through the hell of their suffering.

That was when I felt a sensation of fierceness, of desperation, to think that those evil people who had so astutely caused this result had more strength than my family, which had gone through so many trials so that infamy wouldn't prevail. My mother's horrible shock after confidently wanting to witness the trial, and her annihilation on hearing the verdict, kept going through my mind. Given all of this, my nerves, as so many other times, abandoned me. I broke out in sobs. It was as if I was in a crazed state. The only thing I could think of was to free myself from everything—suicide. End it once and for all.

I couldn't bear so much time with the desperation that had taken hold of me, so immobile in the small cell, thinking of my new suffering, the anguish I was causing my family. If I ended my life, their sorrows would cease in the face of the irremediable, and for me it would be a liberation. I remembered so many life experiences! Such far-away happiness![51]

Malonda's obsession with ending her life so that her family could live again makes her very different from many of the Communist women, who wished to live at all costs. Perhaps because Malonda was not an activist, but instead had followed the path of her Socialist husband by helping the working class, she could not cope with the injustice of her situation. Or perhaps the fact that she wrote her book immediately after the war and still was vividly conscious of the despair that other women had forgotten, or had reconstructed in their minds, made her account different.

Despair, though, is visible in different degrees in all the testimonies. Malonda is by far the most eloquent in her misery and rejection of what she considers an unjust and uncivilized world. When Carlota O'Neill finally comes to grips with the fact that her husband has been assassinated, she falls into the grim abyss of desolation. "It was true, there was no other remedy. This was the frightening part. And that black jail, full of walls and iron bars, was like a sepulcher for me. I only had one desire: to be reunited with Virgilio. I would have made a hole in the stones to bury myself. To feel death arrive slowly, what a consolation."[52]

On a different occasion when she speaks of her desire for death, O'Neill is reproached by another woman who is living the same tragedy, husband gone and children "orphaned."

> So you want to die to make your enemies feel good? Are you going to be such a coward that you want to wait for death without resisting?
> You have to live. Live for your daughters and for us, for all of us, because you have to write what you have seen here someday so that the world knows our suffering—these painful experiences of unknown people like us that will slip by without anyone ever finding out. . . . And the death of our people will be lost in oblivion! You have to do your duty![53]

O'Neill claims that she will never forget these words, and her remembrance of them is obvious when we observe her tenacity in writing and rewriting her prison experiences even after they had been destroyed. Curiously, the majority of the political activists who were of humble origins never spoke of suicide or of a desire for death, but rather reflected the dauntless spirit of O'Neill's friend.

The one known case of suicide among the politicized women is so enigmatic that there is a great deal of doubt about the circumstances involved. Matilde Landa was the quintessential example of solidarity in prison. She had gained experience working with the judicial system when she aided in the liberation of political prisoners during the repression of 1934 in Asturias. She was an activist in the International Red Aid group during the war and helped to organize hospitals and civilian evacuations. She was also involved in disseminating Republican propaganda, and when the war ended she decided heroically to stay in Spain to continue her work.

In 1939 Landa was condemned to death and, as usually happened, her death sentence was commuted to thirty years in prison. She was sent to Ventas. Because she was well known as a Republican activist, members of the regime feared her power as a martyr. They offered to free her if she would publicly renounce her politics. Landa categorically refused and was placed in solitary confinement. She was persecuted assiduously for five years. In spite of all this, she did help some of her fellow prisoners to get their death sentences commuted, by studying their files and appealing to the authorities. She was, as di Febo says, "one of the first examples of the militant legal voice—which later would be integral to the anti-Franco battle by democratic lawyers—who revealed the arbitrary nature of the trials and discovered contradictions within the very laws."[54] Finally, Landa was separated from her companions and sent to the prison in Palma de Mallorca in 1943, where she was badgered by the nuns there to return to the church. Her "suicide" is dated 24 September 1943.[55]

Of interest are the remarks made by Landa's companions in the Ventas prison about her bravery against all odds:

> I would like to pay homage to those who worked in the death row of Ventas, where Matilde Landa, condemned to death, with exemplary abnegation fought with a group of brave companions, and the few elements that military law permitted them, to save the women on death row, at one time 189 of them. This was the positive part. The nucleus of Communist women, all young, fought to reorganize the Communists and their sympathizers.[56]

Landa also managed to get the prison authorities to let the women on death row be visited by their families—which did not happen in any prison but Ventas, according to Antonia García.[57] Landa was taken from Ventas because her cause célèbre had become too dangerous to the regime, as Paz Azati tells us.

> The day Matilde left, there was a great sensation. The eleven thousand women who were in Ventas all prepared to say goodbye. The whole prison was on its feet. They closed off the galleries; they locked us all up. But we stood facing the bars and said goodbye to Matilde singing, screaming, and causing a big racket. They kept us incommunicado for fifteen days for what we had done. But Matilde left in the midst of great acclamation.[58]

Many of the women feel that Landa saved their lives. Rosie the Dynamiter is one; she claims that Landa kept vigil over the women who were on death row and told them to scream if the guards came suddenly to take them away.[59]

Given these testimonies and the fact that my own sleuthing in Palma produced absolutely no information about the celebrated prisoner, the story of Matilde Landa's suicide is certainly somewhat spurious. Her faithfulness in helping other women makes us question whether she was the suicidal type. Even more surprising is a letter to her daughter, written in code, about the six months she had spent in solitary confinement. Using metaphors meant for her censors, she writes:

> My darling daughter:
> I have here the first letter that I have received for such a long time. No matter how much I tell you, I will not be able to explain how content I am with it, and the happiness it gives me to know that you are well and studying.
> I am well. After the treatment the doctors gave me—six months without seeing light—now, since I can have my eyes open, I am enchanted with

the wonderful light and air that come in through the window. This hospital is very cheerful. Anyway, I will not be able to escape without an operation—the doctor says it will be any day now [referring to the trial regarding her death sentence]—but even though it is a delicate one, I am very calm and sure that it will come out all right. You know how resistant I am, and I think the worst is over now (I'm talking about the diet that was so severe, which I told you about). I am prohibited from writing so that I don't strain my eyes, but I am doing it thanks to the benevolence of a sick girl who is in this hospital. She is very kind, and a brother of hers will probably stop to visit you. . . .

In this hospital are some very nice girls and we enjoy ourselves as much as we can. I am more encouraged each day. I sing, and I am even learning how to dance. The worst things are daybreaks: I have a hard time and get very sad.

Now, although I'm in the hospital, I work. I am taking care of the most seriously ill girls. I monitor their schedules and I have been successful in improving their health once the doctors have given up all hope. [This refers to her success at reversing the death sentence for some of the inmates.] It is very painful when they die, but it is a tremendous happiness when, after trying so hard to cure them, they are saved. That's why I don't want them to take me away after my operation. I would feel very bad: I have affection and friendships here that are never forgotten.

Today your aunt came to see me—always so affectionate and so good. She and her children always provide everything for me—even flowers! If you only knew how happy they make me!

A big hug for everyone. For you, many kisses from

Your mother

December 2, 1939[60]

Neither the testimonies about Landa nor this brave letter demonstrate any weakness of character that could have led to her suicide. Of course, when she lost her opportunity to save the other women, perhaps the will to save herself dissolved, as is suggested by her remark about not wanting to be taken from the so-called hospital after she was cured.

This is García-Madrid's theory:

Matilde was a great Communist militant—intelligent, active, and efficient. . . . From the first moment of her detention, the Francoites did everything in their power to give her a bad reputation. They tried to bribe her a thousand times, even promising her freedom if she would renounce her Communist ideas; and because she refused to, she spent a half-year incommunicado in a maximum-security cell in Ventas. Afterward they continued to try to kill in her the paradigm of the antifascist woman and activist. . . . When she was sent to Palma de Mallorca, the pressure on her by the nuns of the jail and even by the highest ecclesiastical authorities of that city was so insistent that she preferred jumping out of a window onto the patio rather than giving in, though there are many doubts about her death.[61]

Landa's is a unique and eloquent testimony of moral fortitude in the face of incessant adversity—and also a macabre indictment of the religious and political repression carried out by the church. The publication that celebrates the first congress of the Union of Spanish Antifascist Women in Paris in 1947 pays tribute to Matilde Landa: "Example of heroism, of modesty, and of love for the Republic. Tortured spiritually and physically in the Franco prison in Palma de Mallorca, she remained firm and faithful to our cause and she helped her jailed companions, who showered her with affection. Matilde Landa, beloved sister, your generous sacrifice will be glorified in our liberated Spain under the folds of the Republican flag!"[62]

Many of the women in prison were less than twenty years of age; most had spent the war years collecting money for "the cause." The most-talked-about case was that of the "Thirteen Roses" or "Thirteen Minors," a group of teenage girls in the Ventas prison who were members of the United Socialist Youth group and who were among the fund-collecting teenagers described by Borkenau. Although all the documentation shows that they were entirely innocent of any war crimes, they were summarily tried and condemned to death for "plotting to kill Franco." The young women were shot before a firing squad two days after their trial on 5 August 1939. What most impressed the other prisoners was their pride and bravery. The testimonies describe their final moments: all of them, dressed in their best, walked with their heads held high to face the firing squad. The women listened as each shot resounded. The story became mythologized; poems were written about the Thirteen Roses. It is said that twenty-four hours after they were shot, Franco's pardon arrived.

All of the stories, nevertheless, coincide on the details of the case. Some are more melodramatic than others, of course; for instance, Juana Doña's version:

At midnight on the fourth, the Falange prison officials went to seek them out in their diverse cells, to lock them in the "chapel."[63] At that time there was still no death row and the Thirteen Minors were dispersed all over the prison. Their names were dramatically repeated throughout the jail. When they called the first one, "Joaquina López Lafitte!," the fourteen thousand women shivered and the news spread like wildfire: "They are going to shoot the minors!" The thirteen girls were grouped together without a tear in their childish eyes, their shaved heads held high. Serene and brave, they said goodbye to their sisters in captivity and encouraged them, those thousands of women who refused to believe that this monstrous crime could be committed. They took them away while they sang "Young Guard," and during the whole night in the "chapel," they sang until the trucks came to pick them up. Their echoes reached even the absolute silence of the prison; those fourteen thousand women held their breath in order to hear them. They could even hear the trucks and the warden locking the door, and little by little the echo of the Thirteen Minors was extinguished forever. After about fifteen minutes the rattle of machine guns could be heard, and fourteen thousand mouths counted the shots: 68! The plot was over.[64]

Even though this was the most lamentable of stories, given the youth and innocence of the girls, the subject of the death penalty, in Ventas prison usually called La Pepa,[65] is the most nightmarish of all the topics brought up in the memoirs and testimonies. Many women were automatically given the death sentence when they entered prison, though often it was commuted to thirty years or less. But death by firing squad became a daily threat, because in the case of Ventas and other prisons, the cemeteries where the inmates were executed were in earshot of the prison, as we have learned from Doña's testimony. Many nights were spent waiting for the sound of shots—always at dawn—and many inmates therefore became obsessed with the death sentence. Often large groups were shot on religious holidays, as a lesson to inmates who did not follow the teachings of the Catholic church.

In 1939 the shots were heard daily and the trials were hasty. The regime saw no reason to prolong the trials; repression was so institutionalized early in the postwar period that anyone could be shot without question. People on the outside were too fearful to intervene. This state of affairs continued into the forties. Gradually, primarily because of Hitler's defeat and because Franco hoped to join the United Nations, the regime became somewhat more careful about committing the genocide prevalent at the very beginning of the postwar period.

Blasa Rojo, condemned to death along with her sister for being a leader and activist in Antifascist Women, describes the sensations of being on death row.

You can imagine what happens with the death sentence, watching them take out your companions and not knowing when it will be your turn. . . . The things that happened to us in the Guadalajara jail . . . when we lived in the school patio! . . . It was a mass of women's flesh. . . . What hunger! What disasters! Because my mother couldn't bring anything, she was outside with my two little children; all she could hope for was that people would give her something for her grandchildren. . . . Imagine what it was like to be condemned to death, in a cell that was so tiny (we were seventeen on death row), and to know that they would come for one of us, but not know which one. My sister, who is much more nervous than I, didn't sleep. She sat in the little window that faced the street and stayed there all night waiting to see if they would come. She stayed there like an animal and suffered while waiting to find out if it was her turn. She would say: "I hope they kill me! They've condemned me to death twice! I want them to kill me!"[66]

Rojo's testimonies of the death sentence go on and on, always in a feverish, obsessive tone. As she explains it, waiting for the death squad "is the worst torment and suffering that a human being can go through."[67]

Even the women who were not condemned to die partook of the living death of their cellmates. Paz Azati eloquently tells of this morbid communion.

There is something that I have always said and I wish to say now: I will never, ever, forget the eyes of the women that they took out to kill, because those eyes would change color, with a special expression that I can't describe . . . the eyes of those women who knew that they were going to kill them that night. I have known women whose eyes have been an obsession for me for years. They were, I don't know, . . . the eyes of someone who sees beyond all of us, as though they were already outside life, but whom you still see alive. I can't explain it . . . and I get nervous when I remember it. It is hard for me to remember such things because they hurt, and it is as though I am still seeing them.

There was that silence of tombs that was created when we knew there would be a raid. And when you knew they were in the "chapel" and you were in your cell and it wasn't you they'd come for, . . . you'd get a feeling that you wished they'd shoot you too along with her to end it once and for all. People would say, "If they're taking her, take me too; let's all die at once and get it over with."[68]

Fidalgo too painstakingly describes those moments of horror and fear.

Anguish, indescribable anguish, arose within us when five o'clock came. Every day a new and frightful trial began with twilight. It was with horror that we saw night fall; and we wished the sun would never set. At eight or nine o'clock at night we all began saying goodbye to one another. Some tied up their bundle of personal belongings with the scraps of linen they possessed and used it for a pillow, as if they had tramped and rested for the last time on that final road. Some had already been parted from their jewels, earrings, wedding rings, religious medals, and little necklaces; they had given them to their relations through the bars of the interview cage, with messages for those soon to be orphans. One can guess with what emotions these knickknacks were received. Others who had not been visited gave up souvenirs of their domestic life—souvenirs of happy days to those among us whom they thought would be the last to follow after them.

For those who had a baby with them, and there were many, . . . the first sign that they were to be taken to the executioner was when their infant was taken from them. All knew what this meant: a mother who had her little one taken from her had only a few hours to live. There were heartrending scenes. The condemned mothers covered their little ones with kisses, pressed them for the last time to their bosom; and it was necessary to tear them away by brute force from their mothers. Then the tears ceased. The women fell into a state of semiconsciousness, of absolute fixity, and of frightening dumbness, having lost all idea of their surroundings. It was in this state that the poor women were led to their death. It happened every night.

I have no recollection whatever of our being spared these dramatic scenes. In the profound silence that we kept, we first heard steps on the staircase, then steps in the corridor, and then the door was opened. Civil Guards and Falangists appeared, who read out names very slowly—with torturing slowness. With the reading of the first name, anguish and terror seized all of us. Those who had been named took their kitbag, gave it to us, and asked us to see that their people got it. Those who, once more, had not been named, uttered a sigh of relief at the thought that they had twenty-four more hours of assured life—a small concession that seemed to us a precious gift.

In order to hear the list better we held our breath, and so that our children should not cry, we gave them the breast. We who had to stay behind, fearing that the murderers would prolong their stay among us, begged the condemned ones not to delay their dressing. They knew, and we knew, that they were about to be killed, and we were all anxious that the scene should come to an end; because if the victims claimed were slow in getting ready, the executioners hurled at us the grossest insults and threatened to take us all. The most tragic aspect was that the unfortunate ones who were going to die understood us very well and so went out quickly, some even without their shoes. However long, however full of change life may be, neither I nor any of the survivors shall ever forget those moments.[69]

It is interesting to note the honesty with which Fidalgo expresses what could be construed as cruel indifference. She wished that the women who would die that night would leave hurriedly. Fidalgo was thankful for one day more of life, unlike many other women, who could no longer keep up the hope for life. Of course, time factors are involved here: Fidalgo spent only eight months in prison, while many of the testimonies in the Cuevas books were by women who witnessed these "raids" for years; the erosion of morale was obviously much more acute after years of such mental torture.

García-Madrid is also adept at representing this frightening aspect of imprisonment after the war. She describes the hopelessness gripping the inmates who were surrounded by grave illnesses that went untreated and by prisoners doomed to die by the firing squad.[70] La Pepa was constantly on the lips of the prisoners, and each day they waited with dread to find out who would be liquidated. García-Madrid bitterly describes the indelible mark this made on her:

> She thought that no matter what she would witness in the future, nothing would impress her as much as what she was living today. If she were lucky enough to get out of this rathole alive, even if she lived a thousand years, it would not be possible to erase this memory from her mind. It was like the ancient sacrifices to the gods. The sacrifices of innocents, the more innocent the better—there couldn't be a finer holocaust.[71]

The fact that García-Madrid wrote her book more than forty years after the events took place demonstrates her continuing morbid obsession with her prison experiences. Her outrage and her urgency in telling of prison life are compelling.

Many women's lives were destroyed because of the years they languished in prison, the illnesses they suffered, and, worse, the way they were treated when they left prison. The majority of the women were scorned and shunned by people on the outside, even by many who had been sympathetic to their cause—not only out of fear but also out of shame, since the regime had discredited them so successfully. Many were unable to get jobs because they had no working papers or "sponsors" who would vouch for their conduct. Often they had nowhere to live and no skills to carry them through the hard times. In many cases leaving prison appeared to be worse than staying there. After all, in prison they had their friendships and many things were predictable. The real world was a hostile often unrecognizable place for women who had spent many years incarcerated. Their freedom, full of hope and fear, was indeed a mixed blessing.

Tomasa Cuevas explains her own predicament; she was to be "exiled" in Barcelona,[72] but wished to visit her family in Guadalajara (near Madrid) before leaving. Though she was prohibited from doing so, her desire to see her family was more overpowering than the risk of being caught (this bravery characterized all of the events in Cuevas' life) so she clandestinely traveled to Guadalajara, then hastily left for Barcelona. She managed to find a job as a maid by lying about her past.

Cuevas' perspective on the sad plight of the ex-prisoner reveals that she was happier in jail because at least she was with her own people, while the street appeared to her to be a larger, more volatile prison. She speaks of those she met while standing in the seemingly interminable lines of ex-prisoners, who were required to check in periodically with their probation officers.

> There were so many ex-prisoners who had to go in on the same day that there were immense lines of men and women to sign the book. It was so sad to see the men, because it was harder for them than for us to get work. We could become maids and survive. Men would go to the factories . . . and when they presented their probation papers, they wouldn't give them a job. So many fainted from hunger; they were badly dressed and totally desperate. As hard as it was to be in jail, some said, "It's better there than suffering this social humiliation in the street, exiled, without families or a home." They slept where they could—in doorways, anywhere. I remember that one day a boy did not appear and we found out he had been arrested for stealing something to eat. A comrade who told us he was in the party was furious and said, "This is what those assassins want, to throw us out of our homes, to have the doors slammed on us when we try to work, so that we will be reduced to stealing."[73]

Many women express a kind of happiness "with a price tag" on leaving prison. Their freedom was marred by the sadness they felt each time they thought about their friends who remained behind. Their freedom seems a crime against those left behind; they speak of the emptiness and loneliness of being without their cellmates, to whom they are bound in so many ways. Others tell of their feeling of alienation in a world not at all reminiscent of the Republican years of euphoria and upheaval, and of the chaos and freedom of the war. The world had stood still in prison, but not outside.

María Salvo, who spent many years in Franco's prisons, makes an astounding observation about the passage of time and her entrance into a world in which she was an alien.

> I won't go on about my emotions in those first days; there were so many
> and they were so diverse that it would take too long to tell. I will only
> say that I realized then that the years had passed. It was another world
> that I had to adapt to. It was a strange way of life for me. I had lost the
> habit of eating with a knife and a fork; this was just one small detail, to
> give an idea of the shocks that I would later receive. I didn't know the
> value of money; in prison they used only cardboard pieces that the prison
> authorities handed out. Everything seemed different, and even the con-
> versation with my family and my friends who were so close to me was
> hard to understand. It was as though a wall existed between us that had
> to be torn down little by little.[74]

Soledad Real's saga of life after prison is a remarkable story of fortitude. Even in the year 1982, when Consuelo García interviewed her, she was very cautious about talking to García in her home. Real explained that her neighbor was a civil guard and that his children would sit at the window and repeat the word "whore" over and over, to humiliate her. Forty-three years had gone by since the end of the war. Women who had been political activists had virtually disappeared from view until the death of Franco in 1975. Yet the neighbor's children were still being indoctrinated with the familiar equation about the leftist women of the Spanish civil war.

Real, like many other women in prison, met her future husband by cor-respondence. He was also in prison and acquired information about her through other inmates. She wrote to him for ten years. He left prison in 1955 and she in 1957, when they immediately married. She tells of her final delib-erations as she left prison after sixteen years of confinement. Speaking as a collective voice, she describes the predicament of her companions.

> It seems very simple: you've completed your sentence and you're leaving.
> But it isn't that simple. Because as your friends leave, the experiences of
> these companions give you an idea of the problems you will have to con-
> front. Because the problems of adaptation are tremendous. There was the

woman who got out and her daughters didn't want to live with her. Or the one who was all alone, so afraid she would commit suicide that instinctively, when she was riding in the subway, just as the train would arrive in the station she would press herself against the wall; that's how afraid she was that she would throw herself under the train. Or the one who had been separated from her husband all these years and now they didn't understand each other. Or the one who suddenly felt so weighed down by family problems and housework that she began to yearn for prison, for our camaraderie.[75]

Real is a quintessential example of the victimization that took place among ex-inmates of her gender. As described by Cuevas, the men had somewhat different and perhaps more practical problems than women. Yet the women were still objects of the sexual prejudice that had characterized the plight of the Spanish female activist. Real's husband, Paco, met with opposition from his family when they married because Real was a widow and therefore "secondhand" and furthermore was older than Paco. In addition, Real had been frank in telling her future husband that she had had a lover after the death of her husband, a young activist who was killed by the regime. This news circulated among Paco's family and neighbors, and that information, along with her status as a former political prisoner, was constantly used to control her.

When Real's husband was sent back to prison for clandestine activities, she became even more vulnerable to the insults and sexual advances of the police, who tested her to find out if she worked (or would be willing to work) as a prostitute, so that they could imprison her again. The police knew that prostitution was one of the few options for many women, because of the countless obstacles they faced in trying to rebuild their lives and survive financially. It was obvious that the regime lay in wait to prove the old equation "activisit = whore."

O'Neill tells of her final day in prison after four years there.

I went back upstairs to get my little bundle. They were all there: white and black heads, brilliant eyes without brillance, and in all of them the wetness of the goodbye. What could I say to them?

A kiss for each one, a kiss close to the face. And there they stayed, united by a chain of years and years of prison.

"Remember us!" came out of those sobs.

That is why I am writing this book . . .

When I walked into Mrs. X's house and sat down at a table with a white tablecloth, I felt inhibited. And my reencounter with a mirror. Yes, that was me. Was that me? As before? In those four years I had looked at myself in little fragments of a pocket mirror. I was in front of myself, my whole body, all of me, and I didn't recognize myself. There was, yes, a woman with a tremendous expression of anguish and a wrinkle, like a scar, between the eyebrows. That woman must have been me.[76]

Malonda wrote a letter to her former companions in prison that gives other insights into the mixed blessings of freedom.

My dear companions:

Would you like to know my impressions after leaving you? I don't know if I will be able to explain myself, because they are very complex. I will try to do so for your sake.

They are very diverse: immense pleasure and immense pain. Physically, I have recovered the joy of life. You know that, luckily for me, I landed in one of the most beautiful corners of the world—the Balearic islands!

After profusely praising the natural beauty of the islands, she continues: "What else can I say of so much natural beauty? I don't know. My pen is inhibited by so much grandeur; I do nothing but enjoy, admire, and be silent. . . . Be silent and remember you all incessantly. You are for me, the memory of you, like a thorn nailed into my heart. That is why I said to you that in the midst of my happiness, I felt immense pain." After describing the anguish of remembering her dead husband, she goes on:

My enemies, ours, must have never known real love, since they don't have a heart for it. They would gloat if that knew that, now when we should be happy to have finally released ourselves from their claws, the moral torture begins to poison us, impeding any complete joy. It would be for those creatures a refinement of their well-tested cruelty.

I come up with the conclusion that we who have suffered the unnamable have so many sad episodes to remember that we will never be happy. With your absence and, in the majority of cases, with the disappearance of loved ones, our homes have been broken and our lives truncated. And our own personal suffering is not the only thing that crosses our imagination; one remembers also the suffering of so many who had the same sad luck. Nevertheless, we feel obliged to make unheard-of efforts to recapture the desire to live and continue, continue forward. "Don't look back," he [her husband] used to say to me. This advice, in theory, is fine, but in reality it is quite impossible to avoid the memories and eliminate from my heart those smoldering embers that burn inside me.[77]

O'Neill and Malonda did not suffer the same economic constraints that the vast majority—like Real, Doña, and Cuevas—suffered; both nevertheless express the intense sense of loss, loneliness, and guilt of being free while their companions remained in prison. They did not have to struggle materially and were not accosted by the police for sexual reasons, but they were still called into the offices of the regime's police; they were always on their toes for fear of another prison experience. In the final analysis, they too are examples of the "urgent solitary voice of collective testimony."

The regime was for these women, as well as for the men, a neo–Spanish Inquisition. Even after the regime ended, many were afraid to discuss their activism and prison sentences. In Cuevas' books of testimonies, a number of women would not give their names. Their reasons always were fear of reprisal for themselves, their husbands, or other family members—even when Franco was gone and the democratic government in Spain was flourishing.

Forty years was not enough for them to forget the repression they had suffered. Hiding and silence were a way of life. So many had been imprisoned for no real reason, or for one that they could not imagine entailed any guilt or caused any human suffering. They had spent from several months to twenty years in prison, trying to survive and trying to maintain their dignity and good faith. But they never felt at ease in the outside world, which had fanatically pursued them.

One of the most interesting insights into the inquisitorial perception of life held by the prisoners is expressed by María del Carmen Cuesta, one of the many teenagers who began her activism at age fifteen during the Revolution of Asturias.

Some six or seven years ago they showed a movie on television . . . entitled "Fahrenheit 451." It had a tremendous impact on me because, if you remember the theme, you know that the plot is about a repressive country where there is a terrible dictatorship against the culture with a special corps of firemen who dedicate themselves to destroying all the books they find. . . . The people flee to the forests and each one—men, women, and children—has committed to memory all they can remember about universal literature, all the works, all the genres. Each one of these people is converted into a human book with the goal and hope that some day those books can be printed again.

When I saw this film it had such an impact on me because I thought, "We were hundreds, more than hundreds, thousands of women, who like that film also stored away in our minds some profound testimonies; testimonies that we also hoped and trusted confidently could some day be revealed and could fill the pages of history, the history that was the longest, blackest, most brutal period of our country: the history of Fascism."

I am telling you this because exactly four weeks ago they showed that movie again on Spanish television and I thought, "When I saw this the first time, we had a tremendous muzzle on us that prevented those testimonies from coming to light." But now when I saw it, the shame, impotence, and pain were consuming me even more because now there wasn't a muzzle. It was an imposing gravestone, which seemed impossible to lift, that was weighing on us. We could call it "political strategy," or perhaps a sort of collective shame that may have arisen from so many years of historical deformation, that now was pressing us to not talk too much about the civil war and the subsequent repression. In order to mitigate historical bitterness and try to calm those dark powers, alleging that the Left forgets, it will be difficult for the new generations to know about the Franco repression in all its intensity.[78]

Cuesta's expressive analogy rings true when one looks at the attitude in Spain today. In her assessment of the history of women in the last two decades, Nash describes this phenomenon of erasing history as a "collective historical amnesia," which was prescribed by the Franco movement for obvious reasons.[79]

The Spanish climate of the 1970s and 1980s, the desire to "forgive and forget," which functioned well for the comfortable, victorious class was a source of silent suffering for the vanquished.

Precisely when female activists—the few who are still alive—finally have their opportunity to tell their stories, they have once again been shamed and silenced by taboos that tell us to forget the ugly past. Yet the small group of women who have joined to create this "urgent voice of collective testimony" and challenge the system have given us their memories of resistance. They have conjured up the past of women who can never forget a period that changed their lives forever. The lost women of Spain's civil war have been found.

Part Four *Exile as Memory*

Ventas Prison in Madrid, the Feast of the Virgin of Mercy. Prison guards, authorities, and members of the Sección Femenina; note the portrait of Franco in the background. *A.G.A. M.C.S.E. Fondo Fotográfico*

Soledad Real. Women sewing at the Segovia Prison, 1955. (Real has placed a circle around her face.) *Personal collection of Soledad Real*

Juana Doña (*front, right*). Prison of Alcalá de Henares, July 1961. Photographs were taken on days that children were visiting or on religious holidays. Prisoners were obliged to "dress up" and were told that if they wanted their pictures taken, they had to appear content. *Personal collection of Juana Doña*

Dolores Medio in 1953. *A.G.A. M.C.S.E. Fondo Fotográfico Dolores Medio*

Dolores Ibárruri and Soledad Real, Yugoslavia, 1975. Photograph taken during a trip for "Ex-Prisoners and Victims of Political Reprisal" sponsored by the Communist Party. *Personal collection of Soledad Real*

Chapter 9   The Exodus

*In moments of collective catastrophe like those we were living, my pain was fused
with the immense common pain. Federica Montseny,* El éxodo, p. 30

Spain is a country that has experienced vast migrations over the centuries,
always for religious or political reasons. None competes with the expulsions of
1492. Between 300,000 and 900,000 arabs were expelled from Spain, and some
185,000 Jews also fled.[1] In 1939 Spain experienced its second largest human
bloodletting, when some 500,000 fled the war-torn country. Spain shares the
Iberian Peninsula with Portugal, but because the Salazar dictatorship was in
full force in 1939, Spain's only link to "mainland" Europe at that time was
France. For decades Spaniards had been traveling through the Pyrenees, over
the Atlantic, and through the Mediterranean to France in search of work or
pleasure. In 1939 that country became the only possibility for survival of the
Spanish resistance; France was for Leftists and Republicans the only hope of
escaping death or incarceration, poverty, and hunger.

The refugees entered southern France primarily on foot. Most who passed
through the ports of entry were from the north of Spain. It was much more
difficult to flee quickly from the central and southern regions, since the exiles
had to leave either by boat or by plane. Some 20,000 escaped by boat from
the southern port city of Alicante in March of 1939. By the end of that month,
though, the insurgents had heard rumors of the evacuation and apprehended
many who were waiting for ships to arrive.[2]

The Spanish exodus into France[3] at the end of the war has been documented by journalists, historians, filmmakers, and photographers. Yet that "ant-
hill of human beings," as Louis Stein described the diaspora, has been evoked
best by those who actually experienced the flight. The fact that France provided
the only access to the free world was to become one of history's great ironies,
for France entered the war in September and Hitler's police had already begun
to infiltrate the country in 1939.

Thousands of Spanish women and children, the aged and the maimed, the injured soldiers, were almost invariably directed into camps, mostly on the Côte Vermeille beaches on the southwestern coast—Saint Cyprien, Argelès-sur-mer, and Le Barcarès.[4] Conditions were lamentable in the barbed-wire camps; gross overcrowding, nonexistent sanitation, food shortages, rampant communicable diseases, and generally inhumane treatment prevailed. Those who complained were sent to punishment camps. Alberto Fernández describes the conditions in the camps that had been set up on the beaches: "The prisoners, nude inside the barbed-wire fences, surrounded by Algerian soldiers . . . spent days and days there, eating half-rations when the full rations were insufficient to sustain them, putting up with verbal abuse."[5]

France has been severely criticized for its treatment of Spaniards, yet it should be emphasized that the financial burden was overwhelming and help from other countries or private organizations was minimal.[6] Neil MacMaster, who has provided us with an excellent oral history of one couple in exile, describes the hostile atmosphere in France in 1939.

> The French authorities were hopelessly ill-prepared to cope with the huge numbers involved and lacked the accommodation, food, clothing, medical aid and technical staff necessary for an emergency relief operation on the scale that was required. This explains in part the appalling conditions under which the Republican exiles were forced to live, but far more crucial was the political climate of hostility and xenophobia which prevailed at the time. The considerable influx of foreign labour during the inter-war period, combined with the unemployment of the world depression, had resulted in widespread racism. The right-wing and gutter press deliberately whipped up the already widespread anti-foreigner sentiment by portraying the Republicans as dangerous "Red" terrorists who would swarm in armed bands through southern France, spreading lawlessness and disease.[7]

The fate of these Spaniards varied. Many would return voluntarily or were sent back to Spain by force.[8] Some of the men enlisted in World War II and died in battle. Others were captured by the Germans and were forced to wear a blue triangle with an "S" on it, not unlike their less fortunate comrades in tragedy, the Jews.[9] The liberation of Paris in 1944 was a high point for the Spaniards in France. Some of them participated, driving into the city in tanks with Spanish names written on them.

One of the great horrors for Spaniards in the period of Nazi occupation was the Mauthausen camp in Germany. Some 10,000 Spaniards were sent there; by the end of the war, only 2,000 were still alive.[10] The Spaniards had been required to complete construction of the prison, build the road into the camp, and work in the quarry. Antonio Vilanova claims the Spaniards suffered more than any other nationals in Mauthausen. Exhausted and sick, they were often beaten to death or died in the constant accidents.[11]

Like the French, who had begun to form resistance groups in 1940, the Spaniards began to organize in France, especially to help their compatriots who had fled. Because the Gestapo was forcibly enlisting men from the occupied zones to work in Germany, many Frenchmen escaped to the mountains and forests. At first, these so-called Maquis did no more than hide, but soon it was obvious that they could not survive without food and clothing, which originally had been provided for them. As their numbers grew, they began to join the French resistance. The Spaniards joined the French guerrilla groups and in 1943 formed the first Spanish Maquis. They sabotaged trains, bridges, electrical plants, arms factories; they attacked the Nazi troops and took prisoners. When the war ended, many of the Spanish Maquis returned to Spain to try their luck fighting the Franco regime. Slowly they were liquidated, and by the late 1940s they had disappeared from Spain's mountains. There were some women among the Maquis, but documentation is scarce. It is an amazing story of bravery: Spaniards who had fought their own war, then France's war, returned to fight in Spain once again.

Only those who succeeded in moving from France to another, safer country had a future ahead of them. The Service of Immigration of the Spanish Republicans (SERE) was founded in 1937 to help Spaniards fleeing the war. In 1939, with the blessing of France and Mexico, its activities were taken over by Juan Negrín, prime minister of Spain in 1937. Expeditions were organized to send the refugees to America; the first to go were the political exiles who had been part of the Republican government. The earliest ships went to Mexico; the Chilean Nobel-Prize-winning poet Pablo Neruda, who had been a great friend to the Republic, sent others to Chile on the *Winnipeg*. Chile's other Nobel poet, Gabriela Mistral, organized homes for Spanish children weary of war. One ship landed in the Dominican Republic; the rest of the SERE ships generally went to Venezuela and Mexico. Another group, established in 1939, was the Aid to Spanish Refugees (JARE); founded by Indalecio Prieto, Negrín's former minister of war, it took over much of the refugee rescue work formerly done by SERE.[12]

Mexico was the country that most generously welcomed the thousands of Spaniards who arrived there.[13] The Mexican president in 1938, Lázaro Cárdenas, had founded the Casa de España in Mexico City, which in 1940 became the Colegio de Mexico.[14] Its first mission was to provide a locus for Spanish thinkers who could no longer work in Spain, given that intellectual life there had come to a virtual standstill. These academicians were invited to lecture in Mexico and later found positions in Mexican universities. After the war, though, many intellectuals arrived even without an invitation from the Colegio.[15] Mexico City became one of the most important seats of Spanish intellectual life in America and still boasts prestigious publishing houses that were established at that time. Many of the cultural organizations established in Spain before the war, such as the Ateneo of Madrid, and several new ones were actively functioning in Mexico City. Under Indalecio Prieto, Mexico also became the seat of the Spanish government in exile between 1939 and 1950.[16] It was to be a safe haven where Spaniards did not have the language difficulties of exiles who had settled in France, England, and the United States.

In addition to the many cafes and clubs where the Spaniards gathered and which served as support groups, many felt at home in Mexico. Isabel de Palencia tells us:

> As I lay in my bed and heard the street vendors call out their wares under my window, I could sometimes almost delude myself into thinking that I was back in Spain. . . . Not the Spain we had now left behind. But the Spain I had known as a little girl in Malaga, with its flat-roofed houses and its beautiful gardens, its parks full of palms and pomegranate and pepper trees and huge hibiscus bushes, and roses and carnations and sweet-smelling lilies and tuberoses. Even the way the Mexicans talked reminded me of home, for they do not use the pure but the harsher Castilian pronunciation. They lisp their words softly like Andalusians.[17]

The treatment of those fortunate Spaniards—often the relatively privileged—who arrived in Mexico cannot be compared to the hostility and tragedy that awaited those in France. The world became a prison for Spaniards who stayed in Spain and for those who went to France. Ironically, it also became a prison for the French, who had unwittingly made the decision to imprison the Spanish behind barbed wire while they themselves were slowly being encircled by the Nazis.

Chapter 10 Memory Texts of Exiled Women

There are many memory texts about exile, most written by men. Nevertheless, a number of women's texts are of great interest for this study. All of the women's autobiographies discussed here reflect the period of most extensive emigration, from February to September 1939.[1] Some deal with the war, then with exile as an epilogue to the war years: Palencia's *I Must Have Liberty* (and, more thoroughly, her *Smouldering Freedom*), de la Mora's *In Place of Splendor,* Castro's *Una vida para un ideal,* and Concha Méndez' *Memorias habladas, memorias armadas.* Several books are almost entirely dedicated to exile: those of the writers María Teresa León and Silvia Mistral, and those of the political figures, Victoria Kent and Federica Montseny.[2] Some creative literature describes exile and the camps. Worthy of mention are Teresa Gracia's play and poetry on this theme,[3] and María Aurelia Capmany's novel.[4]

Exile usually provides a new land and a new life, a possible rebirth. Yet forced exile also raises a constant sad and nostalgic evocation of the past. It is a dialectical process: though it may represent a new life, exile also embodies the death of the former life.[5] María Teresa León sums up exile with her customary poetic melancholy:

> I am tired of not knowing where to die. That is the greatest sadness for the immigrant. What do we have to do with the cemeteries of the countries we live in? One would have to make so many introductions to the other dead people that one would never finish. I am tired of spinning toward death. Nevertheless, do we have the right to conclude the history we began? How many times have we repeated the same words, accepting hope, calling to it, begging it not to abandon us?[6]

In her pensive book, written in the sixties and therefore the product of many years of reflection, León calls her world a lost paradise. "For thirty years we have yearned for our lost paradise, a paradise of our own, unique, special.

A paradise of broken houses and fallen roofs. A paradise of streets in shambles, of the unburied dead. A paradise of demolished walls, of fallen towers and devastated fields."[7]

Silvia Mistral reflects on this birth-death phenomenon at the end of her diary. She has arrived in Mexico, her final destination, in the forties.

> We land on Mexican soil. We arrive with the illusion of beginning a life
> destroyed by the horrors of war. We are all poor. We bring with us only
> the memory of things we were trying to save and that were lost in the
> war or in the exodus. We are left with our souls, elevated and purified by
> the anguish of exile, the desire to recover what was lost to us and to
> those who moan beneath the fatal blanket of tragedy.
>
> As I start my journey, under the sky of the port of Verucruz, in my
> heart is an intense emotion and the memory of those who await, in the
> inhospitable camps of France, the horizon of a free nation.[8]

The strongest emotion is guilt, which Mistral expresses when she speaks of those who await freedom. Unlike the imprisoned or the "prisoners of the street" who remained in Spain or the thousands encircled by French barbed wire, those who actually escaped Spain and then France achieved the best of all possible worlds.

Isabel de Palencia reflects the same sense of guilt, as she describes a group of Spaniards waiting for a boat (which never arrived) to take them into exile.

> Of course I knew that by then the fate of those unfortunates was a thing
> of the past. There was absolutely nothing one could do, and yet I too felt
> bowed down with remorse. Remorse for what I could neither avoid nor
> have prevented? No, not for that. What motivates the remorse so many
> of us still feel rests on the fact that we possess what others have lost. In
> the case of the Spaniards waiting on the pier, their very lives or, in the
> best of cases, their priceless freedom. We and all who got away alive and
> free have had to pay a heavy price. For years our eyes have not been
> allowed to dwell on the land of our birth. Some will never go back to it
> again. But the heaviest price of all is the feeling, latent or active in many
> hearts, that we abandoned Spain.[9]

After the Spanish civil war, though, many viewed their exile as temporary. Some even kept suitcases and trunks packed, as did the family of the Asturian Socialist leader Belarmino Tomás, who was exiled in Mexico.[10] Concha Méndez[11] tells us in her memoirs that when she settled in Mexico, she was prone to buy suitcases rather than household goods.[12] The exiles were in a suspended state of inconclusive banishment, as can be perceived in so many of the comments by memorialists of those days; for instance, the final rhetorical statement of Constancia de la Mora's *In Place of Splendor:* "The fascists cannot make Spain fascist. We are a democratic people. We shall always be a democratic people. I know that Spain will soon again be free. Nothing can prevent it—for the the united people of Spain will make a democracy with their blood and their courage. Viva la República!"[13]

The memory texts to be discussed here—those of Mistral, Kent, Montseny, and León—were written in exile with narrative styles and formats that varied based on the experiences of the authors. Kent fled to Paris, taking refuge in the Mexican embassy, while she was tenaciously pursued by both Franco's police and the Gestapo; later she moved to a flat under the alias Madame Duval. Her philosophical autobiography describes her years of hiding and gives her observations about exiled Spaniards, the Nazi occupation of France, and especially the Jewish extermination camps. Kent was not a writer by trade, as we have seen; her style is analytical, as befits a political figure.

Maria Teresa León had a similar Parisian experience, though she lived more openly than Kent. Her lyrical *Memoria de la melancolía* describes her and Alberti's activism during the war and the odyssey of their exile in France, Argentina, and Italy. Her book is a potpourri of impressionistic fragments of her life.

Federica Montseny, who wrote with obstinate pragmatism in her more traditional autobiographical works, describes her dramatic flight from Spain with her two small children, a dying mother, a debilitated father, a stepsister with a month-old baby, and her mother-in-law. She describes both her individual plight and that of her countrymen.

Silvia Mistral wrote of her final days in Spain, the difficulty of being an exiled woman in France, and her embarkation to America. Unlike the others, she used a diary format,[14] which spans the period January to July of 1939.

Despite vast differences in style, format, and viewpoint in these works, there is a common bond: the women protest, not only the Spanish civil war, the early years of Franco's repression, and the tragic plight of Spaniards in exile, but also the inevitability of World War II and the Nazi horrors. There is vehemence, anger, and desolation in their denunciation of those nightmarish years—which began in 1936, but which in many cases did not end with the civil war, but rather in 1944 when the Allies landed in Normandy.[15] Once again, their common writing bond was "the urgent solitary voice of collective testimony."

We must keep in mind that all of these women, except for Mistral, were very well known, were from the middle class, and were mature women; none of them spent long periods in the camps and eventually all except Montseny were able to relocate in America. By contrast, the vast majority of Spanish women in France suffered long periods of camp life. Nieves Castro, for example, describes how when she refused to return to Spain after the war, she was sent with her baby to Argelès-sur-mer, where she slept in the sand and kept her infant in a vegetable bin.[16] Many were forced to return to Spain.

Few managed to escape to Latin America as quickly as did Mistral, Palencia, de la Mora, and later León. Méndez had been a war correspondent briefly during the war; her husband had been a well-known activist who was briefly interned in a French concentration camp. Concha's first days of exile were spent in Paris with Altolaguirre, in the home of the French writer Paul Eluard. Picasso collected money for them to take one of the boats that sailed with so many Spaniards to Mexico.[17] Others such as Montseny and Kent hid in France during the occupation, disguised and with assumed names. The unfortunate unknowns languished for years in prison in Spain or in camps in France.

As Paloma Ulacia Altolaguirre emphasizes in the introduction to her grandmother's memoirs: "One of the characteristics of the exiles is, without doubt, the sensation that their identity has been lost—which is the reason why their memories become doubly important. Since they have lost the context in which they had evolved, the need to remember surpasses the limits of simple nostalgia, converting itself into the spinal cord of their identity."[18]

Méndez' book was written in collaboration with her granddaughter, not long before she died. Therefore, Ulacia's memories of her grandmother's memories intervene in the text and play a considerable role in the shaping of format and content. Not an autobiography—in spite of the fact that is is recounted in the first person and that, unlike some of the other works, it does concentrate on the author's personal life—or a transcribed interview, the Ulacia-Méndez book is yet another species of "outlaw" literature.

In the prologue Ulacia says that her grandmother, whom she interviewed at age eighty-three, had begun to lose her memory. She also explains that she edited the text, selecting what she considered to be the most important material. Ulacia tells us that she had an agenda: her grandmother had been forgotten as a poet, had been ignored as a member of the Generation of 1927. Ulacia needed to vindicate her. Therefore, this interweaving of the memory of a devoted grandchild into the memory of a feeble grandmother presents us with a double-layered text; the "I" is Concha Méndez, but another subject is implicit in her text. Unlike transcribed testimonies in which the transcriber is unfamiliar with the subject, Ulacia tells the story of Méndez telling Ulacia the story of Mendez' life.

Ulacia, describing this process in the prologue, writes a piece of her own autobiography into the text.[19] Vastly different from some of the other exiled memoirs, this is not an "urgent" text on the part of Méndez. It is, rather, urgent for Ulacia. She tells us that she "felt pain" over the years when writers and journalists would visit Concha, only to ask about her contemporaries such as the poet Luis Cernuda (who lived in her house), Federico García Lorca, and others. The fact that they did not ask Concha Méndez to talk about herself produced "that pain of mine" in Ulacia and promoted her to tape her grandmother's memory text.

In most cases, though, it was from both personal and moral necessity that these voices emerged. Kent explains her intent in writing *Cuatro años en Paris,* as she describes the Jewish extermination camp at Drancy: "Let others write history and tell whatever they like; what I want is not to forget, and since our capacity to forget digests and grinds everything up, what I know today I want to put on paper."[20] Kent's work resembles a philosophical essay, although there is a main character and an ephemeral plot. The chapters are divided by years;[21] toward the end of World War II there are a few dated entries, perhaps to show the tension of the final days. There is practically no action in *Cuatro años;* it is instead the process of a mind ruminating on war and destruction, on the loss of identity, and on fear and loneliness. Kent particularly wants to describe the obliviousness of the French to the tragedy of Spain and its link to World War II, and also to the nightmare that Hitler was creating in France. She philosophizes on the insistent theme of the world as a prison, directing her comments to the French.

> The meaning of our strife will start to be understood when the war—in that cruel phase that civil war usually present—begins to bloody French soil; when the crude reality comes to tell us that the enemies of justice and independence are not only in the other trenches, but rather that you have them here in your very own country, though they are wearing a foreign uniform. Only then will you understand the significance of our war, only then will we attain justice, when it is recognized that the war against oppression and tyranny began in Spain, with an investment of two million men.[22]

Curiously enough, Kent hides behind the mask of a male protagonist, just as she hides in real life behind false identity. Denunciation of war and the tragedy of exile is not her only goal. By using this novelistic format and a male protagonist named Plácido, she succeeds in providing a coldly intellectual analysis of the disasters of war. She also achieves what could be referred to as a psycholiterary goal: psychological survival attained through writing. When Paris is liberated, Kent switches from the third to the first person and now appears as the book's protagonist. She communicates to her fictive character, Plácido, that he has been her only link to reason: "Your sanity has been very useful to me, but I no longer need it."[23] When Paris is liberated, Kent's tone becomes jubilant, as she describes how she goes out on a bicycle to observe the city. She repeats the word "freedom" over and over again. Suddenly the first-person voice takes over. It is now Kent herself who addresses her fictional creation: "Who is calling me by my name, my real name? Oh, Plácido. It couldn't be anyone else. Do I want to go for a stroll with you? Yes, that's fine, don't be afraid. Now I am the one who says, 'Don't be afraid of anything.' Get on, get on the bicycle with me, let's go on this freedom ride."[24] Kent has removed her mask.

Cuatro años en París is a curious testimony of survival through the creation of a fictive character who is nevertheless Kent's rational other.[25] Kent is no longer either Madame Duval or Plácido. The book is a curious testimony of psychological survival through literary creation. Kent was writing her autobiographical novel-essay as she coped with the nightmare of persecution. Yet the novel has very few "literary" elements. The plot is not fictional; it is that of a person who fears capture and death, who lives in extreme isolation and solitude, who observes and recounts the extermination of the Jews and the Nazi occupation.

Kent constantly laments the plight of the Jews, stressing her horror at the obliviousness of the French. In a passage from the 1941–1942 period, she describes how 10,000 Jews are packed into the winter sports arena in Paris for three days, frantic and confused about their destinies. Then they are finally led like cattle into the death camp trains.

> The doors close. The cars are sealed. The locomotive, dragging the sealed cars, takes off for its unknown destiny.
>
> The racetrack act has ended.
>
> I begin my return trip. During the entire trip, which I make on foot, I hear the voice of a German who says gravely, over and over:
> "Some centuries will pass before civilization will penetrate our camps and it can be said, 'A long time ago they stopped being barbarians.' " That German was Goethe. His voice, which I still hear, comes to me confused with the noise of the engine that is dragging the sealed cars.[26]

Kent's book is the account of someone who is coping with the material problems of survival—the shortages of food, gas, and electricity—and who, in soliloquy, debates the moral problems of death and destruction and the concept of freedom. It is a series of essays on existential questions. *Cuatro años* is not a memoir of action, but a static account of a mind contemplating war. Static, that is, until the moment of liberation, when the tone of the book becomes charged with joy and excitement, ending with a cry of hope for Spain's freedom.[27]

León had a similar Parisian experience, though she lived more openly than Kent and left France in 1940. She was a literary figure of some importance, despite her distinctly secondary role to her poet husband Rafael Alberti, one of the notable Generation of 27 writers.[28] León was a Communist activist and a member of the Antifascist Intellectuals' Alliance, which was created during the war for both Spanish and foreign intellectuals sympathetic to the Republican cause. Two congresses of this group, held in Valencia, attracted major intellectuals from throughout the Western world.[29] During the war León had organized the Guerrilla Theater, which traveled to Spanish fronts to entertain soldiers. She was also responsible for saving many of the art works of the Prado Museum. With Alberti, she lived in the Pablo Neruda's home in Paris and worked for Radio France until 1940, when Hitler invaded France and Franco asked the Vichy government for their extradition. León and Alberti fled to Argentina, and Neruda returned to Chile.

Memoria de la melancolía is, on a personal level, the story of León's life—sketches from her childhood, the couple's activism during the war, and their exile in France, Argentina, and Italy. Yet there is another level in this book also, which decries the treatment of Spanish exiles in France. León constantly laments the fact that Spanish exiles were ignored; we find her sorrow in statements such as, "Why haven't more books been written about the men and women who were dying in desolation on the sand?"[30] She elaborates on the fact that Hitler was taking over free Europe and that the French seemed oblivious. "If they had only known that we were from that flea-bitten gang of Spaniards, antifascists who had stood up against Hitler, that owner of central Europe who had all laid out his staff's plans for the invasion of Czechoslovakia, Hungary, Poland, and France . . . ! But no one sees the problems of others, and France had not taken any risks to do anything in the face of our destinies."[31]

In another passage, León decries the fate of her countrymen and women.

A horde of nomads seeking survival was about to extend itself over the land. Hundreds of us, thousands, neither alive nor dead, were going around in a state of uncertainty, as though our feet were numb. We knew we had been expelled from something more than just Spain. The French observed the intruders; some were compassionate and others were angry. These two attitudes crushed our sense of decency as combatants for world freedom. That's how we had gone through the streets of France, dragged by our sorrow, without knowing how to manage, indecisive, though sometimes someone would stop and embrace us and say "Comrades!" and we thus advanced a little farther, getting used to being the banished ones.[32]

Because of her literary background, León describes her war activities and exile experiences from the standpoint of the intellectual in exile and with the literary style of the poetic fiction writer, touching on one episode after another without regard for chronology. León passes with ease from the first person to the second to the third. She insists on her high standing in society, her status as an intellectual and that of her writer friends in exile, while still emphasizing her Communist beliefs. She does not attempt to chronicle her exile with dates and historical facts. "The truth is that nothing I am writing pretends to be perfect or truthful. What I say represents the closed garden of what I feel. At times I am ashamed that I don't say anything better or say more, or scream with anger because the fury subsides like rain washing away the memories or as if someone said to me, 'Why vengeance?' "[33] Since León wrote her book many years after the war, perhaps the emotional scars were no longer so acute.

León is clearly the most poetic memory text writer because of the design of her work; also, of all the exile writers she is the most aware that mnemonic material does not necessarily constitute historical fact. She certainly practices what Susanna Egan has labeled "conscious artistry."[34] Like Kent, León is impressionistic in her selections, yet even more arbitrary. Her accounts of war and exile are similiar to literary postcards. She theorizes about the concept of memory with a characteristic staccato rhythm. Her use of the first person plural implies that she regarded herself as part of the masses that escaped Spain at the end of the war. León's is also a voice of collective testimony, though not as consistently as that of the imprisoned memorialists. No one else conceives of her writing in the purely ontological fashion that León does. She writes with raw emotion, forgoing the analytical observation found in Kent's work.[35]

Montseny, in the prologue to *El éxodo,* explains that she wrote the book to remember, "before the most total oblivion blankets the memory of the drama of the political Spanish emigration and the epic of those who, having forgotten the suffering and aggression, contributed to the liberation of the world against

Nazi oppression."[36] At the beginning of *Cien días en la vida de una mujer*, she tells us, "Simply and humbly, with a constant preoccupation with simplicity and strict truth, I have described this episode of my life, an episode that simultaneously has been the endless tragedy of a people in exodus and of a humanity devastated by the most horrible punishment: war and Fascism."[37]

Montseny, like the others, denounces that double apocalypse—"the endless tragedy"—experienced by the Spaniards in exile. Yet there are essential differences in her works based on her vastly different experience in the flight from Spain. First of all, Montseny was traveling with members of her family, most of whom were incapable of caring for themselves. This caused her to emphasize the hardships she endured as mother, daughter, and sister. Perhaps because of her desire to highlight the dramatic situation that she—and thousands of others—were experiencing, Montseny is the most dogmatic about her story being *absolutely* true.

She writes in a realistic style, though there are poetic moments in her work. As we have observed, her descriptions of the exodus, especially of the helpless wounded men and women with small children, are the most frequent and the most poignant. In one passage Montseny says: "Meanwhile my mother was dying. Meanwhile, thousands of exiles were dying. Meanwhile, I didn't have a father, a husband, a home, or a tomorrow. And with me, thousands of women and children, thousands of men, thousands of families." Elsewhere she tells us that "there were large groups of wounded people, their arms in slings, their legs stretched, lying on the ground, soaked. There were colonies of children, unloaded from trucks, fearful and wet, grabbing each other's hands. There were women who were transporting baskets full of wet clothing on their heads, with four or five crying babies grabbing at their skirts. There was all the misery and desperation imaginable, and some that couldn't be imagined."[38]

Perhaps Montseny's most impassioned description is the following passage:

Who, oh who, will ever forget that spectacle of the mountains full of people camping under the trees, trembling with cold and terror? Thousands of cars and trucks were lined up in an uninterrupted queue that went from Figueras to Cerbère to Perthus. Who, oh who, will forget those hours, the crying of the little ones in the rain, the screams of the women, the curses of the men, the sinister sound of the planes flying above our heads?[39]

Montseny is most vehement and moralistic in her description of the French, exhorting vengeance for their inhumanity. She denounces the employment of

Senegalese mercenaries, who were the jailers of the exiled Spaniards. "I again swore and begged heaven and hell that our pain would be theirs one day. That the chalice of bitterness that we were forced to drink to the dregs one day would burn their lips and their entrails."[40]

Montseny's oft-repeated tone of impassioned vengeance is a far cry from Kent's more remote theoretical analyses or León's Proustian poetic reminscences and lamentations. Montseny is neither particularly literary nor particularly philosophical. Her sole purpose is to relate her story, to provide us with a piece of history, as she tells us in the conclusion to *Seis años de mi vida*. "If all of us who have seen ourselves engulfed in that catastrophe narrated our lives—the pathetic and extraordinary adventure of our existence—a historical document of incalculable value would be put together, one that would surpass whatever the most powerful imagination could have constructed in hours of exaltation or insomnia."[41]

Yet Montseny is not unaware of the literary qualities of her story. She explicitly states that her inventiveness as a novelist aided her in her many real-life metamorphoses when she was pursued by the Gestapo. She explains in rather jocular fashion, for example, that when she felt that her alias during World War II—Fanny Germain—would arouse suspicion, she transformed herself into another character, spontaneously inventing stories about her past. She describes her protean life:

> I lied with complete self-assurance, with the greatest cheekiness, utilizing my novelistic practices. I had to keep playing various roles at the same time. Here I was the wife of a Jew; there I was the possible widow of a hero, killed in the line of duty; for others . . . I was a featherbrained woman who dyed her hair in the absence of her husband to look younger and satisfy some "heretic." What did I care! What I wanted to do was confuse people and bring home something for my children to eat.[42]

In spite of Montseny's ever-present goal of providing historical and political testimony, she is capable of irony, mirth, and even lyrical descriptions of the countryside. Contrasting the tragic diaspora of the Spaniards and the beauty of the view, she says:

> The Loire River descended sweetly among spots of marvelous beauty. On one side, the highway; on the other, the train track. And a bower of greenery, of bushy trees, covered with ivy and honeysuckle.
>
> That memorable second of June was a splendid day, one of those spring days in central France when the air is so sweet, the sky so clear,

the sun so lovely; when your lungs swell and your whole body gives in to the joy of life.

But we could not appreciate the beauty of the view and the day. The anguish that dominated us was too great, and the spectacle before our eyes from the cliff reminded us excessively of the terrible moment in which we were living. The highway that ran parallel to the channel displayed a continuous and incessant parade of civil and military fugitives all mixed together.[43]

Silvia Mistral, about whom we have no biographical information (aside from the fact that she wrote a book of short stories[44] and a diary), was apparently employed in the service of the Republic during the war, according to her account of the final days of Barcelona and the tragic last days of her life in Spain. Mistral went to Cuba in 1940 and several years later settled permanently in Mexico. Perhaps the most poignant and desolate existential statement of her plight while in exile is posed by Mistral as she describes the fall of Barcelona, the last bastion of Republican resistance:

The truth is this: Barcelona falls silently. The matron, milked dry, collapses exhausted, to await the enemies of her freedom, of her language, of her flag. The tie is broken. Some journalists still launch a few mottoes of resistance, when everyone already is obsessed with the border, an obsession that they exhibit without any consideration; and as if they were insane, they argue over a place in the trucks that are going to Gerona and Figueras. The nervous tension elicits paltry actions. Those who have fought in the trenches during the entire campaign come down from the mountains and go their way on foot. The eternal agitators of the rear guard feel a special pleasure in attacking, and their fearful and mean spirit is manifest in the ugliest expression: insolidarity.

I have spent four hours tearing up files and correspondence. A German journalist told me those personal autos-da-fé remind him of the days that followed Hitler's pronouncement after the fire at Reichstag.

At 8:00 p.m. I found myself without means of transportation to get home. There was no worker's train, normal at this hour, from the north station. There were no more buses. The trolleys, abandoned on the tracks, looked like black phantoms. I have gone along the solitary and dark highway on foot, thinking about him at that front that changes each morning. Since my feet hurt, I took off my shoes after three kilometers, and the rest of the way I walked digging my feet into the cold asphalt. My nails painted red stand out against the dirty gray cement. All around me is silence and abandonment. Not one policeman. The windows without light, closed like a mole's eyes. Behind them must in some cases be the silence of emptiness; in others, the tearful goodbye or the piles where books, letters, and papers that mean a lifetime for someone are thrown.

Suddenly the sirens went off and I felt the planes cross above my head. The reflectors, in the shadow, remained blind. The antiair craft cannons, deaf. Some people ran to hide in the black mouths of the shelters. I didn't stop. I arrived home, now late. . . .

In a sort of family council, and while I ate the last of the lentils, it was decided I would leave the next day. Mother is packing my suitcases, gathering up the trifles that I like: books, fans, tapestries, paintings, and knickknacks. Father is looking for a rope to tie up a sack. Neither is crying, but their words keep getting caught in their throats.

This is my last night in my parents' home. It is 2:00 A.M. and I am still wandering about the house as if I were saying goodbye to all the things that are part of it. Me, who fought so much against the family regimen, I feel now such a terrible, profound pain.

Will I return someday?[45]

Mistral's heartrending separation from her family and everything dear to her is eloquently expressed in this unabashedly tender portrait of the excruciating pain of exile. Mistral focuses on the forced rite of passage that the war and the flight from Spain would represent in her life, as she tells us when her "trifles" disappear in her flight to France: "People are sleeping out in the open, beneath the inclement night. We five women have a little meeting. Where shall we sleep? The obsession with our suitcases doesn't permit us to rationalize well. Among the mountains of abandoned bundles, we find some of our suitcases. I can't find my books, my things, my little art objects; and that loss seems to separate my life into two periods."[46]

Mistral's style emphasizes the urgency of the moment. She speaks in the first person and does not try to camouflage her identity; she is not in Kent's or Montseny's predicament, inasmuch as they were among the most important political figures in Spain during the Republic and the war. Mistral makes frequent allusions to contemporary writers, so there is some literary pretension to her diary, but her principal purpose is to describe her plight and that of other exiled women.

Isabel de Palencia's *Smouldering Freedom* is perhaps the most objective account of the Republic, war, and exile, given the fact that she spent most of those years as Spain's envoy to the League of Nations, and later, in 1936, as the plenipotentiary minister for Republican Spain in Sweden. Palencia went into exile in 1939 in Mexico. In her book we find first a summary of the war and then a description of the exodus from Spain, though it is a secondhand account. Like *I Must Have Liberty*, this volume appears to be a book whose exclusive purpose was to inform people abroad (where she gave numerous speeches about the war and its aftermath) of the situation in Spain.

Palencia was not immune to the emotional horror of what was happening in Spain and in France. Her son and son-in-law were doctors at the front lines and were later confined in a concentration camp in France. Her estranged husband, the painter Ceferino Palencia, was able to use his connections to have them released and sent to Paris. In her distant analytical fashion—very different from Montseny's and somewhat similar to de la Mora's and Ibárruri's propaganda-laden accounts—Palencia describes the treatment of Spaniards in France.

> Everybody, of course, realizes that the sudden entrance of half a million refugees into French territory constituted a gigantic problem for the French government. It would have done so for any government—not from an economic point of view, for measures were taken to prevent the maintenance of the refugees from becoming a dead weight on France's public budget, but as a mere question of order. No one would have felt annoyed that such a great mass of people from another country was subjected to special supervision. It wasn't that—what hurt the Spanish Republicans so deeply was to be treated like criminals.
>
> Why should they have been handled roughly? Why could they not have been given a hearing? Why should they have been put under the guard of the semibarbarous Senegalese troops and not the regular French army? As has already been suggested, there was a reason. The French fifth column was on the march, preparing for the time they hoped was near when, with Hitler's help, France would be tied to the bandwagon of the Axis.
>
> There was, besides, another motive that did not concern France herself, but in which the Spanish dictator was keenly interested. If note were taken of all the Spanish refugees who had managed to escape Franco's clutches, it would be easy, when the time came, for the French government to hand over to the Spanish Fascists, upon presentation of a claim, those members of the Republican government and parties who had worked most actively against Franco and his partisans. They were right.

When the moment did come, French Fascists found it a very simple job to single out the most hated Spanish Republicans and offer them to Franco and his followers to be punished.[47]

Though Palencia does interject observations about her own circumstances of exile in Mexico, the main objective of her books on the war and exile is to provide a report of the destiny of Spaniards—she was, after all, a journalist and her style is generally that of a newspaper chronicler. She describes the plight of exiles in Mexico, the hunger of those Republicans left in Spain, the existence in Spanish prisons, and the life of the Maquis. Her impersonal reporting provides a somewhat more objective view of the status of Spain and of Spaniards within and without the country, though it lacks some of the dramatic and lyrical style of the other accounts discussed.

Palencia does provide personal information, which reveals her unflinching stoicism during trying times. It is evident when she speaks of her husband's infidelity, which she accepts with quiet resignation.[48] On a few other occasions, Palencia admits to her emotions. When she is leaving Sweden to be reunited with her family in Mexico (after rescuing her nephew from a camp in Tunis with the help of the Committee to Aid Spain), she tells us:

> I looked at Cefe and saw that he was thinking, as I was, that I must speak a few words too, that I could not go away without once more thanking them all in my own name and in the name of Spain. I knew it was going to be hard to speak just at that moment. However, I did manage to say a few words. Then I jumped up on the train steps, and as we moved out I stood at the window waving my hands, with tears—the first I had shed in public since my arrival in Stockholm—streaming down my face. There is nothing so upsetting as kindness at such times. . . . The bunch of streamers I held—the last visible ties that bound us to Europe, to Sweden, and to Spain—broke one after another in my hands. When the last of the blue and yellow paper ribbons fell into the sea, I covered my face with my hands and sobbed. . . . Only one thing was sure: that although we were all together, the ship was taking us farther from Spain, from the Spain we had loved, from our people who were now prisoners in Franco's hands or in French concentration camps.[49]

Usually the female writers in exile did not specifically focus on the problems of Spanish women. Yet the theme of women in exile has been taken up on numerous occasions by the memorialists. Victoria Kent is perhaps the most explicit in her observations:

It has been said that exile produces deeper pain in a man than in a woman, because for a woman, her country is her home and her home goes with her. It goes without saying that these and others are masculine opinions, in general, of exiled men. Today life for a woman is just as brutal as it is for a man. I would say that she is mistreated more brutally than a man, because a woman is always unarmed in the face of violence. A woman in this war has known all the humiliations and sacrifices possible; she has been spared nothing. Exiled, pursued, ill treated, imprisoned, or deported, her country appears to her as an abandoned home.[50]

Of course, this is the observation of a political career woman, who cannot make a new country out of a few pieces of furniture and a kettle on a stove. But with the brutality of a civil war and the double apocalypse of the Spanish people— in this case, of a visible Spanish woman—Kent's remarks are understandable.

Celia Llaneza, a refugee who fled Spain when her husband was killed at the Oviedo front in 1937, explains that when she crossed the border with some other young widows, they chanted a song. In translation, it sounds something like this: "Spanish women refugees / We arrived in France full of hope / Because we thought we'd find men / And all we found was a heap of straw."[51] Mistral describes the feeling of loss of the women who were separated from their men:

Poor women, abandoned along the roads of France! We would like to say many things to our loved ones who are vegetating in concentration camps. Tell them how we long for their affection, their support, their serenity. Here we seem like lost sheep. One day is just like another; each hour, like the other. If it rains we think of the camps, also if it is windy. If only there were still some hope. . . . But no, nothing, only sad news. When the refugee women return from the post office, they reflect—in their looks, their gestures, their walk—all of their tragedy.[52]

Nonetheless Mistral speaks of the bravery and fortitude of the women in the face of the loss of their families. She notes that the young women were constantly tempted by men who offered to establish them in Marseille or Paris to work as prostitutes. Like the young women who remained in Spain and who at the end of the war were left without families and had to sell themselves, or those who, when they were released from prison, were coerced by the police to engage in prostitution, these women had several choices: to continue their seemingly endless nomadism around southern France, to return to Spain, or to establish themselves in a bordello. This dilemma, we learn, incited Mistral to seek asylum in Latin America with even more energy.

Llaneza explains that the women in the camps who were politicized tried to convince their companions not return to Spain, no matter what their tribulations in France.

> At that time, for us, the political women, the biggest worry was keeping the morale of the other women high, to prevent them from returning to Spain. One day they told us they had to disinfect the camp out of fear that we had diseases. They placed us before the soldiers nude and sprayed us with a water hose. This demoralized many of the women; they wanted to leave. But then we young girls succeeded in preventing it.[53]

Montseny's odyssey through France gives a glimpse into the life of a mother who was responsible for many helpless people, yet was at the same time trying to avoid thinking about the catastrophe that had befallen her. Montseny is the "exceptional" woman who forcefully emphasizes the plight of families and the constant obsession with finding one's loved ones. When her mother dies, she is inconsolable in the midst of so much death and devastation.

> My mother's agony lasted only a few days. She was perhaps one of the first victims. Afterward, how many thousands more died! Children carried off by the cold and misery, dysentery, typhoid, diphtheria. Old people . . . felled on the sands of Argeles by hardships and the lack of medical attention. Young men, in the flower of youth, saw their limbs amputated: how many of those hundreds of wounded whom I saw pressed against the locked border gates lost their arms and legs! For many days, no one took care of their wounds; they got infected and the gangrene followed its course. When at last they were taken to the hospital, it was to save their lives at the cost of their limbs. A legion of wretched creatures, the most pathetic victims of this frightening tragedy. Because the dead people were the most fortunate. Their Calvary had ended: their great night was preferable to our dark twilight.[54]

Montseny also emphasizes a recurrent theme of the autobiographies of Spanish women in France: that many of the Spaniards identified with the Jews, who at that time were beginning their journey into the darkness of genocide. She says of her countrymen in France: "No. They are not yet conscious of what is to be our destiny. They have condemned us to becoming the collective and reincarnated image of the errant Jew. Tossed from our homes, from our country, uprooted from our land, never again will we have a hearth, a mother country, or a place to rest."[55]

Nieves Castro, who like many Spanish men was imprisoned by the Fascists in France and lived alongside the Jews and the French and German leftists, describes her experiences in detail. She became a nurse while in prison and was able to observe closely the reactions of her cellmates before the specter of death. "The worst disasters were visible for the Jews. . . . I have witnessed the death of various compatriots, but I witnessed many more Jewish deaths and I learned to recognize a different kind of agony in them."[56] Castro goes on to compare the experiences of the Jews and tries to understand the evolution of the prejudice against them, which she seems to recognize as the central motivating factor behind the Spanish Inquisition. The important fact is that she was living in the midst of the "double apocalypse" in prison. Castro's was an extreme case because, while trying to care for her cellmates, the victims of Nazism in Europe, she herself was ill and also in danger of losing her life.

Other than Castro's, we have scant documentation of "invisible" Spanish women in the resistance and in prison in France. Castro was finally sent back to Spain and spent many more years in Franco's prisons. Those who have written about their experiences were either in camps or in hiding, as we have observed.[57] MacMaster, however, chronicles the flight of Consuelo Granda, who at age fourteen became a nurse's aid at a Republican hospital in the northern region of Asturias. She had fled with her mother and sister to Barcelona when Asturias fell to the Nationalists; at the end of January 1939 they were advised to flee or be killed as the insurgent troops marched in to take Barcelona. Granda had lost her family—she never saw her younger sister again—and all of her belongings. When she finally could walk no longer because of the cold and the snow and her fatigue, she fell asleep. When she woke, she was frozen. She was dragged across the border by a refugee woman and was put to work in semislavery with a French family. The French, she says, cheated the Spaniards out of their salaries, declaring, "If she's not happy, she can go back where she came from."[58]

Granda ends up in a refugee camp in the department of the Hautes Alps. Pregnant at the time, she tells us that "all the children who were born in the camp became ill and died. They might live for three months and then they died."[59] She is advised by a visiting doctor to "eat, no matter what! Anything! Too bad if it's dirty, you've got to eat. Go where they dump the waste from the kitchen and eat anything you can find, potato peels, bits of carrot, anything."[60] Granda survived and gave birth to a healthy baby.

Her husband, David, who has lost a leg in the war, is confined in a concentration camp with other Spaniards and Jews. When they are transferred, David says: "The Jews who were with us thought they were already on their way to the extermination camps in Germany. . . . It was terrible for them."[61] One Jewish man with whom Granda had previously been interned slit his throat because he knew what awaited him. In one camp that was quickly filling up, David tells us that "all the Spaniards had to go to one side and the Jews to the other. We Spaniards then returned to the hut, while the Jews were put into a small compound inside the camp, which was very heavily guarded by special security police. Several days later you would see a train come into the camp and the Jews were put into wagons—not ordinary passenger trains, but cattle trucks."[62]

The Jewish men were convinced they would be sent to a death camp in Poland. David continues: "There were some in our hut who committed suicide at night; they cut their arteries, they stabbed themselves, it was terrible."[63] In the Spanish camps the Spanish exiles watched babies and children die. In the Nazi camps, they often watched the Jews despair and commit suicide or disappear suddenly. During the German occupation, the experiences of Spanish men and women were often extremely different because some of the camps and prisons were reserved for women, others for men.

Miraculously, the Grandas survived. Consuelo and David were finally reunited after the liberation of France. They thought of returning to Spain, but when they visited in 1954, they found the country depressing and dismal. Consuelo says:

> People were very poor, and it wasn't pretty to see. And talking to people it was as if they had been in a prison for twenty years; they didn't know anything, they were cut off from what was going on in the world. Everything that they heard on the radio or from the priests they believed.
> They would not believe anything you said. They were suspicious toward everyone, to a degree that is hard to imagine. . . . They were frightened of everything. You would ask them something, and they would look around two or three times to see if anyone was listening and they lowered their voices.[64]

The Grandas never returned to live in Spain.

Federica Montseny's description of life in France as a female Spanish exile is our most detailed account of the trials of the resistance, since she lived in the midst of it until the final days.[65] In May 1940, the eve of the German occupation, Montseny was living in Paris. She was apprehended by the police, only to find that they were seeking her advice on where to find the famous Spanish "antitank dynamiters." For by this time the French had come to recognize the diabolical nature of the Nazi takeover and had begun to organize the resistance. Montseny's habitual rancor against the French after the civil war provokes her to launch into a tirade about how they handed her countrymen over to the Nazis or simply returned them to Franco.

Montseny reveals her remarkable ability to survive underground during the Nazi occupation. She talks about other women who were part of the resistance and mentions with frankness that good-looking women fared better than those who were not so handsome. Describing the arrival of two friends in Paris, she says: "They arrived in one piece in Paris. Margot was French and in those days young and attractive, a condition she still maintains. This seems irrelevant, but it was very important in those times, when 'charm' was a weapon like any other, in order to get out of certain tight squeezes."[66]

Montseny's openness about her political prejudices carries over into frankness about sexuality, as we see in her comments above. But her document goes far beyond any other by a woman (with the possible exception of Soledad Real's) in its discussion of women's sexual and biological circumstances. She tells us:

> I got pregnant, a pregnancy I solved with an abortion without any medical assistance, even though I risked infection. But how could I call a doctor in the clandestine situation I was in? It would have been just like calling the police. We were all terrified. Fortunately, I have extraordinary physical resistance and I have been able to survive many hardships that would have ruined health, nerves, or the strongest of hearts.[67]

Montseny, treating candidly subjects that her contemporaries considered taboo, explains that precisely when she becomes pregnant a second time in France, she is hauled off to jail. Once again she explains forthrightly what she tells the police when she is apprehended:

> "You can't put me in jail. I am five months pregnant. The law protects women in my situation."
>
> I had, in fact, become pregnant again. After the anxiety we went through with the abortion . . . we preferred to preserve the life of the little being that was gestating, running all the risks of the tragic future that awaited us. My poor little daughter! We had not wanted this pregnancy.

Nevertheless, it's possible that I owe my life to her. At least we owe to her the fact that we were saved from that terrible test.[68]

Montseny's story is perhaps the most revealing of all the memory texts of exile, in light of her exposure to so many dangers in France. Nevertheless, all of the female voices of exile provide us with a unique perspective on the double apocalypse that befell the anti-Franco population at the end of the Spanish civil war. Without them we would consider only the plight of the male population. Tragic and massive though it was, that experience alone would not give us any sense of the female nomads—their resistance to deportation, to prostitution, to demoralization—and their fight against the persecution that followed them out of Spain and into France in those profoundly tragic years of overlapping wars.

Epilogue

Throughout this text I have outlined the invisibility of the female activists of the war. Simultaneously, I have pointed out that since the 1970s the shroud of silence in which those women lived is slowly being lifted. Of course, the voices and memory texts discussed here represent only a fraction of the women who suffered through the war and its aftermath. Yet those who have spoken as urgent voices of collective testimony have served their sisters well. Not only have they described the war, prison, and exile from a perspective that is unique to Spanish history, but they have also been instrumental in providing for feminist scholars of literature and history a body of work that permits us to broaden our understanding of how gender determines the role of women in times of great strife, and of how exceptional situations such as war make for exceptional insights into the lives of women and men.

It seems fitting to end this text with a tribute to those scholars—primarily from Spain, England, and the United States—who took giant steps beyond the traditional study of history and literature as the patrimony of white males (in this case, of Spanish men from the nineteenth and twentieth centuries). The groundbreaking work began in the mid-1970s with topnotch historical scholars such as Rosa María Capel Martínez, Guiliana di Febo, María Angeles Durán, Lidia Falcón, Temma Kaplan, Mary Nash, María del Carmen Nieto París, Antonina Rodrigo, Geraldine Scanlon, and Joan Connelly Ullman.

Their work continued in the 1980s and they were joined by others: bibliographer Julio Iglesias de Ussel and historians Martha Acklesberg, Concha Fagoaga, Esperanza García Méndez, Robert Kern, Mary Elizabeth Perry, and Jane Slaughter. Among others, María Angeles Durán, Pilar Folguera, María Teresa Gallego Méndez, and María del Carmen Nieto París have provided us with texts essential to the study of women, and were among those who in 1979 inaugurated the Seminar of Studies on Women at the Autonomous University of Madrid, which Durán had founded. Also in 1979, the Autonomous University of Barcelona established the Seminar for the Study of Women.

By 1981, feminist scholars from the Complutense University in Madrid were collaborating with those of Madrid's Autonomous University, which resulted in the creation of the Seminar for Interdisciplinary Research. The Center for Historical Research on Women, founded in 1982 at University of Barcelona and directed by Mary Nash, has been instrumental in retrieving from oblivion the history of Catalonian and other Spanish women; it was also the first institution to offer a master's degree in women's studies (1988).

Many other university seminars followed in the 1980s; after those in Barcelona and Madrid were established, women in Valencia, Granada, and in the Basque country followed suit. Their centers became the nucleus of conferences and publications on Spanish women in the social sciences, the humanities, psychology, medicine, and law.[1] Smaller groups were formed in other cities in Spain.

In the area of literary studies, American feminist scholars—most of whom are members of the Feministas Unidas group, an affiliate of the Modern Language Association—have been among the most active in pioneering the study of Spanish women's literature. In the 1980s and 1990s, Electa Arenal, Alda Blanco, Joan Lipman Brown, Carolyn L. Galerstein, Kathleen Glenn, Roberta Johnson, Susan Kirkpatrick, Linda Gould Levine, Carol Maier, Beth Miller, Elizabeth J. Ordoñez, Janet Pérez, Stacey Schlau, Mirella Servodidio, Sharon Keefe Ugalde, Nöel Valis, Gloria Waldman, and many others have been extremely active in rescuing female writers from obscurity. In Europe, Catherine Davies, Clara Janés, Ana Rodríguez, María del Carmen Simón Palmer, and numerous others have advanced the discussion on Spanish women writers.

Several government-funded organizations have been instrumental in the blooming of feminist studies in Spain. The Institute for Women, established in Madrid in 1983 by the Ministry of Culture and now under the direction of the Ministry of Social Welfare, has published numerous books on women since the 1980s and continues to encourage feminist scholarship throughout the country. Other loci for women's studies are the feminist press La Sal in Barcelona, and numerous bookstores throughout Spain, including the Librería de Mujeres in Madrid. The American International Institute in Madrid has also been an important center for conferences on Spanish women. Feminist journals dedicated to women have become more prevalent in Spain as the debate on feminism becomes more heated. An example is Lidia's Falcon's journal *Poder y libertad,* the publication of Spain's Feminist party.

Specific to the study of women and the civil war, the fiftieth-anniversary celebrations (1986–1989) that took place all over Spain and in other countries, including the United States, were instrumental in finally allowing the public voice of activist women to be heard. These conferences not only produced a number of key publications on women and the war (mostly published by the Ministry of Culture), but also served to vindicate the role of leftist women whose names and roles had been negatively encoded and whose lives had been erased from Spanish history.

Since 1986 university groups for the study of women have proliferated; there are some twenty to date (with forty-three universities in Spain). The number of seminars continues to grow, thanks primarily to the support of the Institute for Women, since neither the universities nor the Ministry of Education have provided funding. (The first and only group supported by the ministry, as of May 1993, is the University Institute for the Study of Women, again at the Autonomous University of Madrid.) Also problematic is the fact that the study of women has not been incorporated into the official curriculum leading to an undergraduate or graduate degree. (The exceptions are the University of Granada, which has a Ph.D. in women's studies and the University of Barcelona, which offers a doctorate in the Latin American history of women.) The process is a slow one. Authorization for a mainstream degree in women's studies must pass through the Council of Ministers; several universities are presently negotiating for such a degree.[2]

The decade of the 1990s looks promising. The study of Spanish women and issues of gender are evident in the plethora of recent titles and in the mobilization of feminist scholarship both inside and outside academe, in Spain and abroad. The public memory and the artistic efforts of Spanish women are for the first time coming to the foreground, thanks to those who have recognized the underpinnings of patriarchy and the urgent need for a reinterpretation of gender roles in both private and public life in Spain.

Notes

1. The Awakening to Rebellion

1. They were influenced by the German philosopher Karl Krause (1781–1832), via Julian Sanz del Río, a renowned professor at the University of Madrid who introduced Krause's utopian pedagogical ideas into Spain.

2. Brenan, *The Spanish Labyrinth*, 87–88.

3. Ibid., 120.

4. See Capel, *El trabajo y la educación de la mujer en España.*

5. Pardo Bazán, *La mujer española y otros artículos feministas*, 192–193. Pardo Bazán (1851–1921), who was the first Spanish feminist, created major scandals in Spain both because of her free lifestyle and her espousal of French naturalism.

6. Scanlon, *La polémica feminista*, 56.

7. Ortega y Gasset, *Ideas y creencias*, 150.

8. For information on the interaction of writers and artists at the residence, especially Buñuel, Dalí, and Lorca, see Sanchez Vidal, *Buñuel, Lorca, Dalí.* For the residence and members of the Generation of 1927, see the following autobiographical writings: José Moreno Villa, *Vida en claro: Autobiografía* (Mexico: College of Mexico, 1944); Luis Buñuel, *Mi último suspiro* (Barcelona: Plaza y Janés, 1982), and Rafael Alberti, *La arboleda perdida*, vols. 1 and 2 (Barcelona: Seix Barral, 1975).

9. The International Institute for Young Ladies in Spain was founded in 1882 in the Basque city of San Sebastián by American Protestant missionaries Alice Gordon and her husband, William Gulick, to compensate for the lack of facilities for the education of foreign and Spanish women. After the Spanish-American war, the couple took refuge in France, making contact with key figures from the ILE. In 1901, with funds from leading pedagogists from Boston, they purchased a building to house the institute in Madrid. After 1910 it became a nonsectarian academy for the education of women, growing in size and stature. It continues to be a locus for symposia on women and today houses several programs for American students abroad. For the complete history of the International Institute, see Zulueta, *Misioneras, feministas, educadoras.*

10. The real Beatriz Galindo (1475?–1534) was a humanist who taught Latin to Queen Isabella and her children and became the queen's confidante. Palencia used this name in many of her journalistic writings, but not in her books.

11. *El Sol*, 21 August 1927; quoted by Campo Alange, *La mujer en España*, 209–210.

12. My reference is, of course, to Gilbert and Gubar, *The Madwoman in the Attic.*

13. General Miguel Primo de Rivera (1870–1930) had a brilliant military career

before he established a dictatorship in Spain, which lasted from 1923 to 1930.

14. León, *Memoria de la melancolía*, 311.

15. Concha Méndez describes a less-than-restrained attitude during her youth in Madrid with her friend the surrealist painter Maruja Mallo (1909–). They would travel the streets in search of mischief, and the only places they seemed to stay out of were the taverns, where women were prohibited. Ulacia Altolaguirre and Méndez, *Memorias habladas, memorias armadas*, 51–53.

16. Janet Pérez, "Vanguardism, Modernism and the Spanish Women Writers in the Years between the Wars," *SigloXX/20th Century*, 6 (1988–89): 41.

17. Gloria Angeles Franco Rubio, "La contribución de la mujer española a la política contemporánea: De la restauración a la guerra civil (1876–1939)," in María Angeles Durán et al., *Mujer y sociedad en España, 1700–1975* (Madrid: Ministry of Culture, 1982), 247–249.

18. Maillard, *Asociación española de mujeres universitarias*, 13.

19. Cambrils, *Feminismo socialista*.

20. See Starcevic, *Carmen de Burgos*.

21. See Kirkpatrick, *Las Románticas*.

22. Created in 1934, the Sección Femenina was to become the major women's organization of the Right during the war and the Franco regime. Inspired by the neofascist ideology of the Falange party and its founder, José Antonio Primo de Rivera (son of the dictator), it would be led by the ideologue's sister, Pilar Primo de Rivera.

23. Fórmica, *Visto y vivido*, I, 12.

24. Ibid., 12–13.

25. León, *Memoria de la melancolía*, 58. León was subsequently expelled from the school. She then studied with her illustrious aunt and uncle, María Goyri (the first female Ph.D. in Spain) and Ramón Menéndez Pidal, both famous for their philological research. Their influence was definitive for León's writing career.

26. Jaraiz Franco, *Historia de una disidencia*.

27. The navy was considered the elite sector of the armed forces in Spain.

28. Jaraiz Franco, *Historia de una disidencia*, 25.

29. While attempting to defend Spain's territory in Morocco in 1921, the Spanish army panicked and more than ten thousand soldiers were killed. The massacre caused still more dissension about the colonization of Morocco. The upshot was a profound parliamentary crisis that resulted in the military takeover by Primo de Rivera.

30. Jaraiz Franco, *Historia de una disidencia*, 27–28.

31. Martínez Sierra, *Gregorio y yo*, 22.

32. De la Mora, *In Place of Splendor*, 10–11. Her story is similar to that of Pilar Jaraiz Franco in that both rebelled against their archconservative birthrights. De la Mora, however, was more outspoken and her life was more public.

33. Ibid., 15.

34. Ibid., 17. One of the earliest and most fascinating stories of the persecution of a writer involved Fernando de Rojas, a Jewish convert and author of the dramatic work *La Celestina*, 1499. See Gilman, *The Spain of Fernando de Rojas*.

35. De la Mora, *In Place of Splendor*, 19.

36. Ibid., 49.

37. Ibid., 51.

38. Ibid., 60.

39. Palencia, *I Must Have Liberty*, 31–32.

40. Gazpacho is a cold soup made of vegetables, vinegar, and oil. At the time of this conversation, Palencia obviously did not understand the underpinnings of Andalusian feudalism and did not realize that absentee landlords had no interest in keeping their workers productive or even alive. As Gerald Brenan points out: "Such a lack of self-interest in rich landowners living in Madrid or Seville may appear extraordinary, but the average aristocrat simply took the advice of

his steward and did not bother his head about estates where he knew no one by sight and which he regarded very much as if they were in some distant colony. . . . Very often, too, the owner did not have the capital to develop the land, and the banks would not lend it to him. . . . There were sometimes special reasons for reducing the area of cultivation. By taking advantage of the unemployment so caused he could knock something off the wages and so reduce the rebellious workers to submission." *The Spanish Labyrinth*, 119.

41. Palencia, *I Must Have Liberty*, 55–56. The testimonies and memory texts repeatedly reveal that all charity or favors of any kind from the dominant members of society required a promise of submission to the Catholic church. This situation was to become an acute and often tragic problem for women in prison.

42. Ibid., 64.

43. Only poor women needed to soil their hands in labor. The teaching profession was the most respectable for women of the upper class, but was a possibility only if the family was in financial straits or if the father had been imbued with Krausist ideology.

44. Palencia, *I must Have Liberty*, 66. Here is the most obvious reason for her use of the pen name Beatriz Galindo.

45. During the flowering of Spanish drama in the seventeenth century, female roles were almost invariably played by males because of the poor reputation of the acting profession. Not much had changed by the early twentieth century, even though actresses had been on stage for several centuries.

46. Palencia, *I Must Have Liberty*, 80–81.

47. Ibid., 81–82.

48. Campo Alange, *Mi atardecer entre dos mundos*, 11–12.

49. Ibid., 17, 19. The finest description of Seville, in all its fanatical Catholicism and inveterate machismo, is provided by Constancia de la Mora. At age thirteen, in about 1920 (the same period depicted by Campo Alange), she went there for the Holy Week festivities:

"Seville awoke twice a year—as far as the women were concerned. Of course I am not thinking of the women who lived in the miserable huts on the other side of the Guadalquivir—those huts whitewashed again and again to deceive the world—and the women singing or brawling with their neighbors, or screaming at their children, to forget, too, that the belly that carries this year's child has received as nourishment a piece of bread with an onion to make it savory. No, these women lived every day alike.

"But the women who lived on the other bank of the river, the rich women; they awoke twice a year for the fair in April and for Holy Week. On these occasions they came out of their old stone houses and lived like human beings. For the rest of the year they dwell behind bars looking across the narrow streets of their ancient city. The streets of Seville are very narrow because the sun burns in the summer and the Arabs who built them did not have motor cars in mind.

"But no one can understand Seville and its women of leisure until he walks through the streets at night—then everything is clear and plain. The same women who walk, in the mornings, with short steps and modestly lowered eyes, dressed in black mantillas, a rosary in their black-gloved fingers, followed by their mothers or old weatherbeaten companions, to the church around the corner; the same black eyes that looked blankly through the glass window of a carriage driving through the park, forget all their modesty and reticence as soon as night comes over the town.

"For every house in Seville has a barred window called a *reja*. The *rejas* are the human safety valves of the inhuman society-code. The mothers of Seville go to bed feeling quite safe about leaving their daughters sitting beside the barred windows on the street level with a piece of embroidery or an innocent novel in their hands. About eleven o'clock, when the big house becomes silent and all the lights are out, the young girls of the family, whose whole lives are lived in this single hour, listen for a tap on the windowpane. They diffidently open the window. And outside stands their suitor, iron bars between him and his sweetheart—but iron bars that sometimes melt under the soft southern night sky.

"The men of Seville find life very different from their sisters or daughters or wives. These men of the south are the perfect type of Spanish *señorito*. Landowners, sons of rich men, officers in the Army, they are only interested in bull or horse breeding. Perfect wine tasters, they also know how to taste women. In the *Calle de la Sierpe*, or at the *Círculo de Labradores*, these men sit in front of the tall, thin wine glasses filled with the golden Manzanilla and thick green olives that come from their own olive groves, discussing the bulls, the horses, and the women. Mostly the women. They talk about the new arrivals at the 'houses,' about the old ones and the new ones. They talk, too, for this is not outside the code of a Spanish gentleman, about the girls of good family who are waiting for them now at the barred windows.

"Then the hour grows later, the wine is finished, the last dishes at the late dinner are taken away. The men of Seville rise: and some of them go to court the girls of good families behind the bars, and some of them go to the famous 'houses' where they need not court but only pay. And whether the men visit the virgins in the narrow streets of the rich houses, or whether they go to one of the 'houses,' they will find women obsessed by piety. For the girls in the brothels are exceedingly religious. In every room of the best institutions there is a reproduction of the famous *Virgen de la Macarena*, adorned with rich jewelry, dressed in silk and satins, just as she looks when she is brought out for the Holy Week processions. For these poor girls believe that the Virgin helps them to attract and keep their customers. Some of the most expensive jewels the Virgin wears in the procession are gifts from grateful women of Seville's underworld."

This cascade of social contradictions and double standards, which corroborates Campo Alange's remarks, is from *In Place of Splendor*, 28–29.

50. See Lerner, *The Creation of Patriarchy*.

51. Campo Alange, *Mi atardecer entre dos mundos*, 19. I assume she refers to the fact that the double standard caused a woman to be considered old at thirty, whereas a man of that age was considered a strapping youth.

52. Martínez Sierra, *Una mujer por caminos de España*. Other aspects of her life will be discussed in the next section of this chapter.

In her book *La mujer española ante la república*, she champions the legal and social rights of women. In other works she attempts to stir Spanish women to action. For example, in the first chapter of *Cartas a las mujeres de España* (attributed to Gregorio) she explains the purpose of the book, though with an ambiguous mixture of the condescension typical of "Gregorio's" tone—a posture taken since the book is supposedly written by him—and the feminism that seems to have characterized Lejárraga's life after 1930:

"Yes, the future belongs to women. . . . Out of their entrails will come the new Europe, kneaded in their blood. And the fruit of their lives—how will they deny them their rights? Oh, feminists! You have won the battle through exaltation of the heroic silent duty, the supreme feminine prerogative. As usual, the equality gained has come at a costly price!

"Women of Spain, my friends, why do I tell you all this? Because, in my humble and respectful opinion, you are somewhat asleep. The hour of truth may also come to Spain. And in less complicated conflicts, though so many, it has arrived. You doubtless will also wish to carry out your duties heroically. But to achieve efficiency within heroism, will is not enough: it is necessary to have the resources with which to be heroic. You have to be prepared; you have to learn a little more; you have to think a little more; you have to rise above the enchanted circle in which you are imprisoned by a few pretty lies told by men; you have to worry a little less about fashions and a little more about life; you have to be swayed less by flirting and more by rights. Isn't it true that we men in Spain give you lamentable examples of frivolity, of cowardice, of ignorance, of a lack of abnegation and patriotism? It is true. But don't accept them; and save us, in spite of ourselves, if you can—if you can!—because from the first moment that woman gave birth to the second man of the world, the future of humanity has been in your hands" (10).

53. Martinez Sierra, *Una mujer por caminos de España*, 34. This extended metaphor produced by the exigencies of reality appears in other female texts about the hunger in Spain before, during, and after the war. Food is, of course, the most palpable and basic measure of privilege. In a civil war, privilege becomes more and more difficult to define as chaos grows and class boundaries become confused, while basic products and luxury items become scarce at all levels. Food, down through the centuries, has often been gathered by women— with the exception of fish and game—and invariably bought, traded, and prepared by them. It is interesting to note the repeated discussions of feeding people and the laments about food's scarcity in many oral and written testimonies of the thirties.

These writers saw themselves as responsible for nourishment, as representative of the women throughout Spain who were trying to sustain their husbands and children without means during the war and during the lean postwar years. This obsession with food becomes more visible in the prison texts, but was coupled to the lack of fuel and fuel-producing products.

54. Ibid., 37.

55. Rusinol was a Catalonian painter and intellectual at the turn of the century.

56. Martínez Sierra, *Una mujer por caminos de España*, 72–73.

57. Ibid., 57–58.

58. Garcia, *Las cárceles de Soledad Real*, 27.

59. Juana Doña, interview with author, Madrid, 17 December 1985.

60. *Milicianos* and *milicianas* were the militiamen and women, who were mainly enlisted foot soldiers. There is even a poem about Sánchez, written by the well-known wartime poet Miguel Hernández, who died in one of Franco's prisons.

61. Incidents of this nature caused many bloody uprisings against the civil guard during the days of the Republic. Rosario Sánchez interview with author, Madrid, 6 February 1986.

62. Maruja Cuesta, interview with author, Madrid, 20 December 1985.

63. Nieves Torres, interview with author, Madrid, 16 December 1985. The feminist remarks of all these women derived from attitudes acquired years after the war, in the sixties and seventies, as Juana Doña was quick to point out when I interviewed her. Doña said her own feminism was "imported from France," where she lived in 1972.

2. Visible Women of the Second Spanish Republic

1. Payne, *Spanish Catholicism*, 155.

2. Sanjurjo, a well-known officer who had fought in the Spanish-American War

and later in the Moroccan War, would later be one of the major figures in plotting the 1936 coup against the Republic.

3. Payne, *Spanish Catholicism*, 151.

4. For more information on the feminist groups that defended female suffrage, see Fagoaga, *La voz y el voto de las mujeres*.

5. Chastity was in reality an institution (called "honor" in Spain), and responsible for a variety of social mores that have been analyzed and scrutinized in many treatises and often portrayed in literature, above all in Spanish drama of the seventeenth century. See Boxer, *Mary and Misogyny*. Also consult Perry, *Gender and Disorder in Early Modern Seville*, an excellent study of the how the church controlled women in early Spain. Lerner finds that the concept of honor was already prevalent in the Neolithic period: "Men in patriarchal societies who cannot protect the sexual purity of their wives, sisters, and children are truly impotent and dishonored." *The Creation of Patriarchy*, 80.

6. Nelken, *La condición social de la mujer*, 203.

7. Nelken, as quoted in García Méndez, *La actuación de la mujer en las cortes de la segunda república*, 26.

8. Quoted by Fagoaga, *La voz y el voto de las mujeres*, 188.

9. García Méndez, *La actuación de la mujer*, 60.

10. As quoted by Campoamor, *El voto femenino y yo*, xii.

11. Campoamor, *El voto femenino y yo*. xiiii.

12. García Méndez, *La actuación de la mujer*, 58.

13. Ibid., 59.

14. Martínez Sierra, *Una mujer por caminos de España*, 65.

15. Campoamor, *El voto femenino y yo*, 176.

16. The Revolution of Asturias, also called the Revolution of October (it took place between 5 October and 18 October of 1934), was a national uprising of workers who were protesting the conservative turn the government had taken in 1933 and 1934. It failed in the major cities—Madrid and Barcelona—but was successful in the northern mining province of Asturias. The head of the Radical party, Alejandro Lerroux, sent the then-young Franco into that province, accompanied by mercenary North African legionnaires, to restore order. The result was a two-week rampage of murder and rape by the mercenaries. Thirty thousand to forty thousand prisoners were taken, thirteen hundred were officially reported dead, and three thousand were wounded. Jackson, *A Concise History of the Spanish Civil War*, 24–27. This bloody affair represented what Brenan, in his classic study of the causes of the war, called "the first battle of the civil war." *The Spanish Labyrinth*, 284.

17. For more information on Campoamor, see Fagoaga and Saavedra, *Clara Campoamor*.

18. As quoted in García Méndez, *La actuación de la mujer*, 37.

19. Ibid., 122.

20. Castilblanco was a bizarre affair that broke out among the hungry peasants in Extremadura, the poorest region of Spain. When the enraged villagers went on strike and four of the famed Civil Guards tried to prevent them, the entire town came out to help murder and mutilate the paramilitary guards. This incident is one of many in which the workers of Spain rose up against the Civil Guards, and is a forerunner of what was to transpire during the civil war.

21. Kern feels that her "adventures as a peasant rebel in the south" in 1934 raised suspicion that "Castilblanco may have been Nelken's effort to reach out and gather a following to match the charisma of her rivals, Dolores Ibárruri or Federica Montseny." Together with her "personal attachment" to Ricardo Zabález, who worked with her in staging the unrest, Kern

suggests that "the incident robbed her of any influence she had in the Cortes." Slaughter and Kern, *European Women on the Left*, 153–158.

22. Matilde de la Torre, unpublished notes entitled "Cortes de la Lonja" (Madrid: Fundación Pablo Iglesias, 30 September 1937).

23. María Gloria Nuñez Pérez, "Margarita Nelken: Una apuesta entre la continuidad y el cambio," *Las mujeres en la guerra civil española* (Madrid: Ministry of Culture, 1989), 165–171.

24. Nelken, *Por qué hicimos la revolución* and *La mujer ante las Cortes Constituyentes*.

25. Ibárruri adopted this pen name when she started her career as a journalist in the 1930s. It had been interpreted sexually by many, since the word "Pasionaria" means passion flower; but it seems that she chose this name because she started writing during Passion Week.

26. Rodrigo, *Mujeres de España*, 169.

27. Montseny in Ibid., 170.

28. Amaro de Rosal, interview with author, Madrid, 14 May 1986. De Rosal has written numerous books that deal with Spanish politics and international labor movements. See, for instance, *Historia de la UGT de España* and *El oro del banco de España y la historia del Vita*.

29. Victoria Kent, interview with author, New York, 6 January 1986. Kent's optimistic appraisal of her innovative experiment has been refuted by the majority of her critics.

30. Kent, "Victoria Kent," 7.

31. Azaña, *Memorias políticas y de guerra*, IV, 383.

32. This Communist and Socialist women's antifascist organization will be discussed in Part II.

33. John Capin, a student in my fall 1983 seminar on Spanish women of the nineteenth and twentieth centuries (Davenport College, Yale University) interviewed Kent, and his account reveals her nostalgia.

34. De Rosal, interview with author.

35. Calderón, *Matilde de la Torre y su época.*

36. Virility used in reference to exceptional women connoted positive strength and character.

37. Martínez Sierra, *Una mujer por caminos de España*, 136–137.

38. Ibid., 137–138.

39. O'Connor, *Gregorio y María Martínez Sierra.*

40. Martínez Sierra, *Gregorio y yo*, 29.

41. She was several years older than Gregorio and in her writing gives the impression that her feelings for him were largely maternal.

42. See Alda Blanco's excellent and timely introduction to the 1989 edition of *Una mujer por caminos de España*, 7–46.

43. Spence, *The Death of Woman Wang*, xii.

44. Scanlon, *La polémica feminista en la España contemporánea*, 276.

3. Two Female Leaders of Revolutionary Spain

1. Ibárruri, *They Shall Not Pass*, 60.

2. Ibid., 61–62.

3. Ibid., 84.

4. Ibid., 298.

5. Thomas, *The Spanish Civil War*, 8.

6. Teresa Loring, interview with author, Madrid, 19 May 1987. Misogyny was internalized among women of the Right, as we shall observe repeatedly.

7. Estruch, "Pasionaria."

8. Borkenau, *The Spanish Cockpit*, 121.

9. Ibárruri, *They Shall Not Pass*, 59.

10. Ibid., 61.

11. Ibid., 43.

12. Nash, *Mujer y movimiento obrero en España.*

13. Quoted by Carabantes and Cimorra, *Un mito llamado Pasionaria*, 37.

14. Mullaney, *Revolutionary Women*, 271.

15. Ibid., 272.

16. She did have a moment of difficulty with Moscow in 1932, when her close friend José Bullejos was reprimanded for defending the Republic and was expunged from the party. Ibárruri wrote an article lamenting Bullejo's expulsion, and because of it was required to make a public statement of self-criticism or suffer the same fate. She complied and was exonerated. Estruch, "Pasionaria," 12–14.

17. Doña's book, *Desde la noche y la niebla,* will be discussed in the section of this book dealing with prison autobiography.

18. Juana Doña, interview with author, Madrid, 17 December 1985.

19. Carmen Camaño, interview with author, Madrid, 16 December 1985.

20. De la Torre, unpublished notes entitled "Cortes en San Cugat" (Madrid: Fundación Pablo Iglesias, 1936).

21. Ibárruri throughout her political career wore the same emblematic attire: black dress and stockings, and small, dangling black earrings.

22. Martínez Sierra, *Una mujer por caminos de España,* 137–139.

23. Her most famous phrase was, "It is better to die standing than to live on your knees."

24. The beginning of the twentieth century was problematic for Federica's parents. Joan Montseny and Teresa Mañé (their pseudonyms were Federico Urales and Soledad Gustavo, respectively) had published both the Anarchist *La revista blanca* and the daily *Tierra y libertad,* both of which were suppressed around the time of Federica's birth in 1905. Both were schoolteachers; Mañé ran one of the first secular schools in Spain and Montseny joined her in the endeavor. When Montseny was implicated in a bomb explosion and incarcerated in the Montjuich fortress overlooking Barcelona, they lost the school too. They went into exile in England for a period, but when they re-turned, Montseny continued his militancy and the defense of fellow Anarchists.

25. The majority of the visible women were writers—mostly journalists, though a few also wrote fiction.

26. The Confederación Nacional de Trabajo an Anarchist organization known as the CNT, was founded in 1911 as a consequence of the "Tragic Week" of 1909. (A general strike had been organized, but only Barcelona saw activity. Unfortunately, the strike disintegrated into chaos, without direction or limits. The strikers burned churches; there were deaths and injuries, and hundreds were indicted.) The CNT was responsible for the revolutionary framework of a new anarcho-syndicalist labor movement. The group was weakened by constant clashes with the government because of the strikes it organized and the imprisonment and exile suffered by many of its members. Still, by 1930 the Anarchists had restructured and, together with their left-wing faction, the FAI, began to gain strength and generate contention leading up to the civil war.

27. Federica Montseny was severely criticized by the Anarchists for joining the government in 1936. According to Shirley Fredricks, she was being pragmatic: when it became clear that the civil war would not mean emancipation of the people, she decided to fight Fascism from within the traditional system. Fredricks, "Social and Political Thought of Federica Montseny," 197. Montseny, in spite of her involvement in the FAI, would during the Republic occupy the middle ground in the battle for power. She served as an arbiter in the unfortunate May 1937 clash between the CNT/FAI and the Catalonian socialists in Barcelona. (The clash would strike a debilitating blow to the Republican war effort.) Montseny was the first and last female minister in Spain until after the death of Franco. She has said that her most important accomplishment as minister of health

was to secure the right to abortion. See the documentary film, ". . . de toda la vida" directed and produced by Carol Mazer and Lisa Berger, 1986.

28. For contemporary remarks on the Spanish church and repression with regard to AIDS, abortion, and birth control, see Alan Riding, "Church and State Spar over Condoms and Cash," *New York Times*, 6 April 1991.

29. Montseny often refers to herself in the plural.

30. Alcalde, *Federica Montseny*, 29.

31. Ibid., 31.

32. Anne Jenkins, student in fall 1983 seminar at Yale, class essay in which she analyzes concepts from Shirley Fredricks' dissertation on Montseny.

33. Kaminski, *Los de Barcelona*, 62–63.

34. Jackson, *The Spanish Republic and the Civil War*, 282.

35. Alcalde, *Federica Montseny*, 31. Of course, even this woman who intervened in "male" politics and war negotiations was largely forgotten when she went into exile; she became, for a period of time, just another mother and housewife trying to keep her family alive.

36. See ibid., 26–46, on women who influenced Montseny. In the Basque country no female leaders other than Pasionaria appear in any important texts or are spoken of. In fact, when I interviewed a Basque politician from the war years, he could not recall one woman who stood out as an activist in the resistance against the Nationalist troops. Yet there appear to have been other important Basque women. Aurora Arnáiz, for example, appears repeatedly in photographs of the war. She was a key figure in the Socialist Youth Group. See Nash, *Las mujeres y la guerra civil*.

37. Alcalde, *Federica Montseny*, 85.

38. Fredricks, in Slaughter and Kern, *European Women on the Left*, 130.

39. Ackelsberg, *Free Women of Spain*, 90.

40. Montseny was a prolific writer. At seventeen she began writing in anarchist publications, under the pseudonym Blanca Montsan. Within a few years she was publishing novels that featured women who choose independence and strive for equality with men. Her most famous novel, *La indomable*, was published when she was twenty-one. It is her most autobiographical book; although her protagonist is an idealized version of herself, Montseny uses elements from her childhood.

Feminist scholars have begun to study her literary work. For instance, see Maria Alicia Langa Laorga's edition of *La indomable*. Her political essays and articles from the *Revista blanca* can be found in the National Library in Madrid.

41. Lerner, *The Creation of Patriarchy*, 200. Montseny died in January 1994. See Mangini, "Mujeres en la guerra civil," and Nash, "Federica Montseny."

4. Toward a Theory of Memory Texts

1. Brodzki and Schenck, *Life/Lines*, 4.

2. Smith, *Subjectivity, Identity, and the Body*, 17–18.

3. On the subject of Spanish autobiography, see Spadaccini and Talens, *Autobiography in Early Modern Spain;* Fernández, *Apology to Apostrophe;* Loureiro, "La autobiografía en la España contemporánea"; Romera, *Escritura autobiográfica;* and Loureiro, "Resisting Autobiography."

4. Georges Gusdorf, "Conditions and Limits of Autobiography," translated in Olney, *Autobiography*, 29.

5. Ibid.

6. See Pascal, *Design and Truth in Autobiography*, 75.

7. Lejeune, *L'Autobiographie en France.* For a feminist theory of gender and reading, see Flynn and Schweickart, *Gender and Reading.*

8. See Craig R. Barclay on recent clinical discussions of memory, "Schematization

of Autobiographical Memory," in Rubin, *Autobiographical Memory.*

9. The bibliography on the postmodern debates is lengthy and the issues involved are politically convoluted. For a recent re-visitation of the scene of the postmodern crime, see Judith Butler, "Contingent Foundations: Feminism and the Question of 'Postmodernism' " in Butler and Scott, *Feminists Theorize the Political,* 3–21.

10. See Nancy K. Miller, "Changing the Subject: Authorship, Writing, and the Reader," in de Lauretis, *Feminist Studies/ Critical Studies.* Also see Barbara Johnson, "Gender Theory and the Yale School," in Showalter, *Speaking of Gender.*

11. Nicholson, *Feminism/Postmodernism,* 1–2. Nicholson, feels that postmodernism is responsible for vindicating what I would call the bettyfriedanism of feminism, although the debate on feminism and postmodernism and their epistemologies continues. In all fairness, I must note that during my experience in the Women's Studies Program at Yale in the early 1980s, the dubious universality of feminist criticism had already been challenged; issues of class, sexual preference, and color were emerging as integral parts of the study of women there and at other institutions. On this subject see also de Lauretis' introduction to *Feminist Studies/Critical Studies.*

12. Nancy K. Miller's work is a particularly good example of this phenomenon. See her *Getting Personal.* In this type of critical writing, Miller is simultaneously the reader/ critic of autobiography and the autobiographical subject of her writing. We find this same phenomenon in the pioneer work of this type: Virginia Woolf's *A Room of One's Own,* published in 1929.

13. Jelinek, *Women's Autobiography.*

14. Stanton, *The Female Autograph,* introduction.

15. See Spivak, *In Other Worlds.*

16. Smith and Watson, *De/Colonizing the Subject,* xiii–xvi.

17. Similar phenomena occurred with women of the Resistance during the Hitler and Mussolini periods in Germany and Italy. When those dictatorships ended, the women—except those who were Jewish—had choices other than to retreat to their homes in silence, or to live in prison or in exile, which was the fate of Spanish women after the war. See Koonz, *Mothers in the Fatherland,* and de Grazia, *How Fascism Ruled Women.*

18. Smith and Watson, *De/Colonizing the Subject,* xiv.

19. This label permits me to subsume under it both testimonials and written texts, which often converge because some of the written texts are transcribed oral testimonies and because I have turned other fragments of interviews into "written" text. In still others texts, such as those of de la Mora, Palencia, and Ibárruri the authors use the format of novel, diary, memoir, and more traditional autobiography.

20. Benstock, "The Female Self Engendered," 6.

21 Caren Kaplan, "Resisting Autobiography: Outlaw Genres and Transnational Feminist Subjects," in Brodzki and Schenck, *Life/Lines:* 115–138. Kaplan includes under this rubric testimonials, prison memoirs, and a mix of autobiographical criticism and autobiography.

22. Ibid., 135.

23. On the subject of "testimonios," see John Beverly, "The Margin at the Center: On Testimonio," in Smith and Watson, *De/ Colonizing the Subject,* 91–114; and Doris Sommer, " 'Not Just a Personal Story': Women's Testimonios and the Plural Self," in Brodzki and Schenck, *Life/Lines,* 107–130. Both feel strongly that autobiography and testimony are very different, with distinct intention and format; both look to the traditional definition of autobiography and therefore logically see testimony as outsider literature.

24. In any event, Louisa Passerini, in her work on the oral history of Fascism in Turin, concludes that history retold is not an accurate account of what truly happened, but rather that "the personal memory combines with the collective memory, and individual mythology turns into a tradition shared by a family, a circle of friends or a political group." *Fascism in Popular Memory*, 19.

25. See Susanna Egan's distinction between "contingent" and "virtual" reality in *Patterns of Experience in Autobiography*.

26. See especially Lifton, *The Broken Connection* and *History and Human Survival*.

27. Lifton describes the phenomenon: "Resembling the psychological defense of denial, and the behavioral state of apathy, psychic closing-off is nonetheless a distinctive pattern of response to overwhelmingly threatening stimuli." *History and Human Survival*. 153. He refers specifically to Hiroshima and the denial of death, though one could extend this loss of memory to other equally painful experiences related to war and devastation.

28. It is curious to observe the current interest in protest literature, such as the Latin American testimonios of women activists, which until recently were completely unknown. Because of the international recognition of Rigoberta Menchú's story upon the publication of *Me llamo Rigoberta Menchú y así me nació la conciencia* (Barcelona: Editorial Argos Vergara, 1983), she became the 1992 Nobel Peace Prize winner. Without the published text of her tragedy, Menchú undoubtedly would have been just one more victim of the systematic genocide that Guatemalan natives have been suffering for many years. Colonized women's voices are obviously more powerful than hitherto imagined. There are a number of similarities between the female Latin American testimonios and many of the voices of Spanish women from the war (for example, the

sense of empowerment that these women felt from writing and speaking). This fact was reconfirmed when in December of 1993 I met with Rosario Sánchez, Juana Doña, and Soledad Real, who continue to be active politically and intellectually. Doña has published a new autobiographical novel, *Gente de abajo*, (Madrid: A Z Ediciones, 1992); Sánchez is now enrolled in the School of Fine Arts in Madrid, has exhibited her paintings, and is writing her memoirs; Real is researching the feminist aspects of Socialist thinkers.

29. Only a few actually acquired an understanding of female oppression and patriarchy many years after their experiences of war and imprisonment.

30. Harlow, *Resistance Literature*, 120.

31. The first female autobiographical treatise in Spain was written by a fourteenth-century aristocrat, Leonor de Córdoba. See Amy Katz Kaminsky and Elaine Dorough Johnson, "To Restore Honor and Fortune: The Autobiography of Leonor López de Córdoba," in Stanton, *The Female Autograph*, 70–80. Saint Teresa of Avila (1515–1582), *Libro de su vida*, is the most famous female Renaissance text. The first female memory text on war was written by the nineteenth-century thinker Concepción Arenal. In a series of loosely woven vignettes she recalls the tragedies she witnessed while nursing soldiers (she had been named secretary general of the Red Cross in Madrid) in the last of the Carlist wars. *Cuadros de guerra* (Buenos Aires: Editorial Nova, 1942; first published 1874).

32. Some of the best autobiographies written by men include the brilliant Arturo Barea, *La forja de un rebelde* vol. 3, *The Clash*, translated by Ilsa Barea (New York: Viking Press, 1972), a book that compares well to de la Mora's *In Place of Splendor*. Other works comparable to some of the prison autobiographies are Jose Leiva, *Memorias de un condenado a muerte* (Barcelona: DOPESA, 1978), and Cipriano Mera,

Guerra, exilio y cárcel de un anarco sindicalista (Paris: Edicions Ruedo Ibérico, 1976). For a fairly complete listing of male autobiographies (a few women are mentioned), see Cuadernos bibliográficos de la guerra de España (1936–1939), vols. 1–3, edited by "La cátedra de 'Historia Contemporánea de España' de la Universidad de Madrid."

33. Dolores Ibárruri and Irene Falcón, interview with author, Madrid, 26 February 1986.

34. Ibárruri, They Shall Not Pass, 347.

35. Ibid., 108.

36. Ibárruri and Falcón, interview with author

37. The book, first published in 1962, created an opportune moment for Ibárruri. (Editions appeared in Spanish, French, English, and Russian in 1962 and in Cuba, Mexico, the United States, France, and Moscow in 1963.) The Spanish Communist party was emerging from its clandestine state. In fact, Ibárruri had been instrumental in staging a general strike within Spain in 1959. Though unsuccessful, it reminded Franco that he still had an important constituency of enemies in exile (especially in France and Latin America—mostly Mexico) who were in touch with their comrades in Spain and were capable of mobilizing them. (Franco was taken aback by this show of strength and immediately increased repressive tactics all over the country.) Most important, the sixth congress of the Spanish Communist party had conceded the presidency to Pasionaria in 1960, and she was carefully reshaping her political image to rid herself of the public scars acquired by party leaders once the truth about Stalin had been released. The book was a step in the right direction to restore Ibárruri as one of the most important figures of political hagiography.

38. Patricia V. Greene discusses the genesis of de la Mora's text in her article "Constancia de la Mora's In Place of Splendor,"

in "Resisting Autobiography," Journal of Interdisciplinary Studies 5 (1993): 75–84.

39. De la Mora, In Place of Splendor, 249.

40. Gilligan, In a Different Voice, 17.

41. De la Mora, In Place of Splendor, 154.

42. Martínez Sierra, Una mujer por caminos de España, 162–163.

43. Medio, Atrapados en la ratonera, 32.

44. Ibid., 115.

5. Women Remembering War

1. Whealey, Hitler and Spain, 11.

2. Jackson, A Concise History of the Spanish Civil War, 31.

3. Franco would learn that the energy and euphoria of youth was a key force in producing war and revolution. He kept close watch on Spanish universities during the entire regime. Even in the 1970s, when the Basque separatist group ETA began a rampage of terrorist activity, there was cavalry at the doors of the University of Madrid because the government feared student rebellion in favor of ETA.

4. See Payne on Spanish fascism in The Franco Regime, chapter 4, "The Nationalist Opposition."

5. Josefina de Silva, child of a wealthy, conservative family, reflects on the polarization and fear that gripped the Spanish Right before the elections. With childlike simplicity, she notes the admiration her family felt for Gil Robles and comments: "I remember seeing caricatures of Gil Robles in newspapers and magazines, which really caught my attention because he always appeared with a pear for a face. I was not convinced that you could feel such devotion for a pear. My first political statement, after tiring of hearing the adults talk about the elections, was, 'I don't care if the Left or the Right wins.' Then they explained to me that if the Left won, they would kill my mother, my grandmother, my uncle, the priest, my aunt the

nun, my godfather who was in the military.
. . . In the face of such solid arguments, plus
the fact that I couldn't go out well dressed,
with how much I loved nice clothes, . . . I
decided, "Well then, let the Right win." De
Silva, *Nosotros, los evacuados* 54.

De Silva's observations, from the perspective of a child, emphasize that the civil war
was a class war. Her observation about
clothes was a reality: during the war the distinction between the rich and powerful
Right and the poor and impotent Left was
seen at every level. The conservatives who
were in leftist territory, such as Madrid and
Barcelona, did not wear suits, ties, and hats
when they walked the streets. The men
dressed shabbily, often in the "revolutionary" uniform—overalls—to hide their class,
and therefore their political sympathies. The
women wore peasant clothes, not tailored
dresses and suits and gloves. Nuns and
priests who had to leave their convents and
churches also disguised themselves by wearing ordinary clothing.

María Manuela de Cora describes the
nuns who were forced to leave their convents for fear of being captured by leftist
troops: "There were a few women near me
who were dressed very eccentrically, one of
them with a huge 1900-style hat. They
looked like rabbits caught in a trap, with
their frightened eyes and their faces dis-
torted and trembling. They were nuns from
a convent located on the outskirts of Madrid. Some of them were crying quietly;
others were praying and trying to console
the most depressed ones." De Cora, *Retaguardia enemiga*, 56. Madrid and Barcelona
were vast panoramas of masquerade and
deceit, not the least of which were the costumes of the wealthy.

6. The Popular Front was to disinte-
grate into chaos and in-fighting, which was
strongly to disadvantage the Left in the war.
The intervention of the Comintern exacer-
bated this problem; their purges of suspicious comrades and their witch-hunt for
unorthodox Marxists were responsible for
the creation of an irrevocable rift within
leftist sectors.

7. Mola was the only general planning
the overthrow who was in Spain at the
time. He was to be the link between the exiled generals and the dissident factions,
which included the Carlistas in addition to
the Falangists and the Catholic groups. In
any event, Sanjurjo was killed in an airline
crash three days after the coup, as he took
off for Spain from Portugal.

8. Franco himself practiced it; he had
his first cousin, a major in Tetuan, executed
for refusing to rebel against the government. Payne, *The Franco Regime*, 212.

9. According to the military historian
Antony Beevor, this was to have been the
first major airlift in history. *The Spanish
Civil War*, 63.

10. Only 7 of the 27 major generals and
20 of the 35 brigade commanders took part.
The others did not act. Payne, *The Franco
Regime*, 99.

11. The strategy for the takeover of Madrid was for Mola to come down from the
north to meet Franco, who would arrive in
the capital from the south.

12. Seville was the pivotal geographic
spot for the organization of the Nationalist
army, since its airstrip was used to receive
forces from Morocco.

13. There were three major Nationalist
strongholds: Burgos, Valladolid, and Salamanca. The last became the most important
international seat of Nationalist power, since
German and Italian leaders had their offices
there.

14. According to Ramón Tamames,
Germany would make 170 trips with arms
to aid Spain. Its troops, the Condor Legion,
numbered approximately 30,000. Germany
spent $400 million on Franco's Holy Cru-
sade. Italy sent 120,000 soldiers, 50,000 of
whom died aiding Franco. Arab troops
numbered 100,000; this included both Foreign Legion and regular troops. The USSR

sent the Republic food and arms costing $578 million, and 1409 planes. Ramón Tamames, *La República: La era de Franco* (Madrid: Alianza Editorial, 1973), 268–280. Stalin came to the aid of the Republic on August 26. Beevor says: "The head of [Russia's] European section, based in Paris, was Willi Muenzenburg, a highly successful publicist and organizer. International Red Help, which was already in existence, started fund-raising drives and collections. The International Committee for Aid to the Spanish People was set up, and many other front organizations were formed." *The Spanish Civil War,* 124. For more information on foreign aid to the Republic, see Fyrth, *The Signal Was Spain;* Kershner, *Quaker Service in Modern War; La Solidarité des peuples avec la république espagnole;* and Wilson, *In the Margins of Chaos.*

15. The International Brigade troops numbered 40,000; some 18,000 died (these figures are controversial; other sources speak of 60,000 troops there). Tamames, *La República,* 281. The brigades came from all over western Europe, some from Canada and the United States, even a few from South America. There were some women, mostly nurses. The largest group was French, numbering about 10,000; there were also around 10,000 Germans, Austrians, and Poles. More than 3,000 Italians and another 3,000 Americans fought in the war. The majority were Communists or became affiliated with the party during the war; most were from the working class. There are countless books on the brigades; see, for example, Johnston, *Legions of Babel,* and Brome, *The International Brigades.*

16. Payne, *The Franco Regime,* 219–220. The literature on the issues outlined here is vast. Thousands of books and articles are available on nearly every aspect of the war; most can be found in the Bolloten collection of the Hoover Institution at Stanford University, one of the most important civil war collections in the world.

17. Higgonet, *Behind the Lines,* 14.

18. Hidalgo de Cisneros (1896–1966) was an aristocrat who was the air attaché during the Republic. During the civil war he became a powerful figure in the Ministry of War, while still carrying out bombing missions. He saw the Communists as the strongest force and joined the party in October 1936. After the war he became a member of the central committee of the Spanish Communist party. His two-volume autobiography, *Cambio de rumbo,* first appeared in France; a Spanish edition was published in Barcelona in 1977.

19. De la Mora, *In Place of Splendor,* 267–268.

20. De la Mora's criticism undoubtedly was also prompted by the bitterness she felt when Indalecio Prieto asked her to resign as chief censor because she refused to follow his orders. Though she was reinstated in her position, Bolloten quotes her as saying in an interview in Mexico in 1940, "Prieto hated me . . . because he believed that I had influenced Ignacio to join the Communist party." (Prieto was extremely fearful of Comintern intervention during the war.) *The Spanish Civil War,* 540.

21. Both were leftist Catalonian groups.

22. Soledad Real, interview with author, Madrid, 18 July 1986.

23. O'Neill, *Una mujer en la guerra de España,* 18–19.

24. Ana María Martín Rubio, sister-in-law of an important local Socialist political figure, Manuel Espada; interview with author, Dos Hermanas (Seville), 6 July 1986.

25. Dulce del Moral, interview with author, Seville, 4 July 1986.

26. Angelina Puig i Valls, "Mujeres de Pedro Martínez (Granada) durante la guerra civil," in *Las mujeres y la guerra civil española,* 41.

27. The only remark about her that I encountered is in Antony Beevor's book: "The defense committee of the town was organized by Anita López, who greatly en-

couraged the ferocious resistance. She was among those killed when Yague's troops finally entered the town that night." *The Spanish Civil War*, 101.

28. Many groups were named after Pasionaria.

29. Nieves Torres, interview with author, Madrid, 16 December 1985.

30. J. Alvarez del Vayo, *Freedom's Battle*, trans. Eileen E. Brooke, 2nd ed. (New York: Hill and Wang, 1971), 184–185.

31. Ibid., 186.

32. Maruja Cuesta, interview with author, Madrid, 20 December 1985.

33. De la Torre, *Mares en la sombra*, 71–72.

34. Ibid., 76–77.

35. Medio, *Atrapados en la ratonera*, 78.

36. Soledad Real, interview with author.

37. Higgonet, *Behind the Lines*, 7.

38. Ibid., 6.

39. Fraser, *Blood of Spain*, 286–287.

40. Beevor, *The Spanish Civil War*, 89. Hugh Thomas has mentioned that there were a "few" milicianas, though he notes that their participation was the exception rather than the rule. "La revolución en la España republicana," *Diario 16* (Sunday Magazine), 23 February 1986, 281.

41. García, *Yo he sido marxista*, 160.

42. One miliciano told the journalist H. E. Kaminski: "When I see a woman in the line of fire, I would like to run and protect her. I think it's a natural masculine sentiment and it is impossible for me to avoid it." Kaminski, *Los de Barcelona*, 210.

43. Trejo, *Lo que vi en España*, 42.

44. Kaminski, *Los de Barcelona*, 209–210.

45. Geraldine Scanlon discusses their participation briefly, suggesting that the negative remarks about the motives of the milicianas were probably "not unfounded." *La polémica feminista*, 295.

46. Nash, *Las mujeres en la guerra civil*, 25–26.

47. There is a book about Odena (Estivill, *Lina Odena*), which is obviously a propagandistic tool to encourage the youth to continue their resistance, given that the copy I possess is a third edition. When I traveled to Asturias to discuss de la Fuente's life with her family, they refused to speak to me and acted ashamed and fearful over the telephone, even after I explained my project. As do many other cases, this one suggests that the Franco regime was very successful in brainwashing the public to think that all milicianas were scandalous and that journalists were still searching for sensationalistic information.

48. Nash, *Las mujeres en la guerra civil*, 27.

49. Rosario Sánchez, interview with author, Madrid, 6 February 1986.

50. Etchebéhère, *Mi guerra de España*, 56–57. Etchebéhère, a French revolutionary, had accompanied her Marxist husband to Spain; when he was killed in the war a month after their arrival, she became a captain of the POUM (Partido Obrero de Unificación Marxista, the Workers' Party of Marxist Unification, a small group of anti-Stalinist Communists), a unique post for a woman in the civil war. She was arrested by the Communists when they were pursuing POUM members, but was rescued from prison. Beevor, *The Spanish Civil War*, 186.

51. Blasco, *Peuple d'Espagne*, is a memory text by one of these mothers.

52. Mary Nash, "La miliciana: Otra opción de combatividad femenina antifasicsta," in *Las mujeres y la guerra civil española* 97–108. Durruti, who died at the front, was a hero among his followers. Hugh Thomas claims Durruti was a bandit and a murderer, and that he was probably killed by one of his soldiers. Thomas also speaks of the milicianas as transporting diseases to the front, and there were some instances of this. *The Spanish Civil War*, 44, 201, 328. In fact, it appears that some of the women who went to fight with the militiamen from

Barcelona actually came from the Barrio Chino, that city's red light district.

53. Nash, "La miliciana."

54. Rosario Sánchez, interview with author.

55. After the Revolution of Asturias, Mujeres Antifascistas (Antifascist Women) was censured by the government and renamed the Proinfancy Group; it helped rescue children from the Asturias purge in 1934. When the war started, the group reclaimed the name Antifascist Women. In 1947, under the direction of Irene Falcón, the Council of the Union of Antifascist Women was held in Paris. The members had regrouped in exile and had made clandestine contact with antifascist women throughout Spain. See *Consejo de la Unión de las Mujeres Antifascistas Españolas,* a curious collection of speeches, stories of famous revolutionary women, letters, songs, and illustrations all pertaining to Spanish women of the Left, especially activists from the civil war and those in prison.

56. Carmen González Martínez, "Mujeres antifascistas españolas: Trayectoria histórica de una organización femenina de lucha," in *Las mujeres y la guerra civil española,* 56.

57. María del Carmen García Nieto París, "Unión de Muchachas, un modelo metodológico," in Folguera, *La mujer en la historia de España,* 321.

58. See *Muchachas,* 2 (20 February 1937).

59. Nash, *Mujer y movimiento obrero,* 244.

60. Correspondence in the National Archives of the Spanish Civil War, Salamanca, Spain. Dolores Ibárruri and Irene Falcón corroborated this information in my interview with them in Madrid, 26 February 1986.

61. Nash, *Mujer y movimiento obrero,* 246.

62. Ibárruri and Falcón, interview with author.

63. Nash, *Mujer y movimiento obrero,* 246–247.

64. Ackelsberg, *Free Women of Spain,* 88.

65. Nash, *Mujer y movimiento obrero,* 85.

66. Letter dated 14 June 1936, found in National Archives of the Spanish Civil War, Salamanca.

67. Comaposada, a lawyer, and Sánchez Saornil, a writer and poet, first met in 1934 at a meeting of the Feminine Cultural Group, a CNT organization created after the October Revolution. They founded the Free Women's group in Madrid. Poch y Gascón, a physician interested in sexuality and the double standard, was active in Barcelona. All three worked on the journal. Ackelsberg, *Free Women of Spain,* 92–94.

68. Nash, "Mujeres Libres," 8.

69. Nash, *Mujer y movimento obrero,* 89.

70. Ackelsberg, *Free Women of Spain,* 135.

71. Quoted in Nash, "Mujeres Libres," 73.

72. Ackelsberg, *Free Women of Spain,* 126.

73. Berenguer, *Entre el sol y la tormenta,* 237–280.

74. Ibid., 11. Berenguer tells us she left school at age twelve, like the majority of proletariat women.

75. Ibid., 12–13.

76. Berenguer is one of the main "characters" in the documentary film ". . . toda la vida," in which women who were militants in the CNT discuss their role in the Anarchist movement and, in some cases, in Free Women. It was filmed in Toulouse (where Federica Montseny still lived), Beziers, France, and Barcelona. The women speak of themselves and their colleagues, so they add a visual element to the memory texts of women from the war. Like many of the Socialist and Communist women whom I have interviewed, these women continue to be

active in politics and in social work. Included in the film besides Montseny are
Maria Battett (who had been at Montseny's
side since before the war and who worked
with Teresa Mañé) and several other extremely active and articulate women: Lola
Iturbe, Concha Perez, Pepita Carpena, Dolores Prat, Soledad Gustavo, and Teresina
Torrellas. Martha Ackelsberg, who interviewed the women, describes repeatedly
how in the 1980s they still spoke with enthusiasm about their participation in the
group and how they felt they had helped
women to recognize their importance. Ackelsberg, *Free Women of Spain.*

77. Like many of the proletariat women
who talk about their background it was usually the father or boyfriend or other male
friend who motivated their political activism. Doris Sommer comments on this tendency in testimonials: "The 'superior' man
may initially be the narrator's object of desire and source of approbation, but she gets
beyond her dependence upon any particular
man. More than a love object, he represents
goals and ideas with which the narrator falls
in love." "Not Just a Personal Story," in
Brodzki and Schenck, *Life/Lines,* 125.

78. Berenguer, *Entre el sol y la tormenta,* 290–291.

79. Iturbe, *La mujer en la lucha social.*

80. Nash, *Mujer y movimiento obrero,*
105.

81. Shirley Fredricks, in Slaughter and
Kern, *European Women on the Left,* 126.
Yet Montseny did not support a separate
feminist movement within Anarchism and
collaborated only marginally with the group.

82. Quoted in Rodrigo, *Mujeres de España,* 169.

83. Gallego Méndez, *Mujer, falange y
franquismo.* It is in fact one of the few
books about the Feminine Section. One
other is Primo de Rivera's autobiography,
Recuerdos de una vida, which is a justification of the Falange and Primo de Rivera's
group. Gallego Méndez' study is an indict-

ment of the fascist nature of the group, as
is Rosario Sánchez López' 1990 book, *Mujer española, una sombra de destino en lo
universal.*

84. Juntas de Ofensiva Nacional Sindicalista was a small party of militant Fascists
with an office in Valladolid. It was affiliated
with the Falange at the beginning of 1934.

85. Gallego Méndez, *Mujer, falange y
franquismo,* 197.

86. This was the Sociedad de Estudiantes Unificados.

87. Primo de Rivera, interview with author, Madrid, 26 July 1986.

88. Ibid.

89. Ibid. The repeated use of the term
"solution" is somewhat eerie, since it brings
to mind Hitler's "final solution."

90. Primo de Rivera, *Recuerdos de una
vida,* 210.

91. Scanlon, *La polémica feminista,*
317.

92. Primo de Rivera, interview with author. Teresa Loring, national secretary of
the Feminine Section, confirms Primo de
Rivera's statements: "Some girls were at the
front lines as nurses and washerwomen. But
most were at home, making clothes, etc. It
never occurred to us to go to fight. The
milicianas had a bad reputation because
they were morally undesirable. I don't even
think they were good soldiers. It isn't appropriate for women to be soldiers, physically even. Women's natural role is to help
men. Their capacities are different from
men's." Loring, interview with author, Madrid, 30 June 1986.

93. Primo de Rivera visited Germany in
1937 to make contact with the Fascist wom-
en's groups.

94. Later renamed Social Help, its purpose was to feed children. It was motivated
by the "thirst for justice and the longing for
true brotherhood which inspire the Spanish
Phalanx." *Social Help.*

95. Thomas, *The Spanish Civil War,*
356.

96. Foronda, *Nueve meses con los rojos en Madrid*, 12.

97. Queipo de Llano, *De la cheka de Atadell a la prisión de Alacuas*, 63. Queipo de Llano is obviously a relative of the ferocious officer who commanded the massacres by the Arab troops in Andalusia, General Gonzalo Queipo de Llano. It is unlikely that the militiawoman was a mulatta, since Spain is not interracial. She was probably Andalusian; individuals from that region are generally darker skinned than their northern neighbors.

98. Marola, *Prisonera del Soviet*, 33.

99. Lerner, *The Creation of Patriarchy*, 212–213.

100. Ibid., 218.

101. As quoted in Scanlon, *La polémica feminista*, 319.

6. The Lost Women of Spanish Prisons

1. For an analysis of the history of prison and punishment, see Foucault, *Discipline and Punish.*

2. See the treatment of this topic in Romeu Alfaro, *El silencio roto.*

3. Cited in Suárez and Equipo 36, *Libro blanco sobre las cárceles franquistas*, 73.

4. Tomasa Cuevas, *Cárcel de mujeres, 1939–1945* (Barcelona: Ediciones Sirocco, 1985), I, 16.

5. Ibid.

6. Suárez and Equipo 36, *Libro blanco sobre las cárceles franquistas*, 63–64. It is impossible to determine the number of executions because the statistics for those years show many assassinations in Spain as "suicides." In addition, the press was not permitted to discuss the existence of political prisoners. It was the "criminals" and "suicidal" types in jail who necessitated all the grave digging. Ramón Salas Larrazábal claims that most of the deaths were due to illness and war wounds and that only 23,000 deaths are attributable to execution between 1939 and 1961. *Los datos exactos de la guerra civil*, 310.

7. In *Estadísticas básicas de España*, the number of women was less than 10 percent of the number of men, which according to this volume was 247,485. Iturbe speaks of 30,000 in *La mujer en la lucha social.* Interestingly, the *Estadísticas básicas de España* claims that in 1953 there were 44,293 women in prison and 219,949 men. The number of men did not differ greatly from 1939, whereas the number of women doubled.

8. Suárez and Equipo 36, *Libro blanco de las cárceles franquistas*, 75. Petra Cuevas, who spent several years in the Ventas prison, claims that she was prisoner number 14,000, suggesting that at least that many women passed through Ventas in the early postwar period. Doña confirms these numbers in *Desde la noche y la niebla.* Guiliana di Febo, in her pioneer study of female activism in Spain, claims that in 1939 alone, between 9,000 and 11,000 women spent time at Ventas. *Resistencia y movimiento de mujeres en España*, 28. Also see Romeu Alfaro, *El silencio roto*, 307–324, on the numbers of women in Spanish prisons.

9. De Grazia, *How Fascism Ruled Women*, 43.

10. María Encarna Nicolás Marín and Basilisa López Gracía, "La situación de la mujer a través de los movimientos de apostolado seglar: La contribución a la legitimación del franquismo, 1936–1956," in Rosa María Capel Martínez et al., *Mujer y sociedad en España, 1700–1975* (Madrid: Ministry of Culture, 1982), 370.

11. See Martín Gaite, *Usos amorosos de la postguerra española*, on repressive tactics used against women during the Franco regime.

12. For a close study of sexual repression during the regime, see Alonso Tejada, *La represión sexual en la España de Franco.*

13. Gallego Méndez gives minute details of the conscription process. It was primarily aimed at the lower classes, especially single working women. At first those who did not

cooperate were fined up to fifty dollars, in those days a considerable sum of money that was, of course, completely inaccessible to proletarian women. By 1945, women who did not complete their social service duties were threatened with loss of their jobs. *Mujer, falange y franquismo,* 91–98. Scanlon also describes the increasingly repressive measures that were used to enlist women in the Feminine Section. *La polémica feminista,* 323–328.

14. The manual was entitled "El libro de las Margaritas." The Margaritas were girls aged seven to ten who belonged to the Feminine Section.

15. Gallego Méndez, *Mujer, falange y franquismo,* 79.

16. Ibid., 155.

17. Ibid., 182.

18. Barbeito, *Cárceles de mujeres en el siglo XVII,* 9.

19. Beatas were "pious women" who often displayed themselves in the streets and were considered mediums for the voice of God. Known in France, Belgium, and western Germany as Beguines, they were, as Sidonie Smith remarks, "unattached groups of celibate women, who were neither subordinated in marriage nor confined in the cloister, remained marginalized, anomalous, and potentially disruptive, their sexuality potentially unrepressed. Such public female activity, unauthorized by the church, threatened the social order." *A Poetics of Women's Autobiography,* 34. See also Perry, *Gender and Disorder in Early Modern Seville,* 97–117.

20. Jackson, *The Spanish Republic and the Civil War,* 377. Unlike the clergy in the rest of Spain, the Basque priests generally sided with the Republic. They supported Basque autonomy, which the hegemonic regime wiped out. *Requetés* were Carlist militiamen who wore red berets.

21. According to Scanlon, 58.2 percent of the female population in 1930 was illiterate. *La polémica feminista,* 50.

22. Carmen Camaño, interview with author, Madrid, 16 December 1985.

23. Joaquín Ruiz Giménez was an important judge during the regime, who later drifted away from Franco's dictatorship and became a liberal political figure.

24. Camaño, interview with author.

25. Gallego Méndez, *Mujer, falange y franquismo,* 45.

26. Teresa Pàmies, filmed interview in "The Spanish Civil War, Part V," Granada Productions, John E. Allen. Pàmies, a self-taught Socialist activist during the war who was strongly influenced by her revolutionary father, wrote war chronicles, delivered speeches, and traveled abroad to aid the Republic. She describes this period in her memoir *Cuando éramos capitanes.* After the war Pàmies joined her father in France, living in refugee camps; she was jailed in Paris, lived temporarily in Latin America, then in Prague for twelve years. Her thirty-year exile was spent principally in France. Much of her life is chronicled in her twenty autobiographical novels, written for the most part in Catalonian.

27. Lifton, *History and Human Survival,* 279.

7. The Intent and Format of the Prison Texts

1. García-Madrid, *Réquiem por la libertad.*

2. Angeles García-Madrid, interview with author, Madrid, 6 October 1985.

3. First discussed in Mangini, "Spanish Women and the Spanish Civil War."

4. García-Madrid, *Réquiem por la libertad,* 12.

5. Doña, *Desde la noche y la niebla,* 30.

6. Ibid., 16–17.

7. Juana Doña, interview with author, Madrid, 11 December 1985.

8. Doña, *Desde la noche y la niebla,* 18.

9. García-Madrid, *Réquiem por la libertad,* 33.

10. García-Madrid, interview with author.

11. Malonda, *Aquello sucedió así.*

12. Lidia Falcón, "Cincuenta años de lucha," *Poder y libertad* 11 (1989): 7.

13. O'Neill, *Una mujer en la guerra de España,* 9–10.

14. Cuevas Gutiérrez, *Cárcel de mujeres,* II, 14.

15. Tomasa Cuevas Gutiérrez, interview with author, Madrid, 26 June 1985. In her dedication to my copy of *Cárcel de mujeres* she writes, "What I wish is that what I have said here will serve a purpose."

16. Cuevas Gutiérrez, *Cárcel de mujeres,* II, 14.

17. García, *Las cárceles de Soledad Real,* 5. It seems that García came from Germany—she is Spanish—to record the voices of imprisoned women. The first activist she met was Real, who impressed her so much that she filled twenty-one tapes of interviews with her and published them exclusively. Real's story is, incidentally, the only example—of all those discussed here—in which the text of an "invisible" activist was published by a mainstream Spanish press. Of course, it was transcribed by a professional journalist, which probably explains this anomaly.

18. Ibid., 9.

19. *Libro blanco* does provide some of this information, as do several of the organizations investigating the prison situation in Spain during the regime. It was very difficult to gain entrance to the prisons. Even as late as as 1967, when repression had supposedly dwindled considerably, Nancy Macdonald expressed frustration because she could not get information or find ways to help the war prisoners. *Homage to the Spanish Exiles,* 222–223. The regime kept a very tight rein on conditions in Spanish prisons; it did not behoove the government to let the world know that it had kept some of Franco's enemies in prison for several decades.

20. Núñez, *Carcel de Ventas,* 12.

21. Castro, *Una vida para un ideal,* 159.

22. Ibid., 104.

23. Ibid., 100. Castro illustrates that since maternity was woman's most important function in life, she and others like her were compelled to justify their activism as convincingly as possible.

24. Fidalgo, *A Young Mother in Franco's Prisons,* 4.

25. Ibid., 32. The term "men" was undoubtedly translated from "hombres," which includes women.

26. Malonda, *Aquello sucedió así,* 170.

27. Ibid., 25.

8. Themes of the Texts

1. García-Madrid, *Réquiem por la libertad,* 92.

2. My own experience indicated that in some cases the women had experienced a psychic closing off, but that in many others they genuinely feared reprisals if they denounced their captors. Even in the 1980s many still seemed afraid to speak, as I have repeatedly illustrated.

3. Angeles García-Madrid, interview with author, Madrid, 6 October 1985.

4. Cuevas Gutiérrez, *Cárcel de mujeres,* II, 98.

5. Ibid., 75.

6. Sender, a Spanish Republican novelist (1901–1981) whose wife had been executed without trial by the Nationalists, wrote novels portraying Nationalist repression. He left Spain during the war and later settled in the United States as a professor of Spanish literature. See *Death in Zamora.*

7. García, *Las cárceles de Soledad Real,* 141. Obviously, the bathroom was where they secretly read.

8. Cuevas Gutiérrez, *Cárcel de mujeres,* II 163.

9. This optimism was, of course, destroyed when it was obvious that Franco would not be driven out of Spain with the

fall of Hitler. When in 1946 the world began to recognize Franco's regime and the United States sent financial aid, the dictator's power was solidified. Yet Franco felt the need to show some semblance of "democracy" at this time, and the number of political assassinations began to diminish.

10. García, *Las cárceles de Soledad Real,* 132.

11. The gender experience for women was devastating. When they finally left prison many of them had lost both youth and beauty. Their hopes and dreams were gone. Many were in poor health and without work; often they had lost boyfriends or husbands in the war. Ostracized from society, they were frequently penniless and helpless.

12. Núñez, *Cárcel de Ventas,* 65–66.

13. Cuevas Gutiérrez, *Cárcel de mujeres, II,* 100–118; Petra Cuevas, interview with author, Madrid, 31 October 1985.

14. Di Febo, *Resistencia y movimiento de mujeres en España,* 34.

15. Ibid., written testimony by Antonia Garcia, 35.

16. Núñez describes how so many babies died that they would pile them up in the bathroom overnight until they could be buried; the mothers would take turns keeping vigil to prevent the rats from eating the little corpses. *Cárcel de Ventas,* 18.

17. Doña, *Desde la noche y la niebla,* 170.

18. Petra Cuevas, interview with author.

19. Malonda, *Aquello sucedió así,* 147.

20. García-Madrid, *Réquiem por la libertad,* 92.

21. Malonda, *Aquello sucedió así,* 102–103.

22. Ibid., 103. Some children from leftist families were sent to Russia during the civil war and endured the severe hardships of World War II there. See, for example, Milagros Latorre Piquer's testimony in Medrano, *Nuevas raíces,* 61–113.

23. O'Neill, *Una mujer en la guerra de España,* 172.

24. Garcia-Madrid, *Réquiem por la libertad,* 172.

25. Cuevas, *Cárcel de mujeres, I,* 171.

26. Ibid., 125.

27. Ibid., 98.

28. García-Madrid, *Réquiem por la libertad,* 190.

29. Núñez, *Cárcel de Ventas,* 93–94.

30. García, *Las cárceles de Soledad Real,* 178–179.

31. O'Neill, *Una mujer en la guerra de España* 101–102. It is unlikely that women less prominent than O'Neill would have been taken to a hospital and treated with such care.

32. Castro, *Una vida para un ideal,* 109–110.

33. García, *Las cárceles de Solidad Real,* 112.

34. Núñez, *Cárcel de Ventas,* 38–39.

35. Ibid., 39–40.

36. Fidalgo, *A Young Mother in Franco's Prisons,* 22–23. Veloria was also responsible for the death of Amparo Barayón, the wife of novelist Ramón Sender. In the 1980s their son, Ramón Sender Barayón, who has lived most of his life in the United States, went on a fact-finding mission to Spain to investigate the mystery surrounding his mother's death. He published the tragic story of her 1936 murder under the title *Death in Zamora.*

37. García, *Las cárceles de Soledad Real,* 149–150.

38. García-Madrid, *Réquiem por la libertad,* 43.

39. Doña, *Desde la noche y la niebla,* 154.

40. Castro, *Una vida para un ideal,* 97.

41. García, *Las cárceles de Soledad Real,* 146.

42. Doña, *Desde la noche y la niebla,* 281.

43. O'Neill, *Una mujer en la guerra de España,* 54.

44. Doña, *Desde la noche y la niebla,* 259.

45. O'Neill, *Una mujer en la guerra de España,* 62.

46. Núñez, *Cárcel de Ventas,* 45.

47. Cuevas, *Cárcel de mujeres, II,* 71.

48. There are two accounts of this affair. Antonia García claims that the Chilean woman was "a lawyer who was going to write a thesis on the prison regimes of all countries." Cuevas, *Cárcel de mujeres, II,* 76. Soledad Real says that she was a journalist writing an article on Franco's prisons. Garcia, *Las cárceles de Soledad Real,* 168. Their accounts do coincide on the details of the episode.

49. For a fascinating and macabre analysis of the Nazi mentality on gender, see Theweleit, *Male Fantasies, vols. 1 and 2.*

50. Malonda, *Aquello sucedío así,* 63.

51. Ibid., 77–78.

52. O'Neill, *Una mujer en la guerra de España,* 77.

53. Ibid., 174.

54. Di Febo, *Resistencia y movimiento de mujeres en España,* 61.

55. Ibid., 60.

56. Cuevas, *Cárcel de mujeres, II,* 18.

57. Ibid., 82.

58. Ibid., 92.

59. Ibid., I, 161.

60. Reproduced in di Febo, *Resistencia y movimiento de mujeres en España,* 101–102.

61. García-Madrid, *Réquiem por la libertad,* 123.

62. *Consejo de la Union de las Mujeres Antifascistas Españolas,* 132.

63. This may be a euphemism for the room where the prisoners waited before being sent to the firing squad. Or the term could be related to the fact that the priests or nuns invariably tried to coerce the inmates into confessing their sins before dying, a tactic which appears to have been largely unsuccessful among the leftist activists.

64. Doña, *Desde la noche y la niebla,* 165–166. See also Romeu Alfaro's account of Julia Conesa, one of the Thirteen Roses, in *El silencio roto,* 267–293.

65. Di Febo describes the term; she also includes a poem that the girls sang about La Pepa. *Resistencia y movimento de mujeres en España,* 96.

66. Cuevas, *Cárcel de mujeres, I,* 64–65.

67. Ibid., 67.

68. Ibid., II, 98–99.

69. Fidalgo, *A Young Mother in Franco's Prisons,* 8–10.

70. García-Madrid herself contracted tuberculosis and was left to die with the terminal patients; probably because she was still in her teens, however, she recovered.

71. García-Madrid, *Réquiem por la libertad,* 113.

72. It was typical, as part of probation, to continue to punish ex-prisoners and others by sending them out of reach of their families and friends. I know of women who were teachers, not activists (though associated by blood or friendship with anti-Franco activists), who were taken out of their urban schools and sent to harsh and isolated mountain villages to teach. The loneliness and the poverty of these primitive locations resulted in an experience that could be equated to a form of prison life.

73. Cuevas, *Cárcel de mujeres, II,* 214.

74. Ibid., 173.

75. García, *Las cárceles de Soledad Real,* 192.

76. O'Neill, *Una mujer en la guerra de España,* 199.

77. Malonda, *Aquello sucedío así,* 158–160.

78. Cuevas, *Cárcel de mujeres, I,* 178–79.

79. Nash, "Two Decades of Women's History in Spain," 382.

9. The Exodus

1. Llorens, *La emigración republicana,* I, 27–28, 39.

2. Giral and Santidrián, *La república en el exilio.* 36–37.

3. The vast majority went to France—some 400,000 to 500,000 between January and February of 1939 alone. There are discrepancies in the figures because some Spaniards returned to Spain soon after their arrival in France; see Wingeate Pike, *Vae victis!* Eduardo Pons Prades claims that 500,000 arrived in France, 75,000 of whom were children, 105,000 women, and 15,000 wounded soldiers. *Republicanos españoles en la segunda guerra mundial,* 35.

The only other alternatives for the refugees were Portugal and North Africa. Those who did cross the border to Portugal were usually sent back to Spain to face a firing squad, given that Salazar's dictatorship was sympathetic to Franco's cause. Soriano, *Exodos,* 21.

Many who entered France were later able to migrate to South America. Spaniards had been entering France since 1936; between 1936 and 1938, Louis Stein documents some 60,000 people who left Spain. The country that welcomed the largest number of exiles was Mexico; Stein believes there were 15,000 to 20,000. *Beyond Death and Exile,* 90. Smaller numbers went to Chile, Cuba, the Dominican Republic, Argentina, Russia, England, Belgium, Switzerland, Venezuela, Bolivia, Central America, Colombia, Ecuador, Panama, Peru, Puerto Rico, Uruguay, Brazil, Canada, and the United States. See Llorens, *La emigración republicana,* for more information. See, also, the testimonies of women in the camps in Medrano, *Nuevas raíces.*

4. Pons Prades claims that there were 80,000 Spaniards in Saint Cyprien, 65,000 in Argeleès-sur-mer, and 35,000 in Le Barcarès. (The figures are very different in Wingeate Pike, *Vae victis!*; see page 55.) The other Spaniards—more than 90,000—were dispersed in camps throughout France. Pons Prades, *Republicanos españoles,* 35. Soriano says that "the men were grouped into concentration camps and the majority of the women and children were distributed in places that were called shelters ['refugios'], disseminated throughout nearly all of France. That implied the painful dispersion of families." *Exodos,* 21.

The same is reflected by Isabel de Palencia in *Smouldering Freedom* (85): "It is only fair to say that the treatment of those women and children, around one hundred and forty thousand in number, did not at first give serious cause for criticism. The sight of such unfortunate, homeless people, the health of many delicate through privation, awoke sympathy in some of the French population to remedy and satisfy their needs. . . . In the men's camps the situation was much worse."

Of the plight of the women who were in prison camps with men, Alberto Fernández says, "The female refugees have had to cohabit in monstrous promiscuity, 'performing their needs' in the middle of the camps, surrounded by other women to try to at least hide their intimate parts from the glances of their male companions in misfortune." *Emigración republicana española,* 9–10.

5. Fernandez, *Emigración republicana española,* 11–12. Women were not usually sent to these camps.

6. Stein, *Beyond Death and Exile,* 69–70.

7. MacMaster, *Spanish Fighters,* 19. Several women speak of the invaluable help they received from the Quakers in France. See Medrano, *Nuevas raíces.*

8. Many had fled out of fear of reprisals, though they had not been responsible for "war crimes." Giral and Santidrián claim that some 200,000 returned once the panic had died down. *La república en el exilio,* 52. Substantial numbers of these people were undoubtedly from the Barcelona area, which had staunchly supported the Republicans and the Left until the bitter end.

9. Although the Franco-German armistice signed in June 1940 required that all anti-Nazi Germans who had fled their country—some of whom had fought in the international Brigades in Spain—be turned over to Hitler, another clause permitted the capture of political undesirables, many of whom were Spaniards. According to Soriano, approximately 7,000 Spaniards died in Nazi camps. *Exodos*, 42. But the figures vary a great deal: many prisoners were executed as soon as they arrived in the camps, before being counted, or their number was given to another prisoner after their death. Javier Alfaya, "Españoles en los campos nazis," *El exilio espanol de 1939* (Madrid: Taurus, 1976), II, 102. See also Roig, *El catalans al campos nazis* and "Mujeres en campos nazis."

10. Alfaya, "Españoles en los campos nazis," 119.

11. Vilanova, *Los olvidados*, 169–172.

12. For further information on international organizations that aided the Spanish refugees, see Macdonald, *Homage to the Spanish Exiles*.

13. Between 1939 and 1949 some 18,000 Spaniards fled to Mexico. Kenny et al., *Inmigrantes y refugiados españoles en México*, 300. Giral and Santidrián claim that altogether some 50,000 Spaniards went to Mexico. *La república en el exilio*, 44.

14. See Lida, *La Casa de España en Mexico*, and Lida and Antonio Matesanz, *El Colegio de Mexico*. For more information on Spanish exiles in Mexico in general, see Fagen, *Exiles and Citizens*.

15. The majority of the prominent writers and artists had been staunch Republicans, and most of them went into exile. The few intellectuals who were sympathetic to the Franco regime were characterized by mediocrity, given their subservience to the religious and political constraints of the dictatorship.

16. Juan Marichal divides the government in exile into four phases: (1) Mexico City and London, 1939–1950; (2) France, 1950–1956; (3) contact with leaders in Spain, 1962–1969; (4) reorganization of parties in Spain, 1969. "Las fases politicas del exilio (1939–1975)," *El exilio español de 1939* 2: 229–236.

17. Palencia, *I Must Have Liberty*, 468. The testimonies of other women who express gratitude to the Mexicans and happiness about their lives in Mexico can be found in Medrano, *Nuevas raíces*.

10. Memory Texts of Exiled Women

1. Stein estimates that some 200,000 to 340,000 had already poured into France from the onset of the war to the end of 1938, including representatives of both sides and those who were neutral. *Beyond Death and Exile*, 6.

2. Mistral, *Exodo;* Kent, *Cuatro años en Paris;* Montseny, *El éxodo, pasión y muerte de españoles en el exilio; Cien días en la vida de una mujer;* and *Seis años de mi vida.*

3. Teresa Gracia, *Las republicanas* (Valencia: Pre-Textos, 1984). Her slim volume ·of poems is entitled *Destierro* (Valencia: Pre-Textos, 1982).

4. María Aurelia Capmany, *La color más azul* (Barcelona: Editorial Planeta, 1984). For more information about the novels written by Spanish women on the subject of the war, see Janet Pérez, "Behind the Lines: The Spanish Civil War and Women Writers," in Pérez and Aycock, *The Spanish Civil War in Literature*, 161–174.

5. Ugarte discusses this concept in *Shifting Ground*. See his Chapter 6, "Exilic Autobiographies."

6. León, *Memoria de la melancolía*, 29.

7. Ibid.

8. Mistral, *Exodo*, 191.

9. Palencia, *Smouldering Freedom*, 64.

10. The Tomás family lived in Mexico until 1975. Immediately after the death of Franco, the survivors, with their children, moved back to their native land.

11. Concha Méndez and her husband, Manuel Altolaguirre, were both active in the vanguard group Generation of 1927, and both were involved in the war effort. They divorced in Mexico; Méndez resided there until her death in 1986.

12. Ulacia Altolaguirre and Méndez, *Memorias habladas, memorias armadas,* 116.

13. De la Mora, *In Place of Splendor,* 42.

14. Diaries, after all, are generally written by young women. Mistral was a young activist, whereas the others were all mature women during the war.

15. According to Stein, for many Spanish men the hardships and battles did not end in 1944. They continued to work in labor camps for the French or Germans, and when they were liberated from the Nazis, they resumed their resistance against Franco. In some cases their underground activity lasted until 1975, when Franco died. *Beyond Death and Exile,* 3–4.

16. Castro, *Una vida para un ideal,* 61.

17. Ulacia Altolaguirre and Méndez, *Memorias habladas, memorias armadas,* 108–109.

18. Ibid., 15.

19. Consuelo García, it should be recalled, does something similar in *Las cárceles de Soledad Real;* though briefly, she also inserts herself into the text in the introduction, when she discusses her reasons for publishing Real's testimony.

20. Kent, *Cuatro años en Paris,* 159.

21. Chapter 1 is divided into four sections: "Four Walls (1940–1941)"; "In the Street (1941–1942)"; "Drops on the Zinc (1942–1943)"; and "Toward Freedom (1943–1944)."

22. Kent, *Cuatro años en Paris,* 125.

23. Ibid., 181–182.

24. Ibid., 181.

25. When I asked Kent if the text is "truly" autobiographical, she responded that she had lived through all of the experiences described in the book. Interview with author, New York, 6 January 1986.

26. Kent, *Cuatro años en Paris,* 100. Curiously, it was in this same arena that Dolores Ibárruri gave a speech in 1938, in which she said, "Spain will never be fascist." Ibárruri, *Speeches and Articles, 1936–1938* (New York: International Publishers, 1938). The book was printed in Moscow.

27. Once again, we are faced with a text that knows no single definition: philosophical treatise, novel, essay, diary, autobiography?

28. This is true of all the women who participated in one way or another in the activities of the Generation of 27. For more information on women writers of the Modernist period, see Levine, Marson, and Waldman, *Spanish Women Writers.*

29. For more information on the Congress of the Association of International Writers in Defence of Culture, see Escolar, *La cultura durante la guerra civil.*

30. León, *Memoria de la melancolía,* 229.

31. Ibid., 216.

32. Ibid., 235.

33. Ibid., 7.

34. Egan, *Patterns of Experience in Autobiography,* 12.

35. Other observations about the autobiographical works of Kent and León (and also those of Doña, García-Madrid, Ibárruri, and de la Mora) can be found in Mangini, "Memories of Resistance."

36. Montseny, *El éxodo, pasión y muerte,* 8.

37. Montseny, *Cien días en la vida de una mujer,* 3.

38. Montseny, *El éxodo, pasión y muerte,* 22.

39. Ibid., 19–20.

40. Ibid., 31.

41. Montseny, *Seis años de mi vida,* 233.

42. Montseny, *Cien días en la vida de una mujer,* 19.

43. Ibid., 10.

44. Silvia Mistral, *Madréporas* (Mexico: A. Finisterre, 1967).

45. Mistral, *Exodo,* 22–24.

46. Ibid., 50.

47. Palencia, *Smouldering Freedom*, 47–48.

48. Palencia, *I Must Have Liberty*, 143–147. Ironically, in spite of Palencia's professional, businesslike way of describing the events of the war and exile, she goes into great detail when she discusses her emotional state on learning of her husband's affair. Most Spaniards of this era would not have broached a subject dealing with sexual matters.

49. Ibid., 462–463.

50. Kent, *Cuatro años en Paris*, 74–75.

51. Quoted in di Febo, *Resistencia y movimiento de mujeres en España*, 107.

52. Mistral, *Exodo*, 95–96.

53. Di Febo, *Resistencia y movimiento de mujeres en España*, 108.

54. Montseny, *El éxodo, pasión y muerte*, 31–32.

55. Ibid., 21.

56. Castro, *Una vida para un ideal*, 115.

57. *Nuevas raíces* includes several testimonies about women's odysseys through France to freedom.

58. MacMaster, *Spanish Fighters*, 121.

59. Ibid., 141.

60. Ibid., 142.

61. Ibid., 153.

62. Ibid., 156.

63. Ibid.

64. Ibid., 195. When I first traveled to Spain in the late 1960s, I found that the situation had not changed a great deal. People were skeptical, suspicious, and fearful that Franco's police might be listening to their conversations. Until the 1970s my friends at the University of Madrid were cautious if more than three of us congregated to speak in the hallways. They said, "More than that is considered a political meeting." Curiously, the specter of the Grand Inquisitors had revisited Spain in 1939, and the blanket of silence and fear had again muffled the entire country for some thirty-five years.

65. In *Cien días en la vida de una mujer*, Montseny describes this period.

66. Montseny, *Seis años de mi vida*, 157. Other oral history accounts of the German occupation allude to this "method" of survival, which was available to women, rarely to men.

67. Ibid., 165.

68. Ibid., 172–73. Montseny suggests that her protest against incarceration saved her life. Maternity is another method women employed to survive; tragically, pregnancy was useless for this purpose to Jewish women.

Epilogue

1. See Castaño, "Women's Studies in Spain," and Nash, "Two Decades of Women's History in Spain," for more information. Both Nash, at the University of Barcelona, and Castaño, at the University of Valencia, have been instrumental in promoting women's studies in Spain.

2. Some of this information was provided to me in December 1993 during an interview in Madrid with María Teresa Gallego Méndez.

Bibliography

Primary Sources

Acklesberg, Martha. *Free Women of Spain: Anarchism and the Struggle for the Emancipation of Women.* Bloomington: Indiana University Press, 1991.

Alcalde, Carmen. *Federica Montseny: Palabra en Rojo y Negro.* Barcelona: Editorial Argos Vergara, 1983.

Alvarez del Vayo, J. *Freedom's Battle.* 2nd ed. New York: Hill and Wang, 1971.

Azaña, Manuel. *Memorias políticas y de guerra.* Mexico: Ediciones Oasis, 1968.

Barbeito, Isabel, ed. *Cárceles y mujeres en el siglo XVII.* Madrid: Editorial Castalia, 1991.

Beevor, Antony. *The Spanish Civil War.* New York: Peter Bedrick Books, 1982.

Benstock, Shari. "The Female Self Engendered: Autobiographical Writing and Theories of Selfhood." *Women's Autobiographies, Women's Studies* 20 (1991): 5–14.

Berenguer, Sara. *Entre el sol y la tormenta.* Barcelona: Seuba Ediciones, 1988.

Bolloten, Burnett. *The Spanish Civil War: Revolution and Counterrevolution.* Chapel Hill: University of North Carolina Press, 1991.

———. *The Spanish Revolution.* Chapel Hill: University of North Carolina Press, 1979.

Borkenau, Franz. *The Spanish Cockpit.* Ann Arbor: University of Michigan Press, 1974.

Brenan, Gerald. *The Spanish Labyrinth.* 8th ed. New York: Cambridge University Press, 1971.

Brodzki, Bella, and Celeste Schenck. *Life/Lines: Theorizing Women's Autobiography.* Ithaca: Cornell University Press, 1988.

Cacho Viu, Vicente. *La Institución Libre de Enseñanza.* Madrid: Ediciones Rialp, 1962.

Callahan, William J. *Church, Politics, and Society in Spain, 1750–1874.* Cambridge, Mass.: Harvard University Press, 1984.

Cambrils, María. *Feminismo socialista.* Valencia: Tipografía "Las Artes," 1925.

Campo Alange, María. *Mi atardecer entre dos mundos.* Barcelona: Editorial Planeta, 1983.

———. *La mujer en España: Cien años de su historia, 1860–1960.* Madrid: Aguilar, 1964.

Campoamor Rodríguez, Clara. *El voto femenino y yo: Mi pecado mortal.* Barcelona: LaSal, Edicions de les Dones, 1981.

Castro, Nieves. *Una vida para un ideal.* Madrid: Ediciones de la Torre, 1981.

Consejo de la Unión de las Mujeres Antifascistas Españolas. n.p.: Consejo Nacional, 1947.

Cora, María Manuela de. *Retaguardia enemiga.* Madrid: Altalena Editores, 1984.

Crispin, John. *Oxford and Cambridge en Madrid: La Residencia de Estudiantes.* Santander: La Isla de los Ratones, 1981.

Crónica de los consejos nacionales de la Sección Femenina. 2 vols. Madrid: FET de la JONS, n.d.

Cuevas Gutiérrez, Tomasa. Cárcel de mujeres. 2 vols. Barcelona: Ediciones Sirocco, 1985.

———. Mujeres de la resistencia. Barcelona: Ediciones Sirocco, 1986.

Diaz, Janet. "Vanguardism, Modernism, and Spanish Women Writers in the Years between the Wars." Siglo XX/20th Century 6.1–2 (1988–89): 40–47.

di Febo, Giuliana. Resistencia y movimiento de mujeres en España, 1936–1976. Barcelona: ICARIA Editorial, 1979.

Doña, Juana. Desde la noche y la niebla (mujeres en las cárceles franquistas). Madrid: Ediciones de la Torre, 1978.

Egan, Susanna. Patterns of Experience in Autobiography. Chapel Hill: University of North Carolina Press, 1984.

Estadísticas básicas de España, 1900–1970. Madrid: Confederación de Cajas de Ahorros, 1975.

Estruch, Joan. "Pasionaria: La verdad sobre Dolores Ibárruri." Historia 16 (Feb. 1986), no. 118: 11–24.

Etchebéhère, Mika. Mi guerra de España. Translated from the French. Barcelona: Plaza y Janés Editores, 1987.

Fagoaga, Concha. La voz y el voto de las mujeres: El sufragismo en España, 1877–1931. Barcelona: Editorial ICARIA, 1985.

Fagoaga, Concha, and Paloma Saavedra. Clara Campoamor: La sufragista española. Madrid: Instituto de la Mujer, 1986.

Falcón, Lidia. Los hijos de los vencidos. Barcelona: Pomaire, 1979.

———, ed. "50 Años de lucha, 1939–1989: Homenaje a las mujeres de la guerra civil española." Poder y Libertad. Special issue (1989).

Fernández, Alberto. Emigración republicana española (1939–1945). Algorta: Zero, 1972.

———. Españoles en la resistencia. Bilbao: Zero, 1973.

Fidalgo, Pilar. A Young Mother in Franco's Prisons. London: United Editorial, 1939.

Fórmica, Mercedes. Visto y vivido. 2nd ed. Barcelona: Editorial Planeta, 1983.

Foronda, Ana María de. Nueve meses con los rojos en Madrid. Avila: Imprenta Católica Sigirano Díaz, 1937.

Fraser, Ronald. Blood of Spain: An Oral History of the Spanish Civil War. New York: Pantheon Books, 1979.

Fredricks, Shirley. "Social and Political Thought of Federica Montseny, Spanish Anarchist, 1923–1937." Ph.D. diss., University of New Mexico, 1972.

Gallego Méndez, María Teresa. Mujer, falange y franquismo. Madrid: Ediciones Taurus, 1983.

García, Consuelo. Las cárceles de Soledad Real. Madrid: Ediciones Alfaguara, 1982.

García, Regina. Yo he sido marxista. Madrid: Editorial Nacional, 1946.

García Durán, Juan. La guerra civil española: Fuentes (archivos, bibliografía y filmografía). Barcelona: Editorial Crítica, 1985.

García-Madrid, Angeles. Réquiem por la libertad. Madrid: Copiasol, 1982.

García Méndez, Esperanza. La actuación de la mujer en las cortes de la II República. Madrid: Ministry of Culture, 1979.

Gilligan, Carol. In a Different Voice. Cambridge, Mass.: Harvard University Press, 1982.

Giral, Francisco, and Pedro Santidrián. La república en el exilio. Madrid: Ediciones 99, 1977.

Gómez Molleda, María Dolores. Los reformadores de la España contemporánea. Madrid: Essic, 1966.

Grazia, Victoria de. How Fascism Ruled Women: Italy, 1922–1945. Berkeley: University of California Press, 1992.

Harlow, Barbara. Resistance Literature. New York: Methuen, 1987.

Higonnet, Margaret R., et al. Behind the Lines: Gender and the Two World Wars. New Haven: Yale University Press, 1987.

Ibárruri, Dolores. *They Shall Not Pass: The Autobiography of La Pasionaria.* New York: International Publishers, 1966.

Ibárruri, Dolores, et al. *Guerra y revolución en España, 1936–1939.* 4 vols. Moscow: Editorial Progreso, 1966.

Iturbe, Lola. *La mujer en la lucha social: La guerra civil de España.* Mexico: Editores Mexicanos Unidos, 1974.

Jackson, Gabriel. *Aproximación a la España contemporánea, 1898–1975.* Barcelona: Ediciones Grijalbo, 1980.

———. *A Concise History of the Spanish Civil War.* London: Thames and Hudson, 1974.

———. *The Spanish Civil War.* New York: New York Times Company, 1972.

———. *The Spanish Republic and the Civil War, 1931–1939.* Princeton: Princeton University Press, 1965.

Jaraiz Franco, Pilar. *Historia de una disidencia.* Barcelona: Editorial Planeta, 1983.

Jelinek, Estelle C., ed. *Women's Autobiography.* Bloomington: Indiana University Press, 1980.

Jellinek, Frank. *The Civil War in Spain.* London: Victor Gollancz, 1938.

Jiménez Fraud, Alberto. *Historia de la Universidad Española.* Madrid: Alianza Editorial, 1971.

Kaminski, H. E. *Los de Barcelona.* Barcelona: Ediciones del Cotal, 1976.

Kent, Victoria. *Cuatro años en París (1940–1944).* Buenos Aires: Sur, 1947.

———. "Victoria Kent: Una experiencia penitenciaria." *Tiempo de historia* 17 (Apr. 1976): 4–10.

Kern, Robert W. *Red Years/Black Years: A Political History of Spanish Anarchism, 1911–1937.* Philadelphia: Institute for the study of Human Issues, 1978.

Kirkpatrick, Susan. *Las Románticas: Women Writers and Subjectivity in Spain, 1835–1850.* Berkeley: University of California Press, 1989.

Lafitte, María. *See* Campo Alange, María.

Lejárraga, María. *See* Martínez Sierra, María.

León, María Teresa. *Memoria de la melancolía.* Buenos Aires: Editorial Losada, 1970.

Lerner, Gerda. *The Creation of Patriarchy.* New York: Oxford University Press, 1986.

———. *The Majority Finds Its Past.* New York: Oxford University Press, 1979.

Lifton, Robert Jay. *The Broken Connection.* New York: Simon and Schuster, 1979.

———. *History and Human Survival.* New York: Random House, 1970.

Llorens, Vicente. *La emigración republicana,* vol. 1. Madrid: Taurus Ediciones, 1976.

López-Morillas, Juan. *The Krausist Movement and Ideological Change in Spain, 1854–1874.* Cambridge: Cambridge University Press, 1981.

Macdonald, Nancy. *Homage to the Spanish Exiles: Voices of the Spanish Civil War.* New York: Human Sciences Press, 1987.

MacMaster, Neil. *Spanish Fighters: An Oral History of Civil War and Exile.* New York: St. Martin's Press, 1990.

Maillard, M. Luisa. *Associación Española de Mujeres Universitarias, 1920–1990.* Madrid: AEMU and Instituto de la Mujer, 1990.

Malonda, Angeles. *Aquello sucedió así.* Madrid: Acofarma, 1983.

Mangini, Shirley. "Mujeres en la guerra civil." *La esfera, El mundo,* 22 Jan. 1994, pp. 2–3.

Marmo Mullaney, Marie. *Revolutionary Women: Gender and the Socialist Revolutionary Role.* New York: Praeger Publishers, 1983.

Marola (pseud.). *Prisionera del Soriet.* San Sebastián: Editorial Española, 1938.

Martínez Sierra, María. *Gregorio y yo.* Mexico: Biografías Gandesa, 1953.

———. *Una mujer por caminos de España.* Buenos Aires: Editorial Losada, 1952.

———. *Una mujer por caminos de España.* Intro. Alda Blanco. Madrid: Editorial Castalia, 1989.

Martín Gaite, Carmen. *Usos amorosos de la postguerra española.* Barcelona: Editorial Anagrama, 1987.

Medio, Dolores. *Atrapados en la ratonera: Memorias de una novelista.* Madrid: Editorial Alce, 1980.

Medrano, Guillermina, ed. *Nuevas raíces: Testimonios de mujeres españolas en el exilio.* Mexico City: Editorial Joaquin Mortiz, 1993.

Mistral, Silvia. *Exodo, (diario de una refugiada española).* Mexico: Editorial Minerva, 1941.

Montseny, Federica. *Cien días en la vida de una mujer.* Toulouse: Ediciones Universo, 1949.

———. *El éxodo, pasión y muerte de los españoles en el exilio.* Barcelona: Galba Ediciones, 1977.

———. *Jaque a Franco.* Toulouse: Ediciones Universo, 1950.

———. *La indomable.* Edited by María Alicia Langa Laorga. Madrid: Editorial Castalia, 1991.

———. *Seis años de mi vida (1939–1945).* Barcelona: Galba Ediciones, 1978.

Mora, Constancia de la. *In Place of Splendor: The Autobiography of a Spanish Woman.* New York: Harcourt, Brace, 1939.

Las mujeres y la guerra civil española. Madrid: Ministry of Culture, 1989.

Mullaney, Maria Marmo. *Revolutionary Women: Gender and the Socialist Revolutionary Role.* New York: Praeger Publishers, 1983.

Nash, Mary. "Federica Montseny: Luchadora, dirigente anarquista y feminista." *La esfera, El mundo,* 22 Jan. 1994, p.4.

———. *Mujer, familia y trabajo en España, 1875–1936.* Barcelona: Anthropos, 1983.

———. *Mujer y movimiento obrero en España, 1931–1939.* Barcelona: Editorial Fontamara, 1981.

———. "Two Decades of Women's History in Spain." In Karen Offen et al., *Writing Women's History: International Perspectives.* Bloomington: Indiana University Press, 1991.

Nash, Mary, ed. *Las mujeres en la guerra civil.* Madrid: Ministry of Culture, 1989.

———. *Mujeres Libres: España, 1936–1939.* Barcelona: Tusquets Editor, 1975.

Nelken, Margarita. *La condición social de la mujer en España.* Barcelona: Editorial Minerva, 1921?

Nicholson, Linda J., ed. *Feminism/Postmodernism.* New York: Routledge, 1990.

Núñez, Mercedes. *Cárcel de Ventas.* Paris: Editions de la Librairie du Globe, 1967.

O'Connor, Patricia W. *Gregorio and María Martínez Sierra.* Boston: G. K. Hall, 1977.

Olney, James, ed. *Autobiography: Essays Theoretical and Critical.* Princeton: Princeton University Press, 1980.

O'Neill, Carlota. *Una mujer en la guerra de España.* Madrid: Ediciones Turner, 1979.

Ortega y Gasset, José. *Ideas y Creencias.* 10th ed. Madrid: Revista de Occidente, 1970.

Palencia, Isabel de. *I Must Have Liberty.* New York: Longmans, Green, 1940.

———. *Smouldering Freedom: The Story of the Republicans in Exile.* New York: Longmans, Green, 1945.

Payne, Stanley. *The Franco Regime, 1936–1939.* Madison: University of Wisconsin Press, 1987.

———. *Spanish Catholicism: An Historical Overview.* Madison: University of Wisconsin Press, 1984.

———. *The Spanish Revolution.* Surrey: Unwin Bros., 1970.

Perinet, Adolfo, and María Isabel Marrades. *Mujer, prensa y sociedad en España, 1800–1939.* Madrid: Centro de Investigaciones Sociológicas, 1980.

Perry, Mary Elizabeth. *Gender and Disorder in Early Modern Seville.* Princeton: Princeton University Press, 1990.

Pons Prades, Eduardo. *Republicanos españoles en la segunda guerra mundial.* Barcelona: Editorial Planeta, 1975.

Primo de Rivera, Pilar. *Recuerdos de una vida.* 3rd ed. Madrid: Ediciones DYRSA, 1983.

Queipo de Llano, Rosario. *De la cheka de Atadell a la prisión de Alacuas*. Valladolid: Librería Santarén, 1959.

Rodrigo, Antonina. *Mujeres en España: Las silenciadas*. Barcelona: Plaza y Janés, 1979.

Romeu Alfaro, Fernanda. *El silencio roto: Mujeres contra el Franquisimo*. Oviedo: Gráficas Summa, 1994.

Ruiz Miguel, Alfonso. "La junta para la ampliación de Estudios." *Historia 16* (May 1980): 85–93.

Salas Larrazábal, Ramón. *Los datos exactos de la guerra civil*. Madrid: Colección Drácena, 1980.

Scanlon, Geraldine. *La polémica feminista en la España contemporánea (1868–1974)*. Madrid: Siglo XXI, 1976.

Sender Barayón, Ramón. *Death in Zamora*. Albuquerque: University of New Mexico Press, 1989.

Silva, Josefina de. *Nosotros, los evacuados*. Barcelona: Plaza y Janés, 1978.

Simón Palmer, María del Carmen. "Escritoras españolas del siglo XIX o el miedo a la marginación." *Anales de la literatura espanola, Universidad de Alicante* 2 (1983): 477–490.

Slaughter, Jane, and Robert Kern, eds. *European Women on the Left*. Westport, Conn.: Greenwood Press, 1981.

Smith, Sidonie. *A Poetics of Women's Autobiography*. Bloomington: Indiana University Press, 1987.

———. *Subjectivity, Identity and the Body: Women's Autobiographical Practices in the Twentieth Century*. Bloomington: Indiana University Press, 1993.

Smith, Sidonie, and Julia Watson, eds. *De/Colonizing the Subject: The Politics of Gender in Women's Autobiography*. Minneapolis: University of Minnesota Press, 1992.

Soriano, Antonio. *Exodos: Historia oral del exilio republicano en Francia, 1939–1945*. Barcelona: Editorial Crítica, 1989.

Spence, Jonathan. *The Death of Woman Wang*. Middlesex: Penguin Books, 1984.

Spivak, Gayatri Chakravorty. *In Other Worlds*. New York: Methuen, 1987.

Stanton, Domna C. *The Female Autograph*. Chicago: University of Chicago Press, 1984.

Stein, Louis. *Beyond Death and Exile: Spanish Republicans in France, 1939–1955*. Cambridge, Mass.: Harvard University Press, 1979.

Suárez, Angel, and Equipo 36. *Libro blanco sobre las cárceles franquistas*. Paris: Ruedo Ibérico, 1976.

Thomas, Hugh. *The Spanish Civil War*. New York: Harper and Row, 1961.

Torre, Matilde de la. *Mares en la sombra*. Paris: Ediciones Iberoamericanas "Norte," 1940.

Trejo, Blanca Lidia. *Lo que vi en España, episodios de la guerra*. Mexico City: Polis, 1940.

Ulacia Altolaguirre, Paloma, and Concha Méndez. *Memorias habladas, memorias armadas*. Madrid: Mondadori España, 1990.

Vilanova, Antonio. *Los olvidados: Los exiliados españoles en la segunda guerra mundial*. Paris: Ruedo Ibérico, 1969.

Whealey, Robert H. *Hitler and Spain: The Nazi Role in the Spanish Civil War, 1936–1939*. Lexington: University Press of Kentucky, 1989.

Wingeate Pike, David. *Vae victis! Los republicanos españoles refugiados en Francia, 1939–1944*. Paris: Ruedo Ibérico, 1969.

Zulueta, Carmen de. *Misioneras, feministas, educadoras: Historia del Instituto Internacional*. Madrid: Editorial Castalia, 1984.

Secondary Sources

ABC, 1936–1939. Doble diario de la guerra civil. Madrid: Editorial Prensa Española, 1979.

Abella, Rafael. *La vida cotidiana durante la guerra civil (la España nacional)*. Barcelona: Editorial Planeta, 1973.

Abellán, José Luis, ed. *El exilio español de 1939.* 6 vols. Madrid: Taurus Ediciones, 1976.

Aguilar, Isabel Calvo de. *Antología biográfica de escritoras españolas.* Madrid: Biblioteca Nueva, 1954.

Alba, Victor. *Historia social de la mujer.* Barcelona: Plaza y Janés, 1974.

Albert Robatto, Matilde. *Rosalía de Castro y la condición femenina.* Madrid: Partenón, 1981.

Alcalde, Carmen. *La mujer en la guerra civil española.* Madrid: Editorial Cambio 16, 1976.

Alcobendas Tirado, María Pilar. *Datos sobre el trabajo de la mujer en España.* Madrid: Centro de Investigaciones Sociológicas, 1983.

Aldaraca, Bridget, "El angel del hogar: The Cult of Domesticity in Nineteenth-Century Spain." In G. Mora and K.S. Van Hooft, eds., *Theory and Practice of Feminist Literary Criticism,* 62–87. Ypsilante, Mich.: Bilingual Press, 1982.

Aldgate, Anthony. *Cinema and History: British Newsreels and the Spanish Civil War.* London: Scholar, 1979.

Alonso Tejada, L. *La represión sexual en la España de Franco.* Barcelona: Luis de Caralt Editor, 1977.

Amelang, James, and Mary Nash. *Historia y género: Las mujeres en la Europa moderna y contemporánea.* Valencia: Edicions Instituto Alfons el Magnànim, 1990.

Anderson, Bonnie S., and Judith P. Zinsser, *A History of Their Own: Women in Europe. vol. 1, From Prehistory to the Present.* New York: Harper and Row, 1988.

Aranguren, José Luis. *Erotismo y liberación de la mujer.* Barcelona: Ariel, 1972.

Arconada, Cesar M. *La guerra en Asturias (crónicas y romances).* Madrid: Editorial Ayuso, 1979.

Arenal, Concepción. *Cuadernos de guerra.* Buenos Aires: Editorial Nova, 1942.

———. *La emancipación de la mujer en España.* Madrid: Júcar, 1974.

———. *The Woman Question in Europe.* New York: Putnam Sons, 1884.

Arenal, Electa, and Stacey Schlau. *Untold Sisters: Hispanic Nuns in Their Own Works.* Albuquerque: University of New Mexico Press, 1989.

Armangué, Josefa. *Una família en exili: Memòries (1935–1965).* Barcelona: Curiel, 1981.

Artís-Gener, Aveli. *La diáspora republicana.* Barcelona: Editorial Euros, 1976.

Atholl, Katharine Marjory. *Searchlight on Spain.* London: Penguin Books, 1938.

Barea, Arturo. *The Forging of a Rebel.* New York: Viking Press, 1972.

Barthes, Roland. *Roland Barthes by Roland Barthes.* Translated by Richard Howard. New York: Noonday Press, 1977.

Benería, Lourdes. *Mujer, economía y patriarcado durante la España franquista.* Barcelona: Editorial Anagrama, 1977.

Benstock, Shari. *The Private Self.* Chapel Hill: University of North Carolina Press, 1988.

Benstock, Shari, ed. *Feminist Issues in Literary Scholarship.* Bloomington: Indiana University Press, 1987.

Berkin, Carol R., and Clara M. Lovett. *Women, War, and Revolution.* New York: Holmes and Meier Publishers, 1980.

Bernis, Cristina, et al. *Los estudios sobre la mujer: De la investigación a la Docencia.* Madrid: Ediciones de la Universidad Autónoma de Madrid, 1991.

Bertrand de Muñoz, Maryse. *La guerra civil española en la novela: Bibliografía comentada.* Madrid: José Porrúa Turanzas, 1982.

Bibliografía de la guerra de España, 1936–1939. Madrid: University of Madrid, 1966.

Bingham de Urquidi, Mary. *Misericordia en Madrid.* Mexico: B. Costa-Amic, 1975.

Bizcarrondo, Marta, ed. *Octubre del 34: Reflexiones sobre una revolución.* Madrid: Editorial Ayuso, 1977.

Blanc, Felicidad. *Espejo de sombras.* Barcelona: Editorial Argos Vergara, 1977.

Blasco, Sofía. *Peuple d'Espagne: Journal de guerre de "La Madrecita."* Paris: N R C, 1983.

Bofill, Mireia, et al. *La mujer en España.* Barcelona: Ediciones de Cultura Popular, 1967.

Borderías, Cristina. "Feminist Studies and Research in Spain." In *Women's Studies, Concept and Reality.* Brussels: Les Cahiers du Grif, 1989.

Borregón Ribes, Vicente. *La emigración española a México.* Vigo: Premio Nacional Marvá, 1951.

Borreguero, María Concepción, ed. *La mujer española de la tradición a la modernidad (1960–1980).* Madrid: Editorial Tecnos, 1986.

Boxer, C. R. *Mary and Misogyny.* London: Duckworth, 1975.

Boxer, Marilyn, and Jean Quataert. *Socialist Women.* New York: Elsevier North-Holland, 1978.

Bravo-Villasante, Carmen. *Vida y obra de Emilia Pardo Bazán.* Madrid: Revista de Occidente, 1962.

Brome, Vincent. *The International Brigades.* New York: Morrow, 1966.

Broué, Pierre, and Emile Témine. *The Revolution and the Civil War in Spain.* Cambridge; Mass.: MIT Press, 1970.

Brown, Cheryl L., and Karen Olson. *Feminist Criticism: Essays on Theory, Poetry and Prose.* Metuchen, N.J.: Scarecrow Press, 1978.

Brown, Joan L., ed. *Women Writers of Contemporary Spain: Exiles in the Homeland.* Cranbury, N.J.: Associated University Presses, 1991.

Bruss, Elizabeth W. *Autobiographical Acts.* Baltimore: Johns Hopkins University Press, 1976.

Burgos, Carmen de. *Misión social de la mujer.* Bilbao: SOCIEDAD "El Sitio," 1911.

———. *La mujer en España.* Valencia: Editorial Sempere, 1906.

———. *La mujer moderna y sus derechos.* Valencia: Editorial Sempere, 1927.

Butler, Judith, and Joan W. Scott. *Gender Trouble: Feminism and the Subversion of Identity.* New York: Routledge, 1990.

Butler, Judith, and Joan W. Scott, eds. *Feminists Theorize the Political.* New York: Routledge, 1992.

Cabanellas, Guillermo. *La guerra civil y la victoria.* Madrid: Ediciones Giner, 1978.

Calderón, Carmen. *Matilde de la Torre y su época.* Santander: Ediciones Tantín, 1984.

Campo Alange, María. *Concepción Arenal, 1820–1893.* Madrid: Revista de Occidente, 1973.

Campoamor, Clara. *Le Révolution espagnole vue par une républicaine.* Paris: Plon, 1937.

Capel, Rosa María. *El sufragio femenino en la Segunda República.* Granada: University of Granada, 1975.

———. *El trabajo y la educación de la mujer en España (1900–1930).* Madrid: Ministry of Culture, 1982.

Capel, Rosa María, and Julio Iglesias de Ussel. *Mujer española y sociedad: Bibliografía (1900–1984).* Madrid: Instituto de la Mujer, 1984.

Capmany, María Aurelia, and Carmen Alcalde. *El feminismo ibérico.* Barcelona: Oilos-Tau, 1970.

Carabantes, Andrés, and Eusebio Cimorra. *Un mito llamado Pasionaria.* Barcelona: Editorial Planeta, 1982.

Carr, Raymond. *The Republic and the Civil War in Spain.* London: Macmillan, 1971.

Carroll, Berenice A. *Liberating Women's History.* Urbana: University of Illinois, 1976.

Casares, María. *Residente privilegiada.* Barcelona: Editorial Argos Vergara, 1981.

Castaño, Lola. *Estudios de las mujeres en las universidades españolas: Década de los años 80.* Valencia: Nau LLibres, 1992.

———. "Women's Studies in Spain." *Women's Studies Quarterly* (Fall/Winter 1992): 127–135.

Castells, Andreu. *Las brigadas internacionales de la guerra de España.* Barcelona: Ariel, 1974.

Castillo, Isabel del. *El incendio: Ideas y recuerdos.* Buenos Aires: Americalee, 1954.

Catalá, Neus. *De la resistencia a la deportación.* Barcelona: ADGENA, 1984.

Centre d'investigacio histórica de la Dona: Memoria, 1983–1986. Barcelona: University of Barcelona, 1986.

Cierva, Ricardo de la. *Bibliografía general sobre la guerra de España y sus antecedentes históricos.* Madrid: General Technical Secretariat of the Ministry of Information and Tourism, 1968.

Cincuenta aniversario del exilio español. Madrid: Editorial Pablo Iglesias, 1989.

Ciplijauskaité, Biruté. *La novela femenina contemporánea (1970–1985).* Barcelona: Editorial Anthropos, 1988.

Colodny, Robert G. *Spain: The Glory and the Tragedy.* New York: Humanities Press, 1970.

Comaposada, Mercedes. *Esquemas.* Barcelona: Publicaciones Mujeres Libres.

Conde, Carmen. *Poesía feminina española (1939–1950).* Barcelona: Bruguera, 1967.

———. *Por el camino viendo sus orillas.* Barcelona: Plaza y Janés Editores, 1986.

Cooke, Miriam, and Angela Woolacott. *Gendering War Talk.* Princeton: Princeton University Press, 1993.

Cortada, James W., ed. *Historical Dictionary of the Spanish Civil War, 1936–1939.* Westport, Conn.: Greenwood Press, 1982.

Cott, Nancy F. *The Bonds of Womanhood.* New Haven: Yale University Press, 1977.

———. *The Grounding of Modern Feminism.* New Haven: Yale University Press, 1987.

Cuadernos bibliográficos de la guerra de España (1936–1939): Memorias, vols. 1–3. Madrid: University of Madrid, 1967–1969.

Cuadernos bibliográficos del Instituto de la Mujer. Madrid: Instituto de la Mujer, 1989.

Davies, Catherine. "Feminist Writers in Spain since 1900: From Political Strategy to Personal Inquiry." In Helena Forsas-Scott, ed., *Textual Liberation: European Feminist Writing in the Twentieth Century.* New York: Routledge, Chapman and Hall, 1991.

Davies, Catherine, ed. *Women Writers In Twentieth-Century Spain and Spanish America.* Lampeter, Wales: Edwin Mellen Press, 1993.

de Man, Paul. "Autobiography as Defacement." *Modern Language Notes* 94 (Dec. 1979): 919–930.

Derrida, Jacques. *Mémoires for Paul de Man.* New York: Columbia University Press, 1986.

Díaz Garrido, María del Carmen. *Los años únicos (andanzas de una niña en el Madrid rojo).* Madrid: Prensa Española, 1972.

Díaz Plaja, Fernando. *La España política del siglo XX.* Madrid: Plaza y Janés, 1972.

———. *La guerra de España en sus documentos.* Madrid: SARPE, 1986.

Díaz Sánchez, Pilar, and Pilar Domínguez Parts. "Las mujeres en la historia de España: Siglos XVII–XX." *Bibliografía comentada.* Madrid: Instituto de la Mujer, 1988.

di Febo, Giuliana. *L'altra meta della Spagna: Dalla lotta antifranchista al movimento femminista, 1940–1977.* Naples: Liguori, 1980.

Dinnerstein, Dorothy. *The Mermaid and the Minotaur: Sexual Arrangements and Human Malaise.* New York: Harper and Row, 1976.

Doña, Juana. *Gente de abajo.* Madrid: A Z Ediciones, 1992.

La Dona: Repertori bibliografic, 1970–1984: Seminari d'estudis de la dona. Barcelona: Department of Sociology, Autonomous University of Barcelona, 1986.

Duby, Georges, and Michelle Perrot. Historia de las mujeres. 5 vols. Madrid: Taurus, 1993.

Dumbach, Annette E., and Jud Newborn. Shattering the German Night. Boston: Little, Brown, 1986.

Durán, María, Angeles. El ama de casa: Crítica política de la economía doméstica. Madrid: Zero, 1978.

———. Desigualdad social y enfermedad. Madrid: Editorial Tecnos, 1983.

———. El trabajo de la mujer en España: Un estudio sociológico. Madrid: Editorial Tecnos, 1972.

Durán, María Angeles, et al. Mujer y sociedad en España, 1700–1975. Madrid: Ministry of Culture, 1982.

Durán, María Angeles, ed. Liberación y utopia. Madrid: Akal, 1982.

———. La mujer en el mundo contemporáneo. Madrid: Autonomous University of Madrid, 1981.

———. Las mujeres medievales y su ámbito jurídico: Actas de las Segundas Jornadas de Investigación Interdisciplinaria. Madrid: Autonomous University of Madrid, 1983.

———. Nuevas perspectivas sobre la mujer. Madrid: Autonomous University of Madrid, 1984.

Eakin, John Paul. Fictions in Autobiography: Studies in the Art of Self-Invention. Princeton: Princeton University Press, 1985.

Ehrenburg, Iliá. España república de trabajadores. 2nd ed. Barcelona: Editorial Crítica, 1976.

Elbaz, Robert. The Changing Nature of the Self. London: Croom Helm, 1988.

Ellwood, Sheelagh. Prietas las filas: Historia de la Falange española, 1933–1983. Barcelona: Editorial Crítica, 1984.

Elshtain, Jean Bethke. Women and War. New York: Basic Books, 1987.

Enciso, María. Europa fugitiva: 30 estampas de guerra. Baranquilla: Litografía Barranquilla, 1941.

Escolar, Hipólito. La cultura durante la guerra civil. Madrid: Editorial Alhambra, 1987.

Espina, Concha. Esclavitud y libertad; Diario de una prisionera. Valladolid: Ediciones Reconquista, 1938.

Estivill, Angel. Lina Odena: La gran heroína de las juventudes revolucionarias de España. 3rd ed. Barcelona: Editorial Maucci, c. 1936.

Fagen, Patricia. Exiles and Citizens. Austin: University of Texas Press, 1973.

Falcón, Lidia. Mujer y sociedad: Análisis de un fenómeno reaccionario. Barcelona: Editorial Fontanella, 1973.

Federn, Etta. Mujeres de las revoluciones. Barcelona: Mujeres Libres, 1938.

Felman, Shoshana, and Dori Laub. Testimony: Crises of Witnessing in Literature, Psychoanalysis, and History. New York: Routledge, 1992.

Fernández, James. Apology to Apostrophe: Autobiography and the Rhetoric of Self-Representation in Spain. Durham, N.C.: Duke University Press, 1992.

Fernández Valentina. La resistencia interior en la España de Franco. Madrid: Editorial Istmo, 1981.

Fernández Quintanilla, Paloma. Mujeres de Madrid. Madrid: Avapiés, 1984.

———. La mujer ilustrada en la España del s. XVIII. Madrid: Ministry of Culture, 1987.

Fleishman, Avrom. Figures of Autobiography. Berkeley: University of California Press, 1983.

Flynn, Elizabeth A., and Patrocinio P. Schweickart. Gender and Reading: Essays on Readers, Texts, and Contexts. Baltimore: Johns Hopkins University Press, 1986.

Folguera, Pilar. El feminismo en España: Dos siglos de historia. Madrid: Editorial Pablo Iglesias, 1988.

Folguera, Pilar, ed. *La mujer en la historia de España (siglos XVI–XX)*. Madrid: Autonomous University of Madrid, 1984.

Foucault, Michel. *Discipline and Punish: The Birth of the Prison*. Translated by Alan Sheridan. New York: Pantheon Books, 1977.

Fourcade, Marie-Madeleine. *Noah's Ark*. London: George Allen and Unwin, 1973.

Franco, Gloria. *La incorporación de la mujer a la administración del estado, municipios y diputaciones, 1918–1936*. Madrid: General Directorate of Youth and Sociocultural Promotion, 1981.

Francos Rodríguez, José. *La mujer y la política españolas*. Madrid: Librería de los Sucesores de Hernando, 1920.

Fraser, Ronald. *In Hiding: The Ordeal of Manuel Cortés*. New York: Pantheon Books, 1979.

Friedman, Ellen G. "El estatus jurídico de la mujer castellana durante el Antiguo Régimen." In *Ordenamiento jurídico y realidad social de las mujeres, S. XVI–XX*. Madrid: Autonomous University of Madrid, 1986.

Fuyola, Encarnación. *Mujeres antifascistas: Su trabajo y su organización*. Valencia: Ediciones de las Mujeres Antifascistas.

Fyrth, John. *The Signal Was Spain: The Spanish Aid Movement in Britain, 1936–1939*. New York: St. Martin's Press, 1986.

Galerstein, Carolyn L., ed. *Women Writers of Spain: An Annotated Bio-Bibliographical Guide*. Westport, Conn.: Greenwood Press, 1986.

García de León, María Antonia. *Las elites femeninas españolas: Una investigación sociológica*. Madrid: Queimada, 1982.

García Durán, Juan. *La guerra civil española: Fuentes (archivos, bibliografía y filmografía)*. Barcelona: Editorial Crítica, 1985.

García Iglesias, Sara. *Exilio*. Mexico: Fondo de Cultura, 1954.

García Luis, Ricardo, and Juan Manuel Torres Vera. *Vallehermoso "El Fogueo,": Toma de conciencia popular, resistencia y represión (1930–1942)*. Santa Cruz de Tenerife, Canary Islands: Ediciones del Centro, n.d.

García-Nieto París, María Carmen, ed. *Ordenamiento jurídico y realidad social de las mujeres: Actas de las Cuartas Jornadas de Investigación Interdisciplinaria*. Madrid: Autonomous University of Madrid, 1986.

García-Nieto, María Carmen, and Javier M. Donézar. *Guerra civil española, 1936–1939*. Madrid: Ediciones Aula Abierta, 1982.

García Oliveros, Leonor. *Recuerdos de lucha y resistencia*. Madrid: Author's edition, 1989.

Gil, Felisa. *¿Qué habéis hecho de España? Contra la traición y sus cómplices*. Mexico City: Artes Gráficas V. Venero, 1954.

Gilbert, Sandra M., and Susan Gubar. *The Madwoman in the Attic: The Woman Writer and the Nineteenth-Century Literary Imagination*. New Haven: Yale University Press, 1984.

———. *No Man's Land*. Vol. 1, *The War of the Words*. New Haven: Yale University Press, 1987.

———. *No Man's Land:* Vol. 2, *Sexchanges*. New Haven: Yale University Press, 1988.

Gilman, Stephen. *The Spain of Fernando de Rojas: The Intellectual and Social Landscape "La Celestina."* Princeton: Princeton University Press, 1972.

Giménez Caballero, E. *Los secretos de la Falange*. Barcelona: Yunque, 1939.

Giral, Francisco, and Pedro Santidrián. *La república en el exilio*. Madrid: Ediciones 99, 1977.

Gluck, Sherna Berger. *Rosie the Riveter Revisited: Women, the War, and Social Change*. Boston: Twayne Publishers, 1987.

Gluck, Sherna, and Daphne Patai, eds. *Women's Words*. New York: Routledge, 1991.

Goldman, Emma. *Correspondencia concerniente a la actuación anarquista en la* guerra civil española. Ann Arbor: University of Michigan Press, 1937.

——. My Second Visit to Spain. Ann Arbor: University of Michigan Press, 1937.

González, Anabel. El feminismo en España, hoy. Bilbao: Zero, 1979.

Gonzáles, Anabel, et al. Los orígenes del feminismo en España. Madrid: Zero, 1980.

González, María Jośe. La nueva historia: Mujer. Málaga: Editorial Atenea Universidad, 1991.

González Martínez, Pilar. Aporías de una mujer: Emilia Pardo Bazán. Madrid: Siglo XXI, 1988.

González Muñiz, Miguel Angel. Problemas de la Segunda República. Madrid: Ediciones Júcar, 1974.

Greene, Gayle, and Coppélia Kahn. Making a Difference: Feminist Literary Criticism. New York: Routledge, Chapman and Hall, 1985.

Grimau, Carmen. El cartel republicano en la guerra civil. Madrid: Ediciones Cátedra, 1979.

"La guerra civil." Historia 16, no. 1–24. Collection of issues on civil war.

La guerra civil española. Madrid: Ministry of Culture, 1983.

Gustavo, Soledad. La sociedad futura. Barcelona: Ediciones de La revista blanca, 1932.

Guttman, Allen. The Wound in the Heart: America and the Spanish Civil War. New York: Free Press of Glencoe, 1962.

Hayton-Keeva, Sally, ed. Valiant Women in War and Exile. San Francisco: City Lights Books, 1987.

Heilbrun, Carolyn G. Writing a Woman's Life. New York: Ballantine Books, 1988.

Hernández Maldonado, Loren. "Antes que el fuego se apague." Unpublished. Madrid: Fundación de Pablo Iglesias, n.d.

Hildegart. La rebeldía sexual de la juventud. 2nd ed. Barcelona: Editorial Anagrama, 1977.

Ibárruri, Dolores. Memorias de Pasionaria, 1939–1977: Me faltaba España. Barcelona: Editorial Planeta, 1984.

——. A las mujeres madrileñas. Madrid: Ediciones del Partido Comunista.

——. Pasionaria: Memoria gráfica. Madrid: Ediciones P C E, 1985.

——. The Women Want a People's Peace. New York: Worker's Library, 1941.

Ibárruri, Dolores, et al. Lina Odena, heroina del pueblo. Madrid: Ediciones Euro-America, 1936.

Iglesias de Ussel, J. Elementos para el estudio de la mujer en la sociedad española, 1939–1980. Madrid: Subdirección General de la Mujer, 1980.

International Brigade Memorial Archive Catalogue, 1986. London: Marx Memorial Library, 1986.

Izquierdo, Justo Vila. Extremadura: La guerra civil. 2nd ed. Badajoz, Spain: Universitas Editorial, 1984.

Jancar, Barbara Wolfe. Women under Communism. Baltimore: Johns Hopkins University Press, 1978.

Janés, Clara, ed. Las primeras poetisas en lengua castellana. Madrid: Editorial Ayuso, 1986.

Johnston, Verle B. Legions of Babel: The International Brigades in the Spanish Civil War. University Park: Pennsylvania State University, 1967.

Kaplan, Temma. Anarchists of Andalusia, 1868–1903. Princeton: Princeton University Press, 1977.

——. "Other Scenarios: Women and Spanish Anarchism." In Becoming Visible: Women in European History. New York: Houghton Mifflin, 1977.

——. "Spanish Anarchism and Women's Liberation." Journal of Contemporary History 6 (1971): 101–110.

Kauffman, Linda, ed. Gender and Theory: Dialogues on Feminist Criticism. New York: Basil Blackwell, 1989.

Keefe Ugalde, Sharon. Conversaciones y poemas: La nueva poesía femenina española *en castellano.* Madrid: Siglo XXI de España Editores, 1991.

Kenny, Michael, et al. *Inmigrantes y refugiados españoles en México (siglo XX).* Mexico: Ediciones de la Casa Chata, 1979.

Kern, Robert W., ed. *Historical Dictionary of Modern Spain.* Westport, Conn.: Greenwood Press, 1990.

Kershner, Howard E. *Quaker Service in Modern War.* New York: Prentice-Hall, 1950.

Kirkpatrick, Susan, ed. *Antología poética de escritoras del siglo XIX.* Madrid: Castalia/ Instituto de la Mujer, 1993.

Kisch, Richard. *They Shall Not Pass: The Spanish People at War, 1936–1939.* London: Wayland, 1974.

Koonz, Claudia. *Mothers in the Fatherland: Women, the Family, and Nazi Politics.* New York: St. Martin's Press, 1987.

Labor cultural de la república española durante la guerra. Valencia: Ediciones Gráficas Vives Mora, 1937.

Lafitte, María. *See* Campo Alange, María.

Landis, Arthur H. *Spain: The Unfinished Revolution.* New York: International Publishers, 1975.

Lauretis, Teresa de, ed. *Feminist Studies/ Critical Studies.* Bloomington: Indiana University Press, 1986.

Lejárraga, María. *See* Martínez Sierra, María.

Lejeune, Philippe. *L'Autobiographie en France.* Paris: Amand Colin, 1971.

———. "Autobiography in the Third Person." *New Literary History* 9 (1977): 27–49.

———. *Le Pacte autobiographique.* Paris: Seuil, 1975.

León, Luis de. *La perfecta casada* (1583). In *Biblioteca de Autores Españoles* 37. Madrid: M. Rivadeneyra, 1855.

León, María Teresa. *Crónica general de la guerra civil.* Madrid: Alianza de Intelectuales Antifascistas, 1937.

Levine, Linda Gould, and Gloria F. Waldman, eds. *Feminismo ante el franquismo.* Miami: Ediciones Universal, 1982.

Levine, Linda Gould, Ellen Engelson Marson, and Gloria F. Waldman, eds. *Spanish Women Writers: A Bio-Bibliographical Source Book.* Westport, Conn.: Greenwood Press, 1993.

Lida, Clara E. *La Casa de España en Mexico.* Mexico: College of Mexico, 1988.

Lida, Clara E., José Antonio Matesanz, et al. *El Colegio de México: Una hazaña cultural, 1940–1962.* Mexico: College of Mexico, 1990.

Lifton, Robert Jay. *Boundaries: Psychological Man in Revolution.* New York: Vintage, 1970.

———. *The Life of the Self.* New York: Basic Books, 1983.

———. *The Woman in America.* Boston: Houghton Mifflin, 1965.

Lionnet, Françoise. *Autobiographical Voices: Race, Gender, Self-Portraiture.* Ithaca: Cornell University Press, 1989.

López, Aurora, and María Angeles Pastor, eds. *Crítica y ficción literaria: Mujeres españolas contemporáneas.* Granada: University of Granada, 1989.

Loureiro, Angel G., ed. "*La autobiografía en la España* contemporánea." *Anthropos* 125. Special issue (Oct. 1991).

———. "Resisting Autobiography." *Journal of Interdisciplinary Studies* 5. Special issue (1993).

Lumen, Nelly. *Dolor y esperanza: Lo que vi en España.* Mexico: Editorial Lumen, 1938.

Macciocchi, Maria Antonia. *La Dona Nera.* Milan: Feltrinelli, 1976.

———. *Elementos para un análisis del fascismo.* 2 vols. Madrid: El Viejo Topo, 1977.

———. "Female Sexuality in Fascist Ideology." *Feminist Review* 1 (1979): 67–82.

———. *Les Femmes et leur maîtres.* Paris: Christian Bourgois Editeur, 1978.

Madariega, Salvador de. *Mujeres españolas.* Madrid: Espasa-Calpe, 1972.

Malefakis, Edward. *Agrarian Reform and Peasant Revolution in Spain.* New Haven: Yale University Press, 1970.

Mangini, Shirley. "Memories of Resistance: Women Activists from the Spanish Civil War." *Signs. Journal of Women in Culture and Society* 17 (Autumn 1991): 171–186.

———. *Rojos y rebeldes: La cultura de la disidencia durante el franquismo.* Barcelona: Editorial Anthropos, 1987.

———. "Spanish Women and the Spanish Civil War: Their Voices and Testimonies." *Rendezvous* 22 (1986): 12–16.

———. "Three Voices of Exile." *Monographic Review* 2 (1986): 208–215.

Manteiga, Robert, Carolyn Galerstein, and Kathleen McNerney, eds. *Feminine Concerns in Contemporary Spanish Fiction by Women.* Potomac, Md.: Scripta Humanistica, 1988.

Marías, Julián. *La mujer en el siglo XX.* 4th ed. Madrid: Alianza Editorial, 1982.

Martínez Bande, José Manuel. *La marcha sobre Madrid.* Madrid: Librería Editorial San Martín, 1968.

Martínez Sierra, Gregorio. *Cartas a las mujeres de España.* Madrid: Compañía Ibero-Americana de Publicaciones, 1930.

———. *La mujer moderna.* Madrid: Compañía Ibero-Americana de Publicaciones, 1930.

Martínez Sierra, María. *La mujer española ante la república.* Madrid: Ediciones de Esfinge, 1931.

Martín Gaite, Carmen. *La búsqueda del interlocutor y otras búsquedas.* Madrid: NOSTROMO, 1973.

Martín Gamero, Amalia, ed. *Antología del feminismo.* Madrid: Alianza Editorial, 1975.

Martel, Carmen. *La guerra a través de las tocas.* Cadiz: Establecimiento Cerón, 1938.

Matthews, Herbert L. *Half of Spain Died: A Reappraisal of the Spanish Civil War.* New York: Charles Scribner's Sons, 1973.

———. *The Yoke and the Arrows: A Report on Spain.* New York: George Braziller, 1961.

May, Georges. *L'Autobiographie.* Paris: Presses Universitaires de France, 1979.

Mayoral, Marina, ed. *Escritoras románticas españolas.* Madrid: Fundación Banco Exterior, 1990.

McKendrick, Melveena. *Woman and Society in the Spanish Drama of the Golden Age: Study of the "Mujer Varonil."* London: Cambridge University Press, 1974.

Menchú, Rigoberta. *Me llamo Rigoberta Menchú y así me nació la conciencia.* Barcelona: Editorial Argos Vergara, 1983.

Méndez, Lourdes. *Cosas de Mulleres, 1940–1980.* Barcelona: Editorial Anthropos, 1981.

Miguel, Amando de. *El miedo a la igualdad: Varones y mujeres en una sociedad machista.* Barcelona: Editorial Grijalbo, 1975.

———. *Sexo, mujer y natalidad en España.* Madrid: EDICUSA, 1975.

Miller, Beth. *Women in Hispanic Literature: Icons and Fallen Idols.* Berkeley: University of California Press, 1983.

Miller, Nancy K. *Getting Personal.* New York: Routledge, 1991.

Miller, Nancy K., ed. *The Poetics of Gender.* New York: Columbia University Press, 1986.

Moller Okin, Susan. *Women in Western Political Thought.* Princeton: Princeton University Press, 1979.

Montero Moreno, Antonio. *Historia de la persecución religiosa en España, 1936–1939.* Madrid: La Editorial Católica, 1961.

Montseny, Federica. *Mis primeros cuarenta años.* Barcelona: Plaza y Janés, 1987.

Mora, Gabriela, and Karen S. Van Hooft. *Theory and Practice of Feminist Literary Criticism.* Ypsilanti, Mich.: Bilingual Press, 1982.

Moreno, Amparo. *Mujeres en lucha: El movimiento feminista en España.* Barcelona: Anagrama, 1977.

Morodo, Raul. *Acción española: Orígenes ideológicos del franquismo.* Madrid: Ediciones Júcar, 1980.

Mosse, George L. *Nationalism and Sexuality.* New York: Howard Fertig, 1985.

"La mujer." Cuadernos para el diálogo. Special issue (Dec. 1965).

La mujer en la nueva sociedad. Madrid: Ediciones del Movimiento, 1963.

Muñiz, Oscar. *Asturias en la guerra civil.* 2nd ed. Gijón: Ayalga Ediciones, 1982.

Nash, Mary. *Més enllà del silenci: Les dones a la historia de Catalunya.* Barcelona: Generalitat de Catalunya, 1988.

Nelken, Margarita. *Elena e Isabel: Diálogos sobre temas feministas.* Madrid: Editorial Paez, 1927.

———. *La epopeya campesina.* Madrid: Ediciones Aldus, 1936.

———. *Escritoras españolas.* Barcelona: Labor, 1930.

———. *La mujer ante las Cortes Constituyentes.* Madrid: Editorial Castro, 1931.

———. *Por qué hicimos la revolución.* 3rd ed. Madrid: Ediciones Europa-America, 1936.

Núñez Pérez, María Gloria. *Trabajadoras en la Seguna República: Un estudio sobre la actividad económica extradoméstica (1931–1936).* Madrid: Ministry of Labor and Social Security, 1989.

Nussbaum, Felicity A. *The Autobiographical Subject: Gender and Ideology in Eighteenth-Century England.* Baltimore: Johns Hopkins University Press, 1989.

Olney, James. *Metaphors of Self: The Meaning of Autobiography.* Princeton: Princeton University Press, 1972.

Olson, James S., ed. *Historical Dictionary of the Spanish Empire, 1402–1975.* Westport, Conn.: Greenwood Press, 1992.

O'Neill, Carlota. *Los muertos también hablan (continuación de Una mexicana en la guerra de España).* Mexico City: Populibros, 1971.

Ordoñez, Elizabeth J. *Voices of Their Own: Contemporary Spanish Narrative by Women.* Cranbury, N.J.: Associated University Presses, 1991.

Pàmies, Teresa. *Cuando éramos capitanes (memorias de aquella guerra).* Barcelona: DOPESA, 1974.

———. *Una española llamada Dolores Ibárruri.* Barcelona: Ediciones Martínez de la Roca, 1976.

———. *Records de guerra i d'exili.* Barcelona: DOPESA, 1976.

Pardo Bazán, Emilia. *La mujer española y otros artículos feministas: Selección y prólogo de Leda Schiavo.* Madrid: Editora Nacional, 1976.

Pascal, Roy. *Design and Truth in Autobiography.* London: Routledge and Kegan Paul, 1960.

Passerini, Luisa. *Fascism in Popular Memory.* Translated by Robert Lumley and Jude Bloomfeld. New York: Cambridge University Press, 1984.

Payne, Stanley. *Falange: A History of Spanish Fascism.* Stanford: Standford University Press, 1961.

Pérez, Janet. *Contemporary Women Writers of Spain.* Boston: Twayne Publishers, 1988.

———. *Novelistas femeninas de la posguerra española.* Madrid: Porrúa, 1984.

Pérez, Janet, and Wendell Aycock. *The Spanish Civil War in Literature.* Lubbock: Texas Technical University Press, 1990.

Personal Narratives Group. *Interpreting Women's Lives: Feminist Theory and Personal Narratives.* Bloomington: Indiana University Press, 1989.

Piera, Dolores. *La aportación femenina en la guerra de independencia.* Barcelona: Department of Agitation and Propagauda of the Unified Socialist Party, 1937.

"Mujeres poetas." Zurgai Special issue (June 1993).

Preston, Paul. *The Spanish Civil War, 1936–1939.* New York: Grove Press, 1986.

Primo de Rivera, Pilar. *Discursos, circulares, escritos.* Madrid: Sección Femenina de FET y de las JONS, n.d.

Ramón y Cajal, Santiago. *La mujer: Conversaciones recogidas por Margarita Nelken.* Madrid: Aguilar, 1932.

Richardson, R. Dan. *Comintern Army: The International Brigades and the Spanish Civil War.* Lexington: University of Kentucky Press, 1982.

Riesenfeld, Janet. *Dancer in Madrid.* London: George G. Harrap, 1938.

Roberts, Helen, ed. *Doing Feminist Research.* London: Routledge and Kegan Paul, 1981.

Rodrigo, Antonina. "Nuestras mujeres en la guerra civil." *Vindicación feminista* 3 (Sept. 1976): 1989.

———. "Rosario Sánchez Mora, 'La Dinamitera'." *Cuadernos hispanoamericanos* 503 (May 1992): 12–26.

Rodríguez de Lecea, Teresa, Francisco Laporta, and Alfonso Ruiz Miguel. "La Institución Libre de Enseñanza." *Historia 16* (May 1980): 67–93.

Roig, Montserrat. *El catalans al campos nazis.* Barcelona: Edicions 62, 1977.

———. *La mujer en la historia a través de la prensa: Francia, Italia, España, siglos XVIII–XX.* Madrid: Ministry of Culture, 1982.

———. "Mujeres en campos nazis." *Vindicación feminista* 11 (May 1977): 15–21.

Romera, José, ed. *Escritura autobiográfica.* Madrid: Visor, 1993.

Rosal, Amaro de. *Historia de la UGT de España, 1901–1939,* vol. 2. Barcelona: Grijalbo, 1977.

———. *El oro del banco de España y la historia del Vita.* Barcelona: Grijalbo, 1976.

Ross, Bruce M. *Remembering the Personal Past: Descriptions of Autobiographical Memory.* New York: Oxford University Press, 1991.

Rossiter, Margaret L. *Women in the Resistance.* New York: Praeger Publishers, 1986.

Rubin, David C. *Autobiographical Memory.* New York: Cambridge University Press, 1986.

Rubio Cabeza, M. *Diccionario de la guerra civil española,* vol. 2. Barcelona: Editorial Planeta, 1987.

Ruíz Giménez, Joaquín. *Iglesia, estado y sociedad en España, 1930–1982.* Barcelona: Editorial Argos Vergara, 1984.

Saiz de Otero, Concepción. *Un episodio nacional que no escribió Pérez Galdós: La revolución del 68 y la cultura femenina.* Madrid: Librería Victoriano Suárez, c. 1929.

Sánchez, Jose M. *The Spanish Civil War as a Religious Tragedy.* Notre Dame: University of Notre Dame Press, 1987.

Sánchez López, Rosario. *Mujer española, una sombra de destino en lo universal: Trayectoria histórica de Sección Femenina de Falange (1934–1977).* Murcia: University of Murcia, 1990.

Sánchez Saornil, Lucía. *Horas de revolución.* Barna: Publicaciones "Mujeres Libres," 1938.

Sánchez Vidal, Agustín. *Buñuel, Lorca, Dali: El enigma sin fin.* Barcelona: Editorial Planeta, 1988.

Sanz Bachiller, Mercedes. *La mujer y la educación de los niños.* Madrid: Ediciones de Auxilio Social, 1939.

Saval, Lorenzo, and J. García Gallego, eds. *Litoral femenino: Literatura escrita por mujeres en la España contemporánea.* Madrid: Litoral, Revista de la Poesía y el Pensamiento, 1986.

Saywell, Shelley. *Women in War.* Ontario: Penguin Books Canada, 1985.

Sebastiá Salat, M. *Thesaurus d'historia social de la Dona.* Barcelona: Generalitat de Catalunya, 1988.

La Sección Femenina: Historia y organización. Madrid: Sección Femenina, 1952.

Segura, Isabel, and Marta Selva. *Revistes de dones, 1846–1939.* Barcelona: Edhasa, 1984.

Semprún Maura, Carlos. *Revolución y contrarrevolución en Cataluña (1936–1937).* Barcelona: Tusquets Editor, 1978.

Serrano y Sanz, Manuel. *Antología de poetisas líricas.* Madrid: Tipografía de la Revista de archivos, bibliotecas, y museos, 1915.

──────. *Apuntes para una biblioteca de escritoras españolas desde el año 1401 al 1833*, vols. 268–271. Madrid: Atlas, 1975.

Servodidio, Mirella, ed. "Reading for Difference: Feminist Perspectives on Women Novelists of Contemporary Spain." *Anales de la literatura española contemporánea* 12. Special issue (1988).

Showalter, Elaine, ed. *The New Feminist Criticism: Essays on Women, Literature, and Theory*. New York: Pantheon Books, 1985.

──────. *Speaking of Gender*. New York: Routledge, Chapman and Hall, 1989.

Smith, Lois Elwin. *Mexico and the Spanish Republicans*. Berkeley: University of California Press, 1955.

Social Help: Auxilio social. Falange Española Tradicionalista y de la JONS. Spain: n.p., n.d. (May be found at the Hoover Institution, Stanford, California.)

La Solidarité des peuples avec la republique espagnole, 1936–1939. Moscow; Editions du Progrès, 1974.

Sonadellas, Concepció. *Clase obrera y revolución en España 1936–1939*. Bilbao: Zero, 1977.

Souchere, Elena de la. *An Explanation of Spain*. New York: Vintage Books, 1965.

Southworth, Herbert. *Antifalange*. Paris: Ruedo Ibérico, 1967.

──────. *El mito de la cruzada de Franco*. Barcelona: Plaza y Janés, 1986.

Spacks, Patricia Meyer. *The Female Imagination*. New York: Alfred A. Knopf, 1975.

──────. *Gossip*. New York: Alfred A. Knopf, 1985.

Spadaccini, Nicholas, and Jenaro Talens, eds. *Autobiography in Early Modern Spain*. Minneapolis: Prima Institute, 1988.

Spain. World Bibliographical Series, vol. 60. Oxford: Clio Press, 1985.

The Spanish Civil War Collection: A Guide to the Microfilm Collection. Woodbridge, Conn.: Research Publications, 1989.

Starcevic, Elizabeth. *Carmen de Burgos: Defensora de la mujer*. Almería: Librería-Editorial Cajal, 1976.

Stimpson, Catharine R. *Where the Meanings Are: Feminism and Cultural Spaces*. New York: Routledge, 1988.

Sulliman, Susan Rubin, ed. *The Female Body in Western Culture: Contemporary Perspectives*. Cambridge, Mass.: Harvard University Press, 1986.

Theweleit, Klaus. *Male Fantasies*. Vol. 1., *Women, Floods, Bodies, History*. Minneapolis: University of Minnesota Press, 1987.

──────. *Male Fantasies*. Vol. 2, *Male Bodies: Psychoanalyzing the White Terror*. Minneapolis: University of Minnesota Press, 1989.

Todd, Janet. *Feminist Literary History*. New York: Routledge, 1988.

Ugarte, Michael. *Shifting Ground: Spanish Civil War Exile Literature*. Durham, N.C.: Duke University Press, 1989.

Ullman, Joan Connelly. *The Tragic Week: A Study of Anticlericalism in Spain, 1875–1912*. Cambridge, Mass.: Harvard University Press, 1968.

Valis, Noël, and Carol Maier. *In the Feminine Mode: Essays on Hispanic Women Writers*. Cranbury, N.J.: Associated University Presses, 1990.

Van Gelder Forbes, John. *Recent Relief Programs of the American Friends in Spain and France (In Spain, 1937–1939)*. New York: Russell Sage Foundation, 1943.

Varner Gunn, Janet. *Autobiography: Toward a Poetics of Experience*. Philadelphia: University of Pennsylvania Press, 1982.

Viñas, Angel. *La Alemania nazi y el 18 de julio*. Madrid: Alianza Editorial, 1977.

Wallach Scott, Joan. *Gender and the Politics of History*. New York: Columbia University Press, 1988.

Weiler, Martine. *Mujeres activas: Sociología de la mujer trabajadora en España*. Madrid: Ediciones de la Torre, 1977.

Weintraub, Karl Joachim. "Autobiography and Historical Consciousness." *Critical Inquiry* 1 (June 1975): 821–848.

Willis, L. *Women in the Spanish Revolution*. New York: Unity Press, 1975.

Wilson, Francesca M. *In the Margins of Chaos: Recollections of Relief Work in and between Three Wars*. New York: MacMillan, 1945.

Women Writers in Translation: An Annotated Bibliography, 1945–1962. New York: Garland Press, 1984.

Women Writers in Twentieth-Century Spain and Spanish America. New York: E. Mellen Press, 1993.

Woolf, Virginia. *A Room of One's Own*. New York: Harcourt, Brace and World, 1929.

Wyden, Peter. *The Passionate War: The Narrative History of the Spanish Civil War*. New York: Simon and Schuster, 1983.

Yates, Frances A. *The Art of Memory*. Chicago: University of Chicago Press, 1972.

Zambrano, María. *Delirio y destino (veinte años de una española)*. Madrid: Mondadori, 1989.

———. *Senderos: Los intelectuales en el drama de España*. Barcelona: Editorial Anthropos, 1986.

Zugazagoitia, Julián. *Guerra y vicisitudes de los españoles*. Barcelona: Editorial Crítica, 1977.

Index

prison, after civil war (continued)
121–123; "prisoners of the street," 122,
156; prostitutes, 131–133; rape, 130;
reasons for, 99–100; release from, 142–
147, 199n11; solidarity, 116–119;
statistics on women, 101, 104–105,
196n7; substandard conditions, 117;
suicide, 135; torture, 127–129; Ventas
Prison, 32, 101, 118, 120, 135, 196n8;
verbal abuse, 129
Pro-Infancia Obrera, 28
"psychic closing off," 62, 70, 107, 189n27

Quiepo de Llano, Gonzalo, 73, 196n97

Ramón y Cajal, 5
Real Soledad: background, 18, 19; on
prison, 118, 126, 127, 129, 130; on
reasons for writing, 113, 114; on release
from prison, 144, 145, 147; on war, 78
Residence for Young Ladies, 6, 33
Residencia de Estudiantes, 5
Revolution of Asturias (Revolution of
October), 28, 30, 36, 40, 67, 68, 135,
184n16
Rojo, Blasa, 139–140
Rosal, Amaro de, 32, 34, 185n28
Rosie the Dynamiter. *See* Sánchez, Rosario
Ruiz, Julián, 39
Russia, 40, 44

Salvo, María, 144
Sánchez, Rosario (Rosie the Dynamiter), 20,
82–83, 84, 136, 189n28
Sánchez Saornil, Lucía, 87, 89, 194n67
Sanjurjo, José, 23, 68, 183n2, 191n7
School for Female Teachers, 4
Sección Femenina. See Feminine Section
Sender, Ramón, 118, 198n6, 199n36
SERE (*Servicio de Emigración Republicana
Española*), 153
Silva, Josefina de, 190–191n5
Spanish civil war, ix, 18; Andalusia, 73–74;
Asturias, 64–65; attire, 190–191n5;
Barcelona, 69, 71, 89, 165; Burgos, 93;
causes, 4, 67–68; Extremadura, 74–75;
foreign intervention, 92, 191n14;
International Brigades, 69, 89, 192n15;

Loyalists, 68; Madrid, 69, 75;
mercenaries, 68, 83; Mérida, 75; military
strategy, 68-69; Nationalists in, 65, 68;
non-intervention pact, 69; orphaned
children, 122; outcome, 68–70; Popular
front, 191n6; Seville, 68, 69, 73–74
Spanish Inquisition, 3, 102, 171
Spanish Republic, First, 3, 5
Spanish Republic, Second ("La Niña
Bonita"); ix, 5, 17, 22, 23, 37; abortion,
46; divorce, 24, 27, 102; female suffrage,
24–27; phenomenon of "Two Spains,"
24, 64; Popular Front, 68; problems, 17,
23–24, 67; separation of church and
state, 23, 95
Student Residence, 5
Student Residence for Young Ladies, 6

"*testimonio*," 56, 82, 188n23, 189n28
Thirteen Minors (*Las Trece Rosas*), 138–
139
Tomás, Belarmino, 156
Torre, Matilde de la, 29–30, 34–35, 44, 45,
77–78
Torres, Nieves, 21, 75
Trejo, Blanca Lydia, 80

UGT (General Worker's Union), 29
Ulacia Altolaguirre, Paloma, 158, 159

Valencia, during civil war, 69, 161
voice of collective testimony, 57, 58, 61, 63,
101, 108, 112, 113, 144, 147, 148, 157, 162

Winterhelp, 93, 195n94
women: aberrance, 37–38; abnegation, 3,
18, 38, 43, 46, 58, 75, 76, 79; after war,
101–103; Alvarez del Vayo on, 75; as
colonial subjects, 55; de la Mora on, 70–
71, 79; de la Torre on, 77–78; economic
situation at turn of century, 4–5;
equation: activist=whore, 9, 74, 104,
106, 129–130, 144, 145, "flash of
freedom," 76; honor, 107, 184n5;
importance of chastity, 184n5;
motivation for activism, 18; organizations
in '20s and '30s, 7, 8, 25, 36; Real on,
71, 78–79